The Cookie That Did Not Crumble

By Cookie Gilchrist and Chris Garbarino

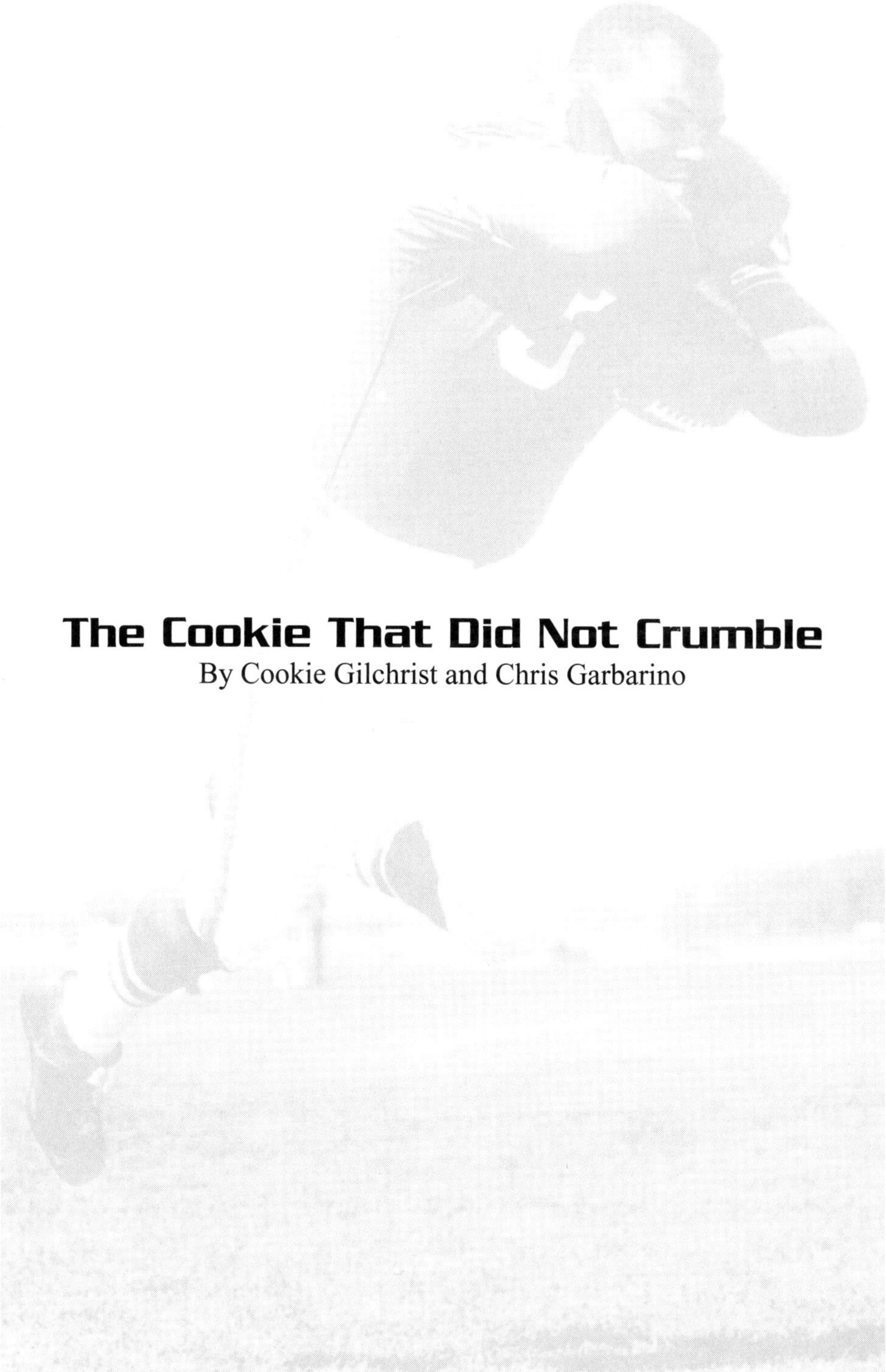

Photo by ©Robert L. Smith Orchard Park N.Y.

For information contact Chris Garbarino, P.O. Box 90415, Staten Island, NY 10309

Library of Congress Control Number: 2011918521

ISBN 978-0-9846885-0-0

Printed in Canada
www.cookiegilchrist.com

For Cookie and all of the former players, who paid the ultimate price making the NFL a success....Chris Garbarino

CONTENTS

Foreword

By Booker Edgerson

Nowadays it would almost be impossible to believe that coaches or trainers would withhold water from players during the heat of summer training camp, but during my rookie year in 1962, that was the case. The lack of water, in conjunction with the summer heat and physical exhaustion brought by the two-a-day practices made training difficult, especially because many of the players were out of shape. In the offseason, many players were forced to work due to inadequate salaries. Players had no time to train, or, if they did have the time, they had no access to training facilities. In rare cases, the trainer or coach would allow a player to have a drink of water because they feared for the player's health. When I snuck water, coach Saban, who treated me like a son, turned a blind eye to my actions.

Then there was the Bills' new acquisition, Carlton Chester "Cookie" Gilchrist, who didn't need to sneak anything. He had unlimited access to water and almost anything else he wanted.

Cookie stood out like a giant. He looked like the Greek god Zeus had chiseled him out of the Rock of Gibraltar. He had a charisma and confidence that could not be mistaken. You also could tell that, despite his laidback attitude when he was among friends, you would never want to meet him in a dark alley. Cookie was well known for his football prowess throughout Canada and New York and was brought in by the Bills to become the franchise.

I was from Rock Island, a small town in Illinois, and had no clue as to who Cookie was because I knew little about Canadian football. It was never shown on TV and had barely been written about in the newspapers.

Well, I soon found out how great a player Cookie was: in fact he was one of the greatest players to ever put on a football uniform. At the time, Cookie was considered the AFL's answer to the great Cleveland Browns fullback, Jim Brown. He never received the accolades or press that Jim Brown received in the NFL, but having seen them both, I contend that Cookie was the better all-around player.

Cookie did so many good things for our football team. He provided constant leadership, often without knowing he was doing it. The assurance and winning attitude that Cookie displayed on the field gave his teammates a confidence that, if they worked together, they would be unbeatable.

When I watched him in practice running plays or providing blocks, I was in awe of what he could do. I also watched the reactions of our other teammates, who were equally impressed with Cookie's ability. Cookie was just doing what came naturally to him on the football field, but he was actually providing inspiration for the entire team.

Cookie was not only a superstar player; he was also a one-of-a-kind personality. He knew how to use his star status to have fun, but more importantly, he used it to influence social change. He was not the bad guy that the press had made him out to be. He refused to take any bullshit from anyone and would speak his mind. He always told me to answer questions honestly, even if the answer was not what people wanted to hear. He would often say the things that other people were thinking, but dared not say out of a fear of being ostracized. His honesty and larger-than-life personality was too much for many people to handle and, I would contend, his only Achilles heel.

When Cookie and I became teammates in 1962, we were both new to the AFL, but he had played professionally for many years in Canada. He took me under his wing and became my mentor. He helped mold me into the man I am today and instilled in me the importance of always standing up for my beliefs. No one could follow Cookie's lifestyle, which was flamboyant, to say the least, but I tried my best to incorporate his teachings into my life. It was my privilege to have him as my teammate, roommate, best friend, and, most of all, brother.

I hope you enjoy reading Cookie's story and getting a behind-the-scenes glimpse into the life and mind of this gridiron great.

A Legend On and Off the Field

Cookie Gilchrist is seen by many who follow the history of football as the greatest all-around player ever to grace the gridiron. He played during the 1950s and 1960s and could dominate at almost every position on the field.

Despite playing more than fifty years ago and well before the media age we now live in, he is still remembered for his larger-than-life exploits both on and off the field. If he had played today he would be one of the NFL's highest paid players and a showman who would have put Deion Sanders and Chad "Ochocinco" Johnson to shame. It was this showmanship and dominance on the field that still bring his name to the lips of football historians.

Cookie's story is a complicated tale, and his life took many twists and turns. While football may be the backdrop to his life story, he lived a life that was so much more than football. During the 1950s, 60s, and 70s, Cookie took part in many major historical events. Unlike the defenses he ferociously barreled through on the football field, these were events through which he moved effortlessly. The one constant at these events would be Cookie, who, like the fictional movie character Forrest Gump, had inadvertently secured himself a front-row seat to some of the greatest moments in history.

Cookie starred in the Canadian Football League before moving on to the Buffalo Bills in 1962 and becoming the first marquee star of the upstart American Football League. During his career he was named an All-Star in 11 of his 14 seasons playing football for the Ontario Rugby Football Union, the Canadian Football League, and the American Football League.

In addition to his exploits on the football field, Cookie became well known for voicing his opinion to anyone who would listen. He would often be labeled as uppity or difficult because he refused to accept second-place status just because he was a black man living through the turbulent times prior to passage of the Civil Rights Act.

Once Cookie's career on the field ended, he foresaw a bleak future for athletes who suffered repeated head trauma and became an advocate for better health care for retirees. Cookie was often told that his ideas for changing the ways in which athletes were treated and followed medically after retirement were sound, but in the same breath was advised that they were not financially feasible.

Almost forty years ago, he unexpectedly dropped out of the public spotlight, and many thought that this was due to his supposed difficult and abrasive personality. Was this the case, or had something else driven him into seclusion?

This is where I became a player in Cookie's story. Through a chance interaction, each of our lives would be changed forever. I had read several books about the history of the American Football League and each chronicled the enigma that was Cookie Gilchrist. In them, he was always described as dominant on the field, and as outspoken as they come off the field. Yet his story seemed to vary greatly in each book I read. I became interested in his story and was driven to find out the truth about Cookie Gilchrist.

I soon learned the reasons behind these variations in his story were due to his reclusiveness. He spoke to almost no one, forcing many writers to re-hash old stories or to rely on the accounts of others for information.

After an extensive search, I finally connected with this legend of the gridiron in one of the most unlikely ways you could imagine. The last few months of his life brought an unforeseen and close friendship between Cookie and I, while also giving me a close-up view of what actually happens to the forgotten greats of the game.

At Cookie's bedside before he died, I promised him that his story would finally be told. The following narrative is constructed from talks during our time together as well as notes left behind in his journals. Each chapter contains Cookie's first person narrative, reconstructed and embellished by his notes and my research, framed by opening and closing statements designed to put the events into historical perspective. This book is the culmination of my promise to my friend, and it's honestly a work of love. I now invite you to read about his extraordinary life story and learn what happens to many of the gridiron greats once the cheering has ended.

Birth of a Gridiron Legend

On May 24, 1935, in Brackenridge, Pennsylvania, Carlton Chester Gilchrist entered this world in the larger-than-life fashion for which he would become so well known. His story will not be remembered for the obstacles and personal misfortunes he suffered, but for the globetrotting and star-studded life he lived in spite of these obstacles.

I was born on Friday, May 24, 1935, at 2:40 p.m. to my parents Rose and Otto Gilchrist. My birth occurred at our family home, 900 Clay Street in Brackenridge and was overseen by the only black physician in the area, Dr. Chester Howell. At birth I weighed in at twelve pounds, thirteen ounces, but was the second smallest child born into the Gilchrist family, which also included my brothers Richard and Robert, as well as my sister, Frances.

My middle name of Chester was given to me in honor of the delivering physician and was the name I preferred over my given first name of Carlton. The name I would be most famously known by was Cookie, which was a childhood nickname given to me by my mother when she realized I had an insatiable appetite for sugary and sweet foods, especially chocolate cake.

The first seven years of my life were spent living primarily with my paternal grandparents, John and Mary Gilchrist. My grandfather and grandmother were both born slaves in 1860. The name Gilchrist, which means "Servant of Christ," came from the surname of the family that owned my grandfather's family.

I still have many fond childhood memories of listening to my grandfather reading the bible and how he regaled the story of how Abraham Lincoln freed the slaves to me. The story of Lincoln always ended with the message that I was born a free man to pursue my dreams in life. Over and over again he told me, "Carlton, you can never ever trust the white man nor ninety-nine percent of the niggers he has working for him," and "You are free to be whatever you want." Considering the conditions that both of my grandparents had been born into, these statements could easily be understood. But at this time in my life the words did not ring true to me. I was still a child more interested in playing Cowboys and Indians with my friends or riding my bicycle. Later in life, having seen firsthand the ugly side of racism, I could understand more clearly what my grandfather was trying to instill in me, even at that early age.

Early in life I also learned that those closest to you could inflict severe mental and physical damage on you. When I was six years of age, my older sister Frances held my hand over an open flame on the stovetop, just for her amusement. Fortunately, my mother stopped her before I suffered permanent damage, but the emotional pain she inflicted never subsided. This incident caused a rift between Frances and me, which lasted the rest of our lives. When she passed away I refused to attend her funeral and just considered that painful chapter of my life closed.

At eight years of age, I moved back into my parents' home on a full-time basis. They were living on Fourth Avenue, a small ghetto in downtown Brackenridge. My father Otto was now working in the local steel mill to do his best to support our family. The neighborhood was extremely poor and, while predominately black, had a few white and Hispanic families. This was the age when I realized that poverty did not discriminate based on race and that it was not just an issue for blacks. Regardless of color, our neighborhood was a close-knit community where everyone looked out for each other like they were family.

I was well aware that my family was poor, but children are resilient and regardless of money will find inventive ways to entertain themselves using only their imagination and ingenuity. When it rained, all the kids around Fourth Avenue would race popsicle sticks or tree branches down the street in the rainwater that flowed along the street curb. The entire neighborhood was eventually razed by the local government under the cover of industrial expansion, but those that lived there still have such a strong bond that a yearly reunion is held to celebrate the lives and bonds formed there. Believe it or not, one of the highlights of these reunions is when the children and grandchildren of those that lived on Fourth Avenue, so long ago, compete in the annual popsicle-stick race.

During my youth I was not an angel by any stretch of the imagination, but I learned early on that doing the wrong thing would have severe consequences. In the second grade I found myself on the wrong side of the law when I stole money from the cash register in the school lunchroom. It was apparent that a life of crime was not in my future when I was caught red-handed. Even before the lunch period ended the whole school learned of my transgression. On the walk home from school, my sister Frances asked me a question: "What kind of birds don't fly?" When I said that I did not know she replied, "Jail Birds, Dummy." It was with glee that Francis told my father about what I had done. The shame I felt, as well as the beating I received from my father for disgracing our family name, made me want to live the rest of my life on the right side of the law.

My mother was also a stern disciplinarian, and she instilled in me a set of values to live by. The words Truth, Honor, Respect, Communication, Goodness and Love signify those values. She taught me that Love was the burning desire to do good for others. Those values carried me throughout my life and no matter what the situation I could always hear my mother's voice in my head reciting those values.

The first football memory I can recall is of my mother giving me a tin can to use as football tee, so I could practice my field goal kicking. She was the one who set me on my path toward the gridiron. While my father worked at the steel mill, she would teach me the basics of playing football. She was a progressive thinker and a woman of action, and I always felt that I followed in her footsteps.

My career in football began when I was only eight years old. From the beginning, I clearly excelled on the gridiron and always wanted to play a full sixty minutes on both offense and defense. The only position I did not play was quarterback because I had not figured out how to throw the ball to myself. The reason I say career was that it was apparent to the coaches and my family, even at this early age, that football would be my ticket to a better life. This would be my way to break the mold of working in the local steel mills like most of the town's men. I took the game seriously from the very beginning because I was now determined to use this opportunity to make a better life for my family and myself.

Cookie was now known locally for his athletic ability and would use his adolescent years to develop the larger-than-life personality and determination that would eventually become his trademark. Cookie would use the values his mother taught him to develop the inner strength needed to overcome the obstacles he would soon face on and off the football field.

A Man Among Boys

Cookie was now primed to become the local football hero for the town of Brackenridge. The Har-Brack High School games brought an escape for the local families, who could spend a few hours a week cheering for their football stars while forgetting the stresses of the outside world. Cookie's larger-than-life personality and ability to dominate on the field were starting to emerge, making him one of the most sought-after college recruits in the nation.

Football really took off for me when I became enrolled at Har-Brack High School and met head football coach Kenneth Karl. Coach Karl took a genuine interest in me as a person and not just as his star football player. In 1952 I was the only sophomore to make the varsity team, but contributed all over the field, playing fullback, linebacker, and kicker. Coach Karl taught me that real men played football for sixty minutes.

Coach Karl and I were very close during my time at Har-Brack, but the relationship started off on the wrong foot. I was not all that interested in attending classes and coach Karl consistently chased after me to make sure that I did not skip school and fail off of the team. After several run-ins with coach Karl over my studies I told him that I quit the team. One of the assistant coaches convinced me to come back to the team, but when I returned to practice coach Karl was still upset with me. During that practice I was sent in to play fullback, with only a quarterback, center and two guards lined up on offense instead of a full complement of players. Coach Karl had put in the entire varsity defense, thinking that I would be overmatched and would have the most difficult practice of my life.

On the first play I ran over everyone for a touchdown. We ran about five more plays and I gained ten to fifteen yards every time I touched the ball. Coach Karl threw his hat down in disgust after I ran in another touchdown, and he had the entire defense run a lap. He even made me run one, too, because I ran over the defense and embarrassed my teammates. Soon after this practice I came to realize that coach Karl was only trying to look out for my best interests and he eventually became a father figure in my life.

The local papers would describe my athletic abilities on the gridiron as a phenomenal display of speed and strength. Even as early as my sophomore year, the local media was talking about the possibility of me starring at nearby Ohio State for fabled coach Woody Hayes.

I was now over six feet tall and weighed a solid 230 pounds. I had been blessed with the gift of good genetics. While other players would have to resort to eating more or spending time in the weight room to increase muscle size, I ate a regular diet and only trained when forced to by the team. Many people are not aware that at this time in football and athletics in general, weight training was not yet recognized as a customary training practice. I realized that I was now on the radar of college football coaches from around the country, due to my package of size, strength, and speed. My games became a regular destination for college coaches and recruiters who were hoping that I would commit to their school. During my junior season at Har-Brack, I was offered 108 scholarships from the top universities in the country. The fact that so many colleges showed interest excited me because I would now have the opportunity to be the first member of my family to attend college. But, being a young man, I sometimes lost focus and became more interested in the fact that young ladies were showing interest in me as well.

My mother and father hoped that I would use football to attend college and make a better life for myself. My father stressed that the colleges would want to use me for my football skills and that I should in turn use them to gather the skills I would need in my post-football life. The ultimate dream was to attend Notre Dame or Michigan to acquire a college degree and later a doctorate in either medicine or law.

I was always considered a good football player, but my junior year of high school was when I began to dominate. The Har-Brack team of 1953 was considered one of the best Pennsylvania high school teams ever and averaged an impressive 43 points per game. The team was christened the "Triple Terror Backfield" by the press and was led by Barry Johnson, Jim Powell, and myself.

The best game I ever played during my high school career came in 1953, a 68-33 win against Vandergrift. In that game I amassed 294 yards rushing on 15 carries for a 19.7-yard average. I also scored five touchdowns and kicked the extra points for all five scores. A 1993 article in the Valley News Dispatch voted that game the number one game in Alli-Kiski Valley football history.

The win against Vandergrift was one of nine straight wins during our undefeated season of 1953 en route to a championship meeting with Denora High School. Both schools would finish the regular season undefeated and would now battle each other for the WPIAL Class AA State Championship. The game was scheduled for November 28, 1953, at Pitt Stadium, which at the time was the largest venue I had ever played in. We played the game under frigid conditions, before a sold-out, standing-room-only crowd of 11,589. Denora's game plan was to focus their entire defense on me in an attempt to shut down my offensive output. I did attempt a 40-yard field goal during the game, but it was short and just missed clearing the crossbar. The game was ultimately determined by the defenses of both teams, who kept the game scoreless, resulting in a 0-0 tie. Har-Brack and Denora shared the WPIAL Championship with identical season records of 9-0-1. This would be the only championship in Har-Brack's history.

Of the 385 points that Har-Brack scored that season I accounted for 189 of them, which at the time was a league record. In 1999, I had the distinction of being voted the fourth best high school player in Valley history by the local sportswriters. I only trailed Valley High School legends Dick Modzelewski, Willie Thrower, and Ed Modzelewski, in the writers' poll.

The end of the season brought several awards, and I was recognized as one of 77 outstanding scholastic players on the seventh annual National All-American High School Football Team. The Wigwam Wiseman of America, who sponsored the award, bestowed the honor upon me. The honorees were voted on by national sports writers, and the award was a sought-after designation. It made me eligible for selection to the East West All Star Football Game, which was being held in Memphis during August of 1954. The All Star game was a real showcase for high school players, and a roster spot on the team would lead to national exposure. That year I also had secured a roster spot on the Allegheny County team, which competed in the Pittsburgh Jaycee All Star game.

I was still reveling in what our team had accomplished when I started to give thought to my senior year. Even though I was only a Junior I knew it was the last time I would play for Har-Brack. I would turn nineteen during my senior season and WPIAL rules stated that I would be too old to play in the league. This was because the maximum age to participate in the league was eighteen. Arrangements were being made for me to attend a private high school, where there would be no age restrictions and I could continue to play football. I planned to continue showcasing my football skills in preparation for my college career.

Following the championship I started my first business venture along with two of my Har-Brack teammates. It was called the Gilchrist, Johnson, and Powell car washing service and we specialized in Cadillacs, Lincolns, and Oldsmobiles. This was because I loved to drive these models around town before dropping them back off with the customers. I always said that once I made some money, the first thing I would buy was a top-of-the-line Cadillac. Once I started to play football professionally I included a Cadillac clause in my contract, which required the teams to lease me a new model Cadillac every season.

In addition to the car washing business I also continued to work odd jobs, which included farm work and newspaper delivery. Whenever I saw an opportunity to make additional money, I took it, in order to help make ends meet at home. My parents struggled financially and I knew that football was going to give me the best opportunity to help them, but expected any chance at playing football professionally to be several years away. I was still filled with thoughts of attending college and one day becoming Dr. Gilchrist. My entire world would soon be turned upside down and all it took was an afternoon visit from Cleveland Browns coach Ed Ulinski.

The spring of 1954 brought great excitement for Cookie and his family. The success he had attained on the football field was now the high point of his young life. The prospect of one day being the first member of his family to attend college now seemed within reach. Unknowingly, Cookie's dream of becoming a doctor or a lawyer was about to derail and he would be sent in an entirely unexpected direction.

Taken for a Ride

Everything in the world seemed to be going well for Cookie. On or off the football field, he felt he could do no wrong. Unfortunately, there were still a lot of closed-minded individuals that felt that this new local celebrity needed to realize that, regardless of what he did on the football field, he was still a black man who needed to learn his place. At this point in his life, Cookie was still a trusting person who saw the goodness in everyone. In the spring of 1954, that was all about to change.

My sophomore year of high school was when I began to date, but I needed to be secretive about who I was seeing. I found white girls attractive, which at the time was a societal taboo. This could cause problems for the young ladies, as well as for me. A scandal like interracial dating would derail my aspirations of attending college on a football scholarship.

The first relationship I had only lasted a few dates. The young lady and I had the misfortune of being caught kissing by her father. Before I knew what was going on I was under attack by her father, who was incensed that his daughter was kissing a black man. He began to wildly swing a large hunting knife at me, but I managed to escape the skirmish with my life. I sustained a few wounds, including a half-moon scar on my chest. This scar became a lifelong symbol of how closed-minded some people could be. Needless to say, that was the end of that short-lived relationship.

On April 24, 1954, I again felt the backlash of racism because I continued to date outside my race. For several weeks I was secretly dating a young female classmate named Betty Ann Richards, who was white. Betty Ann was a popular marching band majorette for Har-Brack. We enjoyed each other's company, but knew that our relationship, if made public, would become a local scandal. We had been out for a leisurely drive on that April night when it all came crashing down.

That evening I had borrowed the car I was using from the father of my friend Harold Edwards. When Betty Ann and I decided to call it a night I drove toward the Colored Elks Club to return the car to Mr. Edwards. As we were approaching the Elks' building I noticed that a New Kensington police car had taken notice of us. When their headlights shined into our vehicle, the officers saw the petite white Betty Ann sitting next to me. They then turned in our direction and began to follow our car.

I pulled the car around to the back of the Elks Club and instructed Betty Ann to stay inside the vehicle with the windows and doors locked. Just as I would not have been accepted by some in her world, if I brought Betty Ann into the Colored Elks Club, she would not have been well received by many inside. I walked around to the front of the building and explained to the doorman that I was there to return Mr. Edwards' car. The doorman allowed me to enter the club, which was now packed with people partying and having the time of their lives. There was loud music, dancing, and a fair amount of drinking going on.

I eventually found Mr. Edwards and returned the keys to the vehicle. Just as I turned to leave, my friend Claude Forston ran up to me and said that the New Kensington Police had just dragged Betty Ann out of Mr. Edwards' car and arrested her.

The entire club spilled out into the street to view what was taking place. When I made it outside, Betty Ann was already handcuffed in the back seat of the police cruiser. One of the officers then addressed the crowd that had gathered around them and asked, "Who does this car belong to?" Harold replied that the car belonged to his father. The officer then asked Harold, "Who was driving the car this evening?" I then yelled out that I was the driver of the car!

The officer then screamed, "You are under arrest, nigger," and proceeded to throw me against the police cruiser. The crowd was aghast at what they were seeing, but no one said a word in defiance. The officers threw me into the back seat of the cruiser with Betty Ann, who was now hysterically crying. Before the officer closed the door I screamed out to Harold that he should call Dr. E. S. Montgomery and let him know that the New Kensington Police had arrested me. When we arrived at the Fifth Avenue Station House, we were both booked and thrown into separate holding cells on opposite ends of the building.

Betty Ann and I were both confused and wanted to know why the police arrested us. We had not committed any criminal offense that we were aware of and the officers refused to inform us of the charges brought against us. Shortly after being fingerprinted, Betty Ann was taken out of her cell and interrogated by a detective. It seemed like she was in the interrogation room for hours, but eventually she was brought back to her cell with tears now streaming down her face. When her father and mother arrived, she was released into their custody.

Betty Ann's parents were aware that she knew me from school and that I was "Cookie Gilchrist," the football player. I had even given her father tickets to several of our games. They had no idea that we were romantically involved and never would have approved. Before Mr. Richards brought Betty Ann home he approached my holding cell, his face red as a beet and in his loudest voice yelled, "Nigger, I hope they throw away the key on your black ass! Don't you know you are a nigger and niggers are not supposed to be with white girls!" This was the man who shook my hand to thank me for football tickets. Now he looked upon me as though I were evil and wanted to destroy his daughter's reputation.

The New Kensington Police Department was predominantly white and only had two black police officers on their force. One of the black officers was O. C. Buckener, who was a friend of my cousin Helen Anderson. Officer Buckener came to my cell and said, "Carlton, I don't know what you have done, but whatever it is, your family will not be able to get you out of it."

I sat in the holding cell wondering what exactly I was being accused of. How was this going to affect my future? The only thought that crossed my mind was that I was a free-thinking and acting young black man in a segregated society. While I continued to ponder my situation Officer Buckener returned and said I was being released to some white gentleman. The sound of the large keys unlocking the cell door rang like church music in my ears because it signaled my release from this personal hell.

Dr. E. S. Montgomery had come to rescue me from the horrible fate of being falsely arrested. I first met Dr. Montgomery when I began cleaning his Cadillac as part of my car-washing business and then began spending time around his farm doing chores for extra money. He began to teach me how to box, in the hope that one day he might mold me into the next heavyweight champion of the world. He had become a positive influence in my life and another father figure for me to lean on.

As we drove away from the police station, Dr. Montgomery told me that he had to pay off the Police Chief, Mayor, District Attorney and Newspaper Editor in order to get me released from custody. This act of kindness by Dr. Montgomery, which erased all evidence of the arrest, left my dream of going to college and playing football intact.

Years later, Betty Ann and I reconnected and she told me how her parents beat her after they left the precinct. They were pressuring her to swear out a complaint of rape so the family name would be spared.

She also detailed how the police detective who interrogated her threatened that swearing out a charge of rape against me would be her only way to avoid criminal charges. To her credit Betty Ann stood up and told the truth when it mattered.

This event would be a wake-up call to Cookie that no matter how special he was on the football field, he was still a young black man in a white-run society. A short time after Cookie's arrest, Emmett Till, a fourteen-year-old Mississippi boy was found tortured and murdered because of allegations that he had whistled at a white woman.

Some might wonder, if Cookie had not been a football star with Dr. Montgomery in his corner, would his story have ended similarly?

Meet Coach Brown

The past year was one of great personal triumph for Cookie. Having just come off of an undefeated season with Har-Brack High and a share of the WPIAL AA Championship, prospects were looking up for the young gridiron star. The finishing touches were being put together for Cookie to continue his dominance on the football field at a private school when newspaper reports started to trickle out that Cookie wanted to forgo his education and jump right into a professional football career. The media reports were far from the truth, but they put into motion events that would change Cookie's life forever.

May 8, 1954, was when I had my first experience with the professional side of football. That was the day I met Cleveland Browns coach Edward Ulinski. Coach Ulinski had first been a player with the Cleveland Browns and was now working as an assistant to head coach Paul Brown. Ulinski came to Har-Brack to present me with the Cleveland Browns' offer of a $5,500 guaranteed contract for the 1954 NFL season. The Browns apparently had caught wind of the newspaper reports that had incorrectly speculated that I wanted to forgo my senior year of high school in favor of playing professional football.

The amount of money that was being offered for the 1954 season was far more than my father had ever made working in the local steel mill. My father spent six days a week grinding steel in the mill to put a roof over our heads. My thought was that this unexpected financial opportunity would be my best chance to help ease my father's work load and allow my family to live a better life.

Neither of my parents was present during this contract offer and I knew they would never have approved of my choice to leave school. But the opportunity to help my family was something I could not pass up and I signed the contract coach Ulinski presented me with that afternoon. Thoughts about how I would use the money to change my family's life flooded my mind, and I could not wait to tell anyone who would listen that I was now a Cleveland Brown.

Coach Ulinski could see that I was bursting at the seams and before we parted, he told me that I could not tell anyone about the contract. That included my parents because the Browns did not want the news to leak out to the press before the team announced my signing through a press release.

On May 19, the Browns made a formal announcement that they had signed me to my first professional contract. Once the news broke, my parents were crushed to find out that I would not be the first person in our family to attend college. I tried to explain my decision to my parents by saying that I wanted to be able to help them financially. This was my way of ending the need for my father to work himself to death in the mill six days a week. My father's response was that he would work every day of the week with a smile on his face, just so I could get my college education. He knew better than I did that a professional football career was short and that I needed a college degree for my life after the game.

The contract had already been signed and any thoughts of attending college were now dashed. The pain and disappointment that my parents felt regarding my decision were as visible as the numbers on my football jersey. Ultimately, I was the one that had to live with the decision and my family did their best to put on a brave face and support my decision.

The summer brought the start of Browns training camp in Hiram, Ohio. It was a who's who of football superstars, including future Hall of Fame players Otto Graham, Marion Motley and Lou "The Toe" Groza. This was going to be my chance to show the NFL what I could do. I had a great camp and even remember out kicking Lou Groza in a field goal competition.

The relationship I would start with Marion Motley, who was considered the Jackie Robinson of football, was the best thing to come out of my Browns experience. Marion was considered the first player to cross the color barrier in professional football. He was a tremendous player on both sides of the ball. As a linebacker on defense, he was a ferocious tackler, and as a fullback on offense, he would steamroll over anyone foolish enough to step in front of him.

When I arrived in camp I was clearly there to be Marion's replacement, but, putting team first, he took me under his wing. Meeting Marion would be one of the few times in my life that I would be starstruck. He had been one of my football heroes, and I tried to emulate his playing style on the field and his professional demeanor off the field. I remember his instilling the importance of pass blocking for a fullback, which I took great pride in from that point forward.

After I retired, Marion and I ran into each other on the banquet circuit and I still felt like I was talking to my older brother. Marion was asked during an interview what he remembered about meeting me for the first time that summer in Browns camp. His reply was, "Cookie was a real good-looking player that could run and block with the best of them, but I was more amazed at how much ice cream he ate."

Eight weeks into my training camp experience I was called to coach Brown's office. I was unaware of why I was being called to the coach's office because I was having a great camp. This type of meeting was ominous as it usually signaled that a player was being let go by the team. Once inside coach Brown asked me to sit down and then said that I was indeed being cut. The explanation I was given was that I was not yet ready to compete at the NFL level, but they thought enough of my talent to keep me on the practice squad, and I would be paid $100 per week for the season's twelve weeks of games.

I had signed a contract that guaranteed me $5,500 and now I felt I was being taken advantage of with this lower offer, which was some $4,300 less than I had been promised.

The other option I was presented with was that I could try playing in Canada with the Winnipeg Blue Bombers. The Blue Bombers were coached by former Philadelphia Eagles quarterback Allie Sherman, and they had a working relationship with coach Brown. Once I attained the seasoning as coach Brown put it, I would be shipped back from Winnipeg to play for Cleveland.

I knew the cover story that my skills were not up to par was a farce. The real story was that Art Rooney Sr., the Pittsburgh Steelers owner had become upset when he heard the news that I signed a contract with the Browns. The Steelers were the professional football team near my hometown and they were well aware of what I was capable of on a football field. Art Rooney knew something that I didn't when I signed the contract with Cleveland. The NFL had a rule that limited players from being signed unless their college class would have already graduated. Mr. Rooney felt that coach Brown was not following the league rules and that Cleveland would be gaining an unfair advantage by signing me straight out of high school. The Steelers, stating that the Browns were trying to circumvent the NFL rules and thereby creating an unfair advantage, had filed a grievance regarding my contract with NFL Commissioner Bert Bell.

Bert Bell and Art Rooney knew each other very well, as they had co-owned the Steelers until Bell left the organization to assume the position of League Commissioner. Bell and Rooney's long-term private and professional relationship was going to make it difficult for coach Brown to come out a winner against the Steelers' claim of unfair labor practices.

Commissioner Bell ruled that my contract was indeed in violation of the NFL's age requirement and that I would be unable to compete in the League until my college class would have graduated. My first thought upon learning the real reason why I was let go by the Browns was that

I would go back and finish high school. I could then attend college and play football as originally planned. I was then informed that I would be unable to qualify for any of the scholarships that had been offered to me. The fact that I had signed a professional football contract, even though the Commissioner voided it, showed my intent to become a professional athlete and thus permanently voided my student athlete status with the NCAA.

On August 4, 1954, I was placed on waivers and left to my own devices. Several newspaper stories were planted by the Browns stating that I was not yet equipped to play with NFL caliber of talent. The newspaper also commented that coach Brown felt I needed further seasoning in Canada.

I rejected Coach Brown's offer to play for their Canadian affiliate in Winnipeg. My rejection of his offer was based on the fact that the Browns never paid me one cent of the promised $5,500 in my contract and also had destroyed my chance to get my college education. If the team went back on their word once, why should I start trusting them now? Coach Brown was not really looking for me to get more seasoning in Canada; this would just be his way to keep me under his control until I became old enough to play in the NFL. I decided to pursue football in Canada, but on my own terms, with no help from coach Brown or his associates.

Cookie's plan to secure financial security for his family was now dashed due to coach Brown's desire to get ahead no matter what the cost. Coach Brown was a leader in the NFL and was fully aware of all of the League's rules pertaining to the signing of new players. Cookie was just another pawn on the League's chessboard. Coach Brown knew that if his plan to circumvent the age requirement came to light, the only person that would face any punishment would be Cookie. It was well known that the "Old Boys Club" of the NFL protected their own and would never acknowledge misconduct done by one of their most respected coaches. As proof of this "Old Boys Club" mentality, neither coach Brown nor the Cleveland Browns were ever fined for their actions. The only apparent loser in coach Brown's scheme was Cookie, who never saw one cent from the promised $5,500 contract and was denied a chance to accept any of the 108 college scholarships that had been offered.

Despite all of these setbacks, Cookie was primed to take his future by the reins, and would now set the Canadian football world on fire.

The Ontario Rugby Football Union

Cookie was now left to pick up the pieces of his life, which had been shattered by coach Brown and the NFL. Once Cookie's contract was found to have violated the league's age requirement rule, he was left without the financial security coach Brown had promised. Though the NFL voided the contract, it did not matter to the schools that had offered Cookie scholarships. He was now seen as a professional athlete by these institutions and no longer eligible to accept their scholarship offers.

Cookie's family could not afford to send him to college on their own, and he knew that without an education or the chance to play in the NFL, his opportunities in life would be limited. He knew that playing football in the United States was out, at least until he met the NFL's age requirement, so he decided to take his skills north of the border.

My father and mother pushed me to pursue playing football in Canada. They were concerned that if I did not take the opportunity to play football, I would wind up working in the steel mill like the majority of the town's men. Working in the mill was honest work, but my parents felt that I had a special opportunity and wanted to make sure it was not wasted because of what had transpired with coach Brown and the NFL.

It was already well into the first week of August and I knew that if I wanted to catch on with a Canadian team, I needed to hurry up, because their season started in late August. My parents scraped together enough money to get me started on my journey. I remember leaving home with a small bag of clothes and a shoebox filled with fried chicken my mother had packed for me. This was my first time outside the United States, and I knew nothing of Canada or the Canadian people.

The Sarnia Imperials of the Ontario Rugby Football Union were the first team to offer me a tryout. The Ontario Rugby Football Union was considered a semi-pro league at the time and following the 1954 season would stop competing for the Grey Cup Championship.

While the skills needed to play in the ORFU were the same as American Football, the rules were somewhat different. Each team possession consisted of three downs in the ORFU compared to the four that the American game used. Also touchdowns in the ORFU only counted for five points at the time, compared to the six points used in American football. The playing field in Canada was also ten yards longer, but I felt the differences in the rules were minimal. I was confident in the fact that I possessed the skills to compete at this level.

Following the tryout I was offered a roster spot with the Imperials for the 1954 season and had to quickly get up to speed because the first game of the season was just around the corner. The Imperials played a twelve-game regular schedule with two additional exhibition games mixed in between the regular season games. Sarnia's equipment manager could not find shoulder pads or other equipment big enough to fit me and was forced to drive to Detroit to obtain larger equipment from the NFL's Detroit Lions.

Sarnia opened the season at home on August 25, 1954, against the Kitchener-Waterloo Dutchmen, in front of a capacity crowd of five thousand. I scored my first touchdown that game by leaping over a pile of players at the goal line. That touchdown was enough for Sarnia to come away with a 23-19 win over the Dutchmen. In addition to playing halfback, I also played several different positions on defense and was the team's kicker.

One of the highlights of the season came on October 23, 1954, and once again against the Dutchmen. The game ended when I kicked a 44-yard field goal as time expired, securing a 17-17 tie. A kick of that distance was unusual for that time and well before the more accurate soccer-style kickers came along in the mid 1960s.

We finished the regular season with a record of seven wins, four losses, and one tie. The playoff system was a best of three format and we lost two consecutive games against the Dutchmen to close out our season.

At the end of the season I was named to the All-Star team at halfback and won the Jimmy Shanks Memorial Trophy, which was awarded to Sarnia's Most Valuable Player. I scored 73 points for the season, which was second in the league and only four points behind Dutchmen halfback and league leader Paul Amodio. I finished with 118 rushing attempts for 845 yards and eight touchdowns and also led the league with my 7.1 yards per attempt average.

I was happy with my season, especially considering the fact that I was now playing against older, more experienced players and was still able to lead the league in rushing.

While I was running on the Canadian gridiron, my peers were home attending their senior year of high school. It was amazing how fast my life had changed in just a few months.

I was enjoying my new life in Canada because I felt less of a need to be concerned about race. The Canadian people were more progressive than Americans regarding race relations. The Canadian people for the most part were gracious towards me and made my adjustment to being away from home easier.

Following the season I returned to Pennsylvania to decide whether to return to Sarnia the next season or accept a contract offer that was extended by the Winnipeg Blue Bombers of the Canadian Football League. The Bombers were coached by former Philadelphia Eagle quarterback Allie Sherman, who also happened to be a close friend of coach Paul Brown. The Bombers and Cleveland Browns had a working relationship, and if I signed with the Bombers it would be coach Brown's way of keeping tabs on me. Once I met the NFL age requirement he could then easily bring me back to play for Cleveland. The Bombers offer was attractive, and the part that had me so excited was that they offered me a job in the off-season as well.

At that time a player needed to work in the off-season to make ends meet and did not have that time available to train like today's athletes do. The Bombers' off-season job offer was to work at the Winnipeg Free Press. I found this job offer more appealing than anything else that I could find because of the fact that I had not finished high school. I had been turned down for several jobs I had applied for that winter and was becoming discouraged. One particular crushing incident was when I applied to work with kids in an organized sports program back home. I thought that my reputation as a star high school player in the area, as well as the fact that I could speak to the kids using my experience as a player in Canada, would give me an edge in getting the job. In fact they would not even interview me, just because the position required prospective applicants to have their high school diploma. This was the first time I could recall regretting not having finished my education.

Even though I did not trust coach Brown, the opportunity with the Bombers intrigued me, so I traveled to Winnipeg to discuss the opportunity further with coach Sherman. Coach Sherman explained that I would be starting for the Bombers and said that he would make me the focal point of the team's offense and the star of the league.

Following my meeting with coach Sherman, a Bombers team official showed me around town and arranged for a tour of the Winnipeg Free Press so I could see where I would be working in the off season. The next morning I woke up and found my car frozen solid from the extreme Winnipeg weather. After it took me an hour to gain access to my car,

I started to have second thoughts about living year-round in Winnipeg. Still, I took to heart coach Sherman's promise to make me the focal point of the offense and decided that I would play the 1955 season for the Bombers.

I called coach Sherman and told him that I accepted his offer to play for the team and added how excited I was to play for him. The next thing I told him was that I was declining the off-season job opportunity and would be returning to Pennsylvania. Coach Sherman said the offer would still be there if I changed my mind, but I could sense that he could tell that the cold Winnipeg weather had played a role in my decision to return to Pennsylvania for the off-season.

Early that summer I received a call from the Bombers coaching staff telling me to report for the start of that season's training camp. I started driving from Pennsylvania towards Winnipeg for the Bombers' training camp when I ran out of money. The first person I called was coach Sherman and I asked him for a small advance so I could make it to training camp. My request was flatly refused and I decided that they did not want me if they could not advance me the few dollars to make it to training camp. Now out of money, I looked for other options and realized I was close enough to make it to Sarnia's training camp. The fact that I led the league in rushing the previous season gave me hope that they would welcome me back.

Not knowing yet how the business end of football worked, I just headed over to the hotel where Sarnia players were housed for training camp and took a room. When I arrived it was late in the evening and I never checked in with the coaching staff. The next morning I showed up to camp with the rest of the team, and the coaching staff asked me why I was there because they thought I was going to play for Winnipeg that season. I was too embarrassed to tell them that I was there because I ran out of money and tried to say that I was there out of a sense of loyalty to my Sarnia teammates.

The coaching staff had already replaced me on the roster and the team was full at the halfback position. If I was going to play for Sarnia that season, I would have to switch to tight end, which was not my strongest position. While grateful for the offer I felt that if I did not play halfback I would not be able to show teams in the CFL and NFL what I could do best, which was run the football. This season was going to be my audition for the larger leagues and I needed the scouts that watched my game film to see me at my best.

I thanked the coaches for the offer of a roster spot, but explained my thoughts on switching positions and told them that I would be moving on.

As I cleared out my things and went to leave the hotel, the front desk clerk stopped me. He advised me that the team was charging me for the one night I slept at the hotel. The fact that I was broke is what brought me back to Sarnia in the first place, and I could not have paid the bill if I wanted to. Local law enforcement was called when I could not pay the bill and the whole incident became quite an embarrassment.

The local court ended up dismissing the matter, and, upon hearing of my misfortune, the Kitchener-Waterloo Dutchmen stepped in to offer me a starting position on their team. The Dutchmen played Sarnia several times every season and thought they could have no better advantage in those match-ups than to have me starting for them with an obvious chip on my shoulder against Sarnia.

Playing for the Dutchmen was where I met coach Harvey Johnson. Harvey respected my playing ability and would later be the one who would bring me back to play in the States when he worked for the Buffalo Bills. For the Dutchmen I played halfback, defensive back, linebacker, and kicker. As I had the previous season with Sarnia, I played 60-minute football. Several opposing players started to call me a headhunter on defense, but at the time it really was an anything-goes mentality on the field.

I recall that this was the season where opposing players started to really up the trash talk and racial comments toward me. In a way I took it as a compliment, because the fact that I was playing so well bothered them to the point where they felt getting into my head was the only way to win the game. The derogatory racial names yelled throughout the game were troubling, but the real problems would start after a tackle. If I were at the bottom of the pile I would get punched, kicked, eye gouged, etc. The opposing team would try anything they thought would work to get me out of the game or disrupt my play. Often if the referee did see one of these incidents they looked away and acted like it never happened. Whenever I was called a name like "nigger," I would call the guy a "nigger" back and then proceed to call him that throughout the game. The puzzled looks these white men would get from my response would throw them off balance and I would come barreling through on the next play and knock them on their asses. I tried to let my play on the field be my retaliation for their closed-minded behavior.

There was one game in particular on September 25, 1955, against the Toronto Balmy Beach Beachers where I was punched square in the face during a pile up. That day I'd had enough and, as soon as I got up, I walked over to the Toronto Bench and challenged the entire team to a fight. This was because I did not see who had thrown the punch and yelled for the person that threw the punch to step up and fight me while my arms were not pinned to the turf. As usual the coward that threw that punch was not man enough to stand up and fight a fair fight.

That season the Dutchmen dominated the ORFU and finished with a regular season record of 10-1-1, beating Sarnia in the playoffs for the League Championship. Following the season I was named to the All-Star team at halfback, after again leading the league in rushing. I finished the season with 806 yards on 129 attempts for a 6.2 yards per carry average and added ten touchdowns. My final point total for the season was 61 points and placed me third in the league, only behind Gino Cappelletti's 63 for Sarnia and the 71 by my Dutchmen teammate and league leader Bill Graham. Cappelletti would later move to the AFL and become a star for the Boston Patriots. He would also lead the AFL and later the NFL in scoring on five separate occasions. Winning the ORFU Championship was a thrill, but I was ready for the next level of competitive football in Canada, the Canadian Football League.

Cookie dominated the Ontario Rugby Football Union and won a championship, in addition to leading the league twice in rushing. Looking for a new challenge on the field, he saw that opportunity with the Hamilton Tiger-Cats of the Canadian Football League.

The hotel bill incident in Sarnia should have been a warning to Cookie that although he was playing a game, professional football was a big business and the owners and managers of the league would treat it as such. The big kid from Pennsylvania who loved playing football was going to have to learn that lesson the hard way.

The Hamilton Tiger-Cats and Grey Cup Glory

Cookie had dominated in the Ontario Rugby Football Union and was now poised to join the more competitive Canadian Football League. He was offered a one-year contract with the Hamilton Tiger-Cats and jumped at the offer to play with and against some of the best football players in the game.

During these years, Cookie would learn that, despite being a gifted athlete, if he did not conform to what was expected of players and especially of black players in that era, he would find himself on the outside looking in. This would be the start of his vagabond career as one of the best all-around football players to ever play the game.

In 1956, I was offered a contract to play for the Hamilton Tiger-Cats of the Canadian Football Council, which would be renamed the Canadian Football League in 1958. The Tiger-Cats were in the Interprovincial Rugby Union, which was referred to as the "Big Four" and also included the teams located in Montréal, Ottawa, and Toronto. The Western Division of the league was called the Western Interprovincial Football Union and was composed of teams located in Edmonton, Winnipeg, British Columbia, Saskatchewan, and Calgary.

The Tiger-Cats general manager, Jake Gaudaur, offered me a $4,800 base salary contract with performance incentives that would allow the contract to top out at $6,200. The contract's incentives, which included monetary increases for rushing performance and All-Star recognition, seemed easily attainable to me based on my two previous seasons in the Ontario Rugby Football Union. Gaudaur had informed me that I would be playing on both offense and defense for the Cats and would also be called upon to kick. Based on the fact that I was going to be playing several different positions, I asked for separate contracts for each position, but was flatly refused. I figured it was worth a shot anyway - I always believed in the saying, "Nothing ventured, nothing gained."

At that time there were no player agents, and players had to negotiate their own contracts. For the most part teams held all of the cards in the negotiations, and players had little recourse if they did not like a team's offer. Only the top players of the day held enough clout to force the owners to even consider listening to a player's counteroffer.

I eventually accepted Gaudaur's offer because I had no resume at this level of football and needed this opportunity to show the league what I could do. I was determined to prove my worth to Gaudaur and the rest of the league by giving it my all on the field. The next time I had a contract come up for renewal, I would make sure I had the football resume to negotiate terms that were on par with my true value to the team. This first contract with the Tiger-Cats would be the last time that I would just accept a team's offer without putting up a fight for what I felt was appropriate compensation for my services.

Jim Trimble was coaching the Tiger-Cats for the 1956 season, and he was also a Pennsylvania transplant living in Canada. This was Trimble's first head coaching experience in Canada and came on the heels of his firing from the same position with the Philadelphia Eagles of the NFL following the 1955 season. Trimble would later become famous not for his coaching ability, but for the invention of the Y or slingshot-style goal posts that are used in today's football.

Following training camp that summer, coach Trimble named former Baltimore Colts running back Zollie Toth as the Tiger-Cats starter for the season opener. I would be relegated to being his back-up, even though I and other members of the team felt I had outperformed him in training camp. At the time I kept my displeasure to myself and hoped that my play on the field would force Trimble to change his mind and make me the starter.

Eventually, my play on the field merited a starting position, but coach Trimble and I continued to have our differences of opinion. On September 12, 1956, the Cats were at home playing the Toronto Argonauts. We were losing 22-21 in the final minutes, but had possession of the ball and were within striking distance of a go-ahead score. During that game I had suffered severe cramping in my hamstring and was having difficulty running the ball with authority. At the end of the game, Tiger-Cats quarterback Nobby Wirkowski mishandled the handoff and fumbled the ball, ending our chances for a win. Nobby walked back to the sideline and, fearful of Trimble, blamed the fumble on me. Nobby's allegation caused an argument between coach Trimble and I, which carried over into the next day.

The next day, the team held practice, and I was still feeling the effects of the cramping I suffered the day before. I advised the coaching staff of the issue and watched the beginning of practice from the sideline bench. Coach Trimble called for me to get on the field and play linebacker during practice despite the fact that I was not feeling well enough to participate.

When the practice play was called I did not react and stood on the field motionless. Trimble began to scream, "If you are not going to even bother, then go back to the locker room where you belong."

A heated exchange ensued, and I told Trimble that I would rather quit than play for him as I walked toward the locker room. I always gave it my all on the field and felt that Trimble was treating me unfairly now that I was not at full strength. As I was showering Trimble came into the showers with assistant coach Ralph Sazio and challenged me to a fight. Trimble said, "Young man, I have handled bigger men than you. If you want to fight, I will accommodate you."

My reply was that, since he was the coach and a much older man, he should throw the first punch. Trimble did not take me up on my offer, but left the shower making this final comment, "You will never play football anywhere ever again."

Trimble spoke with Jake Gaudaur and they placed me on suspension and even refused to pay me my weekly game check. The other Tiger-Cats players held a meeting following my suspension and voted 27-1 to have me reinstated to the team.

Trimble's hand had been forced on this issue, but this would not be the end of our disputes.

The Tiger-Cats finished the 1956 regular season with a record of 7-7 and a date with Ottawa in the IRFU semi-finals. On November 7, 1956, we defeated the Ottawa Rough Riders by a score of 47-21, led by my first three-touchdown game.

The win over the Rough Riders set up a showdown with Montréal in the IRFU Finals. Prior to the first game against Montréal, I was informed that my aunt Mary Gilchrist-Perry had passed away and that I needed to return home for the funeral. I called Jake Gaudaur and informed him of the loss of my aunt and the need to return home for the funeral. I promised that I would only be gone for the day of the funeral and would return prior to the first playoff game against Montréal.

To this day I still do not know the reasons behind his decision, but when Jake Gaudaur was interviewed prior to the first game against Montréal he was asked about my missing practice prior to a playoff game. He stated to the reporter that he did not know where I was and had no idea why I would knowingly miss practice.

Was this payback for my run in with Trimble and a way to portray me in a poor light with the fans? I would never learn the true reasons behind those comments, but many of these incidents with Trimble and Gaudaur soured my opinion toward the CFL management and contributed to my decision to decline induction into the CFL Hall of Fame in 1983.

I returned in time and played in both losses against Montréal in the IRFU Finals. Montréal went on to face the Edmonton Eskimos for the 1956 Grey Cup, which Edmonton won by a final score of 50-27.

I finished the season with 31 points on three rushing touchdowns, two receiving touchdowns and one single. I rushed for 832 yards on 130 carries with my longest run of the season being 79 yards. That season I also intercepted two passes on defense and returned kickoffs on special teams. I was named to the IRFU's All-Star team at halfback and won the Tiger-Cats MVP award.

The summer prior to the 1957 season found me across the desk from Jake Gaudaur in another contract negotiation. This time I planned on actually making this a back-and-forth negotiation instead of the take-it-or-leave-it offer he presented to me prior to the 1956 season. After a back and forth regarding what my worth was to the team I negotiated a $7,000 base salary with a $500 signing bonus and other performance incentives that could eventually have the salary top out around $10,000 for the season. After the contract was signed Jake and I discussed how we both thought that this would be the Tiger-Cats' year to win the Grey Cup, and, as an extra incentive, he promised me a $500 bonus if the Tiger-Cats won it that season.

My 1956 season in Hamilton had been successful on the field, and I also had moderate success off the field with a local restaurant I opened named Uncle Tom's Cabin. The restaurant specialized in barbecue spareribs and fried chicken.

But the real success I found during my Hamilton years was not on the field or in business, but in a relationship I started with a young Canadian beauty named Gwendolyn.

Gwen and I started dating during my time in Hamilton, which would not seem out of the ordinary for two young people. The issue was that Gwen was white, and, although Canada was more progressive about racial issues than the States, there were still those who voiced disapproval of our relationship. Toward the end of the 1956 season I had again been contacted by the Cleveland Browns and asked if I wanted to return to the United States to play for them in 1957. I already had reservations about dealing with coach Paul Brown due to the way I was treated during my time in Brown's training camp prior to the 1954 season. As far as I was concerned, the man had lied to me once already, and he was the reason that I was unable to attend college.

Unbeknownst to me, the Browns had been keeping track of me while I was in Canada, and their offer to play in the NFL came with one provision.

It was that I must end my relationship with Gwen, as the NFL would not accept interracial relationships. Our relationship would be a public relations nightmare for them, and that was a take-it-or-leave-it condition of their offer.

While I would have loved to play back home on the NFL stage, I realized that I loved Gwen more and saw a better future for us in Canada.

After I declined the Browns' offer, they used their first round pick in the 1957 draft on a fullback from Syracuse named Jim Brown.

The 1957, season was when I started to get the reputation of rolling out of bed late and just making it to the field in time for practices or games. Many teammates would say that when I woke up on the wrong side of the bed, the opposing team was in trouble. It became a bit of a superstition, and teammates would predict a win if they heard I had been out partying the night before a game. This superstition would follow me throughout my career, and I can recall that Buffalo Bills teammate Billy Shaw would always check to see what I had done the night before a game to judge what type of day he could expect me to have on the field. If he heard that I stayed out late he would let out a yell in his southern drawl that our opponents won't know what hit them because Cookie's been out all night and is raring to go. My fondness for late evenings would also be one of the main problems I would have with coaches and the reason for several suspensions and fines.

In 1957, I continued to play both offense and defense, while averaging fifty-eight minutes a game. I started the season slow, but in the third game came through with two touchdowns in a 35-8 win over the Toronto Argonauts.

The Tiger-Cats had a new backfield coach named George Terlep who helped me improve my game by teaching me the importance of studying game film and by talking to me instead of down to me as many of my previous coaches had. I would credit Terlep with helping me become more than just a gifted athlete; he had now made me a student of the game.

In week ten of the season, the Tiger-Cats were playing a home game against Montréal, which we won by a final score of 18-15. In that game I scored two touchdowns, but the newspaper article talked about how I was still in hot water from reporting late to a game two weeks prior. The fact that the Tiger-Cats were in first place in the Big Four with an overall record of 8-3 did not seem to matter.

That article I would refer to as the Genesis article, which would be the first to obscure the real story of the day and instead highlight my portrayal as a troublemaker. Just about any article that followed talked about my run-ins with team management instead of just talking about what I had done on the field. From that point on, I was Cookie Gilchrist the troublemaker first, and Cookie Gilchrist the football player second. This is when I realized that controversy sells newspapers better than rushing statistics.

The Cats finished the regular season in first place with a 10-4 record and secured a first round playoff bye entering the East finals. The Cats swept Montréal on consecutive November Saturdays in the best-of-three game format with final scores of 17-10 and 39-1.

The following Saturday, November 30, 1957, would bring the Grey Cup Championship game between the Tiger-Cats and the Winnipeg Blue Bombers. The game was a Tiger-Cats blowout, as we went up 32-0 over Winnipeg before they added a late fourth quarter score to make the final score 32-7. I had two touchdown runs of five and 16 yards respectively and added 78 all-purpose yards on offense. The Tiger-Cats were now Grey Cup Champs, and all of Canada was able to watch our victory because this was the first football game broadcast nationally on Canadian television.

This game would go down in Grey Cup history not just for the Tiger-Cats victory, but for one of the most bizarre moments in its history. Tiger-Cats defender Ray Bawel intercepted a Bombers pass and was running down the sideline when a fan entered the field and tripped him. The Bombers were penalized half the distance to the goal, and the ball was placed at the Bomber 21 yard line. Two plays later I ran in for my 16-yard touchdown. The fan that had tripped Bawel slipped back into the stands following the incident and left undetected.

In 1957, I finished the season with 54 total points and nine rushing touchdowns. I rushed for 958 yards on 204 carries with the longest run being for 57 yards. I also added three pass interceptions on defense. My season totals landed me fourth in the league in total points and second in rushing yardage. The press voted me as a Big Four Offensive All-Star and starting fullback of the Eastern (IRFU) All-Star team.

We returned home to find 25,000 fans cheering us in Hamilton Market Square, which was a thrilling sight, but not nearly as thrilling as when I found out soon after that Gwen was pregnant with our first child. I was very much in love with Gwen and thrilled with the prospect of being a father. We immediately set up the apartment with a nursery and made plans to marry.

Several of my businesses had failed, including the restaurant, and despite my large salary for that era, I was in financial trouble. The rent on the apartment was due, and I had taken the baby furniture on credit. The $500 bonus Jake Gaudaur had promised was now needed to pay these bills and to hold me over until the next season.

When I approached Jake for the bonus, he refused and alleged that he never promised the bonus. We went round and round on the issue, and the baby furniture including the crib was repossessed. This incident added fuel to the fire when it came to my uneasy relationship with Jake Gaudaur.

Gwen and I were married on March 17, 1958, in Mexico. Through loans, which I secured on my future earnings, I kept a roof over our heads.

My relationship with both coach Trimble and Jake Gaudaur seemed beyond repair. I found out that assistant coach Terlep was leaving to become the head coach of the Saskatchewan team in the Western Division. I knew that without Terlep to be a buffer between Trimble and myself, things would only get worse for me in Hamilton.

Jake Gaudaur called me early that off-season to negotiate my contract for the 1958 season. Having reached all of my incentives in 1957 I earned $10,000 and asked for a base salary of $12,000 for the coming season. Jake Gaudaur sat behind his desk stone-faced and offered me a $7,500 base salary and fewer incentives, making the offer worth approximately $8,700 if I met all of the incentives. Jake knew that I would not take less money than I had been paid for the prior season, and this was his way of pushing me out of Hamilton.

Coach Terlep heard of my contract dispute and moved quickly to acquire me in a trade between Hamilton and his new team the Saskatchewan Rough Riders. Saskatchewan met my contract demands and paid Hamilton $5,000 to complete the trade. The Roughriders would eventually receive $2,500 of the amount back if I stayed with them for at least two seasons.

I always thought this was Jake Gaudaur's way of trying to keep me in the Western Division and away from competing against the Tiger-Cats in the East. Jake knew that I now had a chip on my shoulder against Tiger-Cat management and would like nothing better than to face them on a regular basis.

Following the trade to Saskatchewan, I had secured financial security for my expanding family and had escaped the perpetual doghouse I was in with both coach Trimble and Jake Gaudaur. The new contract and fresh start were both much appreciated and welcomed, but the biggest thing I had secured in the trade was being able to continue my professional relationship with coach Terlep.

Cookie was now a Grey Cup champion and had done it competing against the best players Canadian football had to offer. At every level of football, he won a championship, but still had the competitive drive and desire to want to become one of the best to ever play the game. Cookie hoped that by continuing under the tutelage and direction of coach Terlep, he would continue to flourish on the field. This next season would be one of Cookie's best both personally and professionally, and it would bring him one step closer to being considered among the elite in all of professional football, not just in the CFL.

Following Cookie's death an article from former Buffalo beat writer Larry Felser was published in which Felser recounted a conversation he had with coach Jim Trimble in the mid 1990s. Felser was hosting a sports radio show in Buffalo and mentioned on the air that Cookie Gilchrist was the best all-around football player he had ever seen during his years covering professional football. Upon hearing Felser's comment, Trimble, who was listening in Southern Ontario, felt obliged to call the show just to say that he agreed with Felser's assessment of Cookie's abilities, and added that Cookie Gilchrist was the best football player that he ever coached or had to coach against. It's too bad that it took the passage of so much time for Trimble to see what had been right in front of him.

Shuffle off to Saskatchewan

Cookie had secured a new contract from the Saskatchewan Roughriders and was starting to come into his own as a star of the CFL. Playing for the Roughriders would enable him to continue playing for coach Terlep, whom he credited with making him a student of the game.

Cookie continued playing sixty minutes a game as a stalwart on both offense and defense, but was learning to read offenses and defenses better through game film study and improved pre-game preparation. In the past, Cookie had relied on his God-given athleticism to overcome opponents, and that had been enough to make him a perennial All-Star; but with the addition of what coach Terlep taught him about the Xs and Os of the game, Cookie was about to become a one-man wrecking crew on the gridiron.

The summer prior to the 1958 season I made the trip out to Saskatchewan from my home just outside Toronto. My Wife Gwen stayed back east awaiting the birth of our first child. She wished to stay close to her family and friends, and also wished to continue using the obstetrician who had followed her throughout the pregnancy. I made arrangements to split the rent on a house with fellow Roughrider teammate Mike Hagler.

Mike and I were going to split time in the Roughrider backfield with fellow halfback Bobby Marlow. I had already seen instances where the backfield-by-committee principle did not work because one halfback or fullback would get hot and then take the majority of the carries. The working relationship Mike, Bobby, and I had was the exact opposite, as our playing styles complemented each other, allowing for all of us to thrive professionally.

In football you were only as good as your last season, sometimes forcing players to have a "me first" attitude and putting personal statistics before the needs of the team. One poor season on the field and a player could find himself out on the street with no way to support his family. While all three of us wanted to put up big statistics to ensure a new contract at the end of the season, this season was more of a brotherly competition where we cheered for each other to succeed and put the team first.

On Monday, July 21, 1958, I was out on the practice field at training camp when coach Terlep approached me and presented me with a box of cigars. Coach Terlep had been in the office when the call came in from home that Gwen had given birth to a healthy baby boy, whom we named Jeffrey Carlton Gilchrist, and wanted to be the first to congratulate me.

I immediately ran from the field to call Gwen, and told the coach to give the cigars out to the team. The fact that I was so far away from home was difficult for me, but I knew it was nothing compared to Gwen being back home and taking on this great responsibility alone.

While I was committed more than ever to playing football, I looked for other financial opportunities off the field. The local radio station offered me an opportunity to host a one-hour show each week where I would play my favorite jazz records. The program, which ran during the 1958 season, was called "Cookie Gilchrist Swings over CKCK Regina." My shows went over well with the listeners, but I was never able to perfect a successful radio catchphrase like most of the disc jockeys of the era. Nothing sounded quite right so I went with the catchphrase that had worked so well for me on the football field, "Lookie, lookie, lookie, here comes Cookie."

I enjoyed being on the radio and thought that the experience would be helpful once I retired from football, but was well aware that I was only offered the opportunity because of what I had done on the football field. It was a win-win situation as far as I was concerned, because I used the radio station for post-football employment experience and they used my name to draw listeners.

The Roughriders closed out the season with a 29-14 win over the Edmonton Eskimos, giving us a 7-7-2 regular season record. In the final game, Eskimos halfback Johnny Bright secured the League rushing title with a then-record 1722 rushing yards for the season. I finished a distant second with 1254 rushing yards, but felt that if I was going to take a back seat to anyone, I was glad it was a player that I respected like Johnny Bright.

Johnny had played college football at Drake University and was the earliest mobile black quarterback I could remember, and the precursor to modern-day running quarterbacks like Randall Cunningham and Michael Vick. In college and later in the CFL, Johnny was a scoring machine and one of the first black players that I could recall having his name mentioned as a candidate for the Heisman Trophy.

A game that Drake played in on October 21, 1951, against Oklahoma A&M would become known as the "Johnny Bright Incident." In that game Johnny entered the game leading the NCAA in total offense and was targeted and savagely attacked by the Oklahoma players, often well after the plays were over. He was knocked unconscious three times in the first ten minutes of the game, suffering a broken jaw. Johnny stayed in the game for a few more plays following the broken jaw, even completing a 61-yard touchdown pass. Drake lost the game 28-14 and it was the first time in three years that Johnny had not compiled at least 100 all-purpose yards in a game.

The courage that Johnny showed by continuing to get back up despite the vicious punishment he was taking moved me beyond words. A news reporter named Bob Spiegel photographed the hits Johnny suffered and documented the fact that they all came well after the plays had ended. Spiegel's graphic photographs of the event won him the Pulitzer Prize and showed the violence that men would do just because of the color of someone's skin. That game would lead the NCAA to institute the use of face masks on helmets and would make several types of blocks illegal, but more importantly, the game showed the ugly side of racism to a large-scale audience.

Johnny was drafted by the Philadelphia Eagles as the fifth overall pick in the first round of the 1952 NFL draft, but chose to instead play in Canada because he was unsure how he would be accepted by a lot of the southern players that now made up the NFL. One of the best all-around football players had been exiled from his home country due to the racism he had seen up close and personal during his college career.

Johnny Bright would be one of the best players I ever played against and would be one of the players that I aspired to be like both on and off the field.

The Roughriders met the Edmonton Eskimos the following week in the Western Playoff Semi-Finals, which was a best-two-out-of-three game format. On consecutive Saturdays the Eskimos defeated the Roughriders by scores of 27-11 and 31-1.

The Winnipeg Blue Bombers were the eventual Western Division Champion and met my former team the Hamilton Tiger-Cats for the 1958 Grey Cup Title. Winnipeg won the Grey Cup by defeating the Tiger-Cats with a final score of 35-28.

Prior to the game Hamilton coach Jim Trimble predicted that the Tiger-Cats would handily defeat Winnipeg. Winnipeg player Bob Hobert was quoted in the newspaper following the Bomber's win saying, "Trimble's big mouth gave us the incentive to win."

I had called a number of my former Tiger-Cats teammates to wish them luck in the game and felt bad that they had lost, but had no such feelings for Tiger-Cats management. Trimble's public guarantee of a Grey Cup win was one of the first cases I could recall of a team publicly slighting an opponent in the press and thereby supplying an additional incentive to win. Today teams call this supplying an opponent with "bulletin board material" and it comes in many forms now that players and coaches can release information instantaneously on the Internet using social media platforms like Facebook and Twitter.

I can't imagine the trouble I would have gotten into if while I was playing I had been able to immediately release a thought or opinion to the entire world. Despite the trouble I might have found myself in, I definitely would have had more followers than Chad Johnson or whatever he calls himself now.

My final statistics for the season were some of the best of my career. I finished with 1254 yards on 235 attempts for a 5.3 yards per attempt average and added five touchdowns. The fact that I placed second in the league in kickoff average and fifth in returning kicks showed how I was becoming a better all-round football player under the continued direction of coach Terlep. My total points for the season were down from 54 the previous season to 30, but the rest of my statistics were now among the league leaders. The end of the season also brought a Western All-Star designation as the team's halfback.

Even though I enjoyed playing for coach Terlep as a member of the Roughriders, the fact that I was separated from my family had become too much of a distraction. Following the season, I met with coach Terlep and explained that for the benefit of my family I needed to play back in the Big Four of the East. While meeting with the coach I made sure to let him know how much I appreciated his friendship and how much he helped me progress as a player.

Coach Terlep worked out a trade with the Toronto Argonauts general manager Lew Hayman where I would be awarded to Toronto, and the Roughriders would receive Tex Schreider and four other players in return. Playing for the Argonauts would allow me to live with my family year-round and would also bring me back to the familiar surroundings of Toronto and the Big Four Division.

Once the trade was completed with the league I made my way back home with a smile on my face, not just because I was going home to Gwen and young Jeffrey, but also because I would now play for the Toronto Argonauts on the grandest stage in Canada.

The fact that Cookie was back playing in the Big Four would now pit him against his former team the Hamilton Tiger-Cats on a regular basis. Tiger-Cats general manager Jake Gaudaur had hoped to keep Cookie out of their division when they traded him away to Saskatchewan in the Western Division.

It would have benefited coach Terlep to keep Cookie in Saskatchewan for many reasons. The coach had invested time and effort developing Cookie into an elite player, and it would have been in his best interest to keep Cookie on the Roughriders. The Roughriders had also paid $5000 to the Tiger-Cats in the original trade for Cookie, with a provision agreeing that if the Roughriders kept him under contract for at least two seasons, they would receive a $2500 refund from The Tiger-Cats. That was Jake Gaudaur's financial incentive to Roughrider management to keep Cookie from competing against the Tiger-Cats in the Big Four.

But, being a fair man, coach Terlep did what he felt was in the best interest of Cookie and his family by trading him to Toronto. Cookie was excited to be getting a chance to play in the biggest media market in Canada, and hoped he would be able to finish his career in his adopted hometown. However, Cookie would now be dealing with Toronto Argonauts general manager Lew Hayman, and he would soon realize that coach Terlep's gentlemanly approach to matters was the exception and not the rule of professional football.

Back in the Big Four

Cookie's trade to Toronto in 1959 brought him back home to his family and to the Big Four of the Eastern Division. Cookie had been an All-Star while playing for the Tiger-Cats in the Big Four, but was now returning with another year of experience and the overwhelming desire to show how far he had progressed during his time out west. This was going to be Cookie's breakout year and his first chance to set down roots both professionally and personally.

I was excited that I was going to be playing for the Argonauts in 1959 and now had the opportunity to play with fellow running back and All-Star Dick Shatto. The Argonauts had not been all that competitive prior to my arrival, but I hoped the new pairing of Shatto and me in the Argonauts' backfield was going to be enough to turn the team around.

The Argonauts were owned by media mogul John Bassett, but were clearly run by general manager Lew Hayman. Anything football-related had to run through Hayman, who had been brought in to make the Argonauts into a winning franchise.

Prior to coming to the Argonauts in 1956, Hayman had founded the Montréal Alouettes of the CFL, and in addition to being part owner, also acted as the team's general manager and coach. The Alouettes had won only one Grey Cup title during Hayman's nine-year reign, but they always fielded a competitive team. Under Hayman, the Alouettes were the first CFL team to break the color barrier when the team signed Al Trawick, a black lineman from Kentucky State University. Many considered him a progressive football mind because in addition to the Trawick signing, he was also the first to suggest televising CFL games, playing night games, and playing games on Sundays.

When I arrived in Toronto I viewed Hayman as a forward-thinking person based on his previous track record. I hoped that we would have the same type of open working relationship that I had shared with coach Terlep in Saskatchewan.

The head coach for the 1959 season was Hampton Pool, who previously coached the Los Angeles Rams. During his tenure with the Rams he had an outstanding winning percentage going 23-10-2, but resigned in December of 1954 over disputes with his players and amid allegations of dirty play from his team. He came to the CFL in 1957 and along with Hayman was trying to turn the Argonauts around.

In the preseason we faced the Chicago Cardinals of the NFL in an exhibition game on August 5, 1959. The game was played at CNE Stadium, and this was the first season that the Argonauts would call CNE Stadium home. Later CNE would become known for its poor weather conditions due to its proximity to Lake Ontario and be called "The Mistake by the Lake."

We jumped out to an early and unexpected 13-1 lead under the play calling of our quarterback Ronny Knox. The size and speed of Chicago became too much to handle after we lost several first-string players to injury, including Don Caraway and Norm Stoneburgh. The final score of the game was 55-26 with Chicago embarrassing us in front of our home crowd.

We started the 1959 regular season campaign by scraping out a 21-20 win against Ottawa on Ronny Knox's TD passes, but followed that up with three straight losses. On Sunday, September 13, I connected on four field goals against Ottawa, setting a Big Four record for most field goals converted in one game. Dick Shatto added a touchdown, enabling us to secure our second win of the season with a final score of 19-6. We lost the next two games to Ottawa and Hamilton by the scores of 28-1 and 34-17 respectively.

After starting the season 2-5, head coach Hampton Pool was replaced by assistant coach Steve Owen on September 21, 1959. Coach Owen was a former offensive tackle and head coach for the New York Giants. He was known for implementing the A-Formation and Umbrella Defense during his tenure with the Giants and would later be enshrined in the Pro Football Hall of Fame for his accomplishments.

While I did not dislike coach Pool, I preferred the easygoing demeanor of the perpetually tobacco-chewing coach Owen.

The team came out playing hard for coach Owen and we won his first game as head coach with 39-9 victory over Montréal, behind the excellent play of recently acquired quarterback Al Dorow. The next week we won for the second week in a row with a 37-14 win over Montréal. In that game I rushed for two touchdowns and finished with 19 points for the day after converting a field goal and four points after. Dick Shatto rounded out the Argonauts scoring by adding two touchdowns.

The team was playing loose under coach Owen and even though we still had a losing record at 4-5 we felt confident that we had turned the corner and were now on a winning path.

That feeling was short-lived as we lost our remaining five games, finishing with a final record of 4-10 and out of the playoffs. Coach Owen was not retained following our disappointing end to the 1959 season and was replaced by Michigan State defensive line coach Lou Agase.

I ended the season scoring 75 points and was the leading scorer in the Big Four. To put it into perspective the Argonauts scored a total of 192 points that season and I accounted for 75 of them. I rushed for 496 yards on 87 carries for a 5.7 per attempt average and five touchdowns. My longest run from scrimmage that season was 69 yards, but where I excelled that season was kicking. My 2,105 yards on kickoffs for a 52.6-yard average was good enough for second in the Big Four and I also added nine field goals, 16 points after, and two singles. On defense I added four intercepted passes for an additional 66 yards and was named the Big East halfback on offense.

I had won a scoring title and was now close to home. All seemed to be going well in my life.

Looking back, I continued to stay out late more than I should have, and it started to have a negative effect on my relationship with Gwen. Even though I was living at home I was always looking for an opportunity to go out on the town and play the role of local celebrity, and it would eventually catch up with me.

In addition to Gwen noticing my late nights, Lew Hayman also took an interest in the fact that I would stay out many game nights beyond the team curfew. While I was playing well, he was willing to look the other way or he might make me pay a minimal fine, but eventually he would make an issue of it once my production declined slightly.

The 1960 season would bring the Argonauts back to respectability and also mark the start of the Lou Agase coaching era. Agase being a new coach and not quite comfortable with his new position would often defer to Lew Hayman's experience. This included how best to handle me on and off the field.

In the preseason, coach Agase told me that we were going to become a more pass-oriented team, and that would require me to pass block instead of running the ball. I was told that in addition to playing fullback I would also continue to kick, play linebacker, and fill in at defensive tackle from time to time.

At first I thought that playing in a pass-first offense would hurt my personal statistics and damage my ability to negotiate a new contract at the end of the year, but behind the arm of former NFL quarterback Tobin Rote, the Argonauts were about to have a breakout season.

Once again we were slated to play a home exhibition game against an NFL team. This season the Pittsburgh Steelers came into CNE stadium on

August 3, 1960. Once again we were overmatched by the NFL talent and lost by a final score of 43-16. I was able to score a touchdown in the third quarter, but by that point the game had already been decided.

Most of the team questioned even having these exhibition games because we were now embarrassed two years in a row and lost several players to injuries all for a meaningless exhibition game. Tobin Rote injured his knee in that game, but luckily was able to play through the injury and started in the regular season opener.

We won our first three games based on the passing ability of Tobin Rote. I was asked to pass block and give him the time he needed to find the open receiver. He was throwing the ball all over the place and passing for multiple touchdowns in every game. As long as we were winning, I was happy doing my part and the fact that our opponents now expected our team to pass first made my ability to run the ball easier. They would now be caught off guard when I would take a hand-off from Rote, and my season average of 7.5 yards per carry was a clear indication that the entire offense was benefiting from this new play-calling system.

During one game that season, I scored the most unusual touchdown of my career. Rote handed the ball off to me and I broke a couple of tackles around the line of scrimmage and was now looking for the end zone. An opposing defensive player tried one more tackle in the secondary, and instead of tackling me, he ripped off my pants. I continued running in all my glory until I crossed the goal line and even celebrated the score for a few moments before realizing that I needed to make my way to the locker room for a new pair of pants.

Week four brought a game against my old team the Hamilton Tiger-Cats. In that game I led all scorers with 18 points on two touchdowns, three point-after conversions and a field goal. Rote continued to throw touchdowns and we won by a final score of 32-21 and were now 4-0 and in first place.

Over the next few weeks we were up and down, but consecutive loses to Ottawa early in the season put us into a first-place tie with them, with both teams having identical 6-2 records entering week eight.

On October 1, 1960, Tobin Rote exploded for a then-record seven touchdown passes against Montréal, securing a 50-15 win. Dick Shatto scored on three of Rote's passes, and Dave Mann, Boyd Carter, Ed Ochiena, and I scored the others.

Our loss on October 10 against Hamilton, in which I was ejected from the game for fighting with Hamilton defensive back Harry Lunn, put us back into a first place tie with Ottawa. I easily outweighed Lunn by 70 pounds, but he repeatedly made what I felt were cheap shots during the game and I hauled off and threw a punch. We both were ejected and I hoped that my ejection and the subsequent loss by the team would not haunt us at the end of the season. The fact that we were now contenders was big news in Toronto and we were no longer considered the easy win on the schedule.

The rest of the way was going to be a battle. We entered the twelfth game of the season still tied with Ottawa for first place with an 8-3 record. The next two games we would face Ottawa at home and then away. In the home game we won 37-13 in front of a sold-out CNE Stadium and were led by Rote's three touchdown passes, but I capped the game with a 59-yard touchdown run.

The following week in Ottawa we were dismantled by a final score of 38-1. Now that we had split the home and home series, we were going to enter the final week of the season tied at 9-3, with the division title on the line.

Entering the last week of the season, we had a home game against Montréal. Prior to the game, I stood up in the locker room and told the team that we had a chance to be the best in the division and that I was not going to pass up this opportunity. The team came out on fire, and Rote threw another seven touchdowns while I set a team record by scoring 27 points in the game. The final score was 63-27, but despite scoring 27 points Montréal never had a chance against our fired-up squad.

My old team the Tiger-Cats defeated Ottawa by a final score of 26-24 on a late field goal block and helped us secure first place in the Big Four and a first round playoff bye.

In the Eastern Finals we were again matched up against Ottawa. The two best teams from the East met for the right to play for the Grey Cup, but unfortunately Ottawa had our number. We lost on consecutive November Saturdays by scores of 33-21 and 21-20, giving Ottawa the series by a final of 54-41. Ottawa went on to defeat the Western Champion Edmonton Eskimos for the 1960 Grey Cup Title by a score of 16-6.

At the end of the season I was the runner-up to Jackie Parker for the League MVP. I was named to the 1960 Eastern offensive team at halfback and to the defensive team as a linebacker. This was the first time that I was honored by the league on both offense and defense. The 115 points I scored led the entire CFL, and I rushed for 662 yards on 88 carries with the longest being 74 yards. I also caught 25 passes for 346 yards with the longest being 42 yards.

Many people were unaware that I was nearsighted and always wore glasses off the field, but when I played I wore nothing to correct my vision. A lot of those passes came at me as a blur, but I was able to haul them in. My season scoring was rounded out by kicking five field goals, 43 point-after conversions and nine singles. On defense I intercepted one pass and returned it 16 yards while amassing numerous tackles, which were not yet kept as a statistic.

I was disappointed that we had not won the Grey Cup, especially bearing in mind the terrific seasons that Tobin Rote and I had. He had thrown for a then-record 38 touchdowns and was the second CFL player to ever pass for over 4000 yards in a season. I had led the CFL in points and had also set an Argonauts record with 27 points in one game. These accomplishments were not enough for the Grey Cup, but this was the first time that the Argonauts had finished in first place since 1937.

During the season Gwen told me that we were expecting our second child late that spring and I was very excited. I had my best season since arriving in Canada and thought that I was in a prime spot to negotiate the biggest contract of my career. The new American Football League had just started play in 1960 and they appeared to be more open toward race issues. I thought this might give me additional bargaining power in the contract negotiations. Lew Hayman knew that the NFL would not offer me a contract due to my interracial marriage, but he could not be so sure about the AFL. They were playing to survive against the established NFL and needed to put the best product on the field. They could not be so concerned with issues regarding race if they wanted to survive. The AFL owners were starting to recruit from predominately black schools and were willing to think outside the box, while the NFL owners laughed at their actions and assumed that the AFL would eventually fold due to lack of interest. The CFL and NFL owners would now have more competition for the best football talent, and athletes would have additional opportunities to choose where they would play and how much they would be paid.

May 7, 1961, would bring the arrival of a second healthy baby boy, Scott Richard Gilchrist. Our family was living well in Toronto, but I had made several poor business decisions and was looking for a big contract to help get myself out of the financial hole I had created. The Argonauts had a contract option for the 1961 season, but I wanted a multi-year deal to secure my financial future and to also secure a permanent home base for my family.

I had leaked to the press that I was willing to play out my option with Toronto and would then move on to another team. Never before had that tact worked, as any player who had played out an option was never offered a contract from a competing team. This was because there was an unwritten rule among all professional football team owners that you don't go after a player that played out a contract option with another team. Ottawa linebacker Larry Hayes played out his option and was coveted by other teams, but in a show of solidarity no other team dared to offer him a contract. By having this unwritten rule, the owners could in effect prevent what would be free agency and keep their players bound to them like slaves. I knew I was playing a dangerous game of chicken with Lew Hayman, but hoped that my excellent play on the field would force another team to make an offer.

In July of 1961, I came to terms with Lew Hayman on a five-year agreement where I would be paid an average salary of $20,000 per year. I had originally asked for slightly less money guaranteed, but also wanted a percentage of the food and merchandise concessions, as well as ticket sales. Hayman refused and said that if they paid me those percentages, I would own the team before long. I joked that I was okay with that and added that as long as I owned the team he would always have a job. He somehow did not see the humor in my comment and I signed off on the team's five-year offer. At that time it was one of the largest and longest contracts in CFL history. The contract gave me a sense of security that I had not felt during my previous seasons within the league. I thought the contract signified that I would finish out my career in Toronto and we would annually compete for the Grey Cup Title.

The 1961 pre-season brought another exhibition game against the NFL's Cardinals, who had relocated from Chicago to St. Louis. On August 2, 1961, the two teams met in Toronto and we lost for the third year in a row by a score of 36-7. The stadium was packed, even though it was a pre-season game, with many fans looking to see former CFL super star Sam Etcheverry who was now suiting up for the Cardinals at quarterback.

Our quarterback Tobin Rote had injured his hand in the prior pre-season game, and coach Agase was forced to use backup quarterbacks Nobby Wirkowski and John Henry Jackson in his place. Wirkowski was the backup quarterback, but was also working as an assistant coach. He had not planned on playing in that game, and dressed in slacks for his role as a coach. Agase, worried that we would again have a horrible showing against the NFL, asked Wirkowski to suit up and play quarterback.

During the game Wirkowski was being tackled by a Cardinals lineman and tried to straighten his leg so he would not fall in an awkward position. Unfortunately, I had been knocked down during the same play and pinned Wirkowski's leg in that awkward position, tearing his knee ligaments and putting an end to his playing career. Every player that has ever suited up knows the dangers of playing the game and that your career could end on the next play, but we all assume that it will never happen to us. The fact that I inadvertently contributed to the end of Wirkowski's career bothered me greatly and followed me as a constant reminder of how quickly it all could end.

I continued to do what I always did, and that was play hard on and off the football field. For years I was known to roll out of bed just prior to practices and games, but always gave it my all on the field. Now that the team was coming off a winning season, some of my teammates started to follow my lead, and our team became known as a bunch of late-night playboys who frequented Toronto's bistros.

While in the past my late nights and late arrivals to practice were just considered by team management the cost of doing business with "Cookie Gilchrist," the thought of having a team full of players that followed my lead was more than coach Agase and general manager Lew Hayman could bear. The easiest way to get everyone in line would be to make an example of me. As the season went on I was repeatedly fined and unflattering information was leaked to the newspapers by team management.

Hayman and Agase were well aware of who I was and the way I operated when they signed me to the contract extension. I felt betrayed when they all of a sudden had a problem with me. The same way that they had looked the other way when I showed up late, either due to a late night out or an off-the-field business commitment, I looked the other way with some of the less-than-gracious treatment I received from team management, which I felt was directly related to race.

Black players were treated better in Canada, but we were still treated differently. At team hotels we had to share rooms with other black players. At the time blacks and whites did not share rooms and this often prompted teams to have an even number of black players, as players were two to a room on the road. The even number would keep them from having to pay for a room for only one black player and would keep them from having to even consider rooming a black and a white player together.

At different times I had also felt that I was taken out of games in favor of white teammates to give the white players the opportunity to score. Early in my career I did my best to break off long runs for touchdowns, as I feared that I would be pulled out of the game for a white player once we were within scoring distance. Star players like Johnny Bright and I forced the CFL to deal with the issue of race, and our talent could not be ignored, but I felt if they had to choose between a black player and a white player of equal talent, they would always choose the white player. Many general managers or coaches, including Hayman and Agase, would have their favorite players or personal reasons for playing one player over another. My play to that point had dictated that I would play over these allegiances or personal feeling, but that would all change during the 1961 season. While the issue of race was not as overt in Canada, it was still there lying just below the surface.

Tobin Rote, Dick Shatto, Dave Mann, and I were expected to anchor the Argonauts' offense in 1961 and we were looking to bring the team a Grey Cup Title. The season did not start off as expected and we lost our first two games of the season. Entering the third game against Montréal, I did my best to end our losing streak by scoring a rushing touchdown and adding three field goals. We won the game by a final score of 15-10, and I hoped that we would now go on an extended winning streak.

The 1961 season would prove to be an up-and-down season with alternating weeks of wins and losses. The team started to get some bad press saying that we preferred to be out on the town instead of on the field. Our team was extremely talented, but we now gained a reputation in the press of mailing it in and having lapses where we seemed almost disinterested in the games we were playing in.

Following a 37-10 loss against Hamilton, our team was now 5-5-1 on the season and playing well below where we should be, considering the team's talent level. The week prior to the next game, coach Agase called me into his office and told me that I was only going to be playing on defense for the rest of the season.

Up to that point I had rushed for 709 yards on 105 carries for a 6.7-yard per attempt average. I had scored 41 points on three touchdowns, five point-after conversions, five field goals and three singles. My numbers had been among the league leaders and despite my abbreviated season on offense I would finish 11th in the East in scoring.

Agase told me that he was going to feature the two other running backs on offense, Bobby Kuntz and Dick Shatto, and that I would best serve the team on defense. I was already playing both offense and defense and felt that I was removed from offense for a different reason. Kuntz and Shatto were both white and the thought that I was removed due to the color of my skin did come to mind. Shatto was a gifted athlete and would play no matter what color his skin was, but the move to feature Kuntz puzzled me. Kuntz was a good player, but I had just won two scoring titles and felt that the team had ulterior motives for my demotion. Not wanting to make waves, I accepted my defensive assignment and went about helping the team prepare for the next game.

On October 21, 1961, prior to our game against Ottawa, I stood up in the locker room and talked to the team about turning the season around and bringing home a Grey Cup Title. During my speech I threatened to kick the asses of any player that did not hold up their end on the field. Putting the team first, I made sure to speak with Kuntz in the locker room and gave him my full support, even though he had replaced me on offense.

Rote and Kuntz led the scoring that day, giving the Argonauts a 21-7 win. We split the last two games of the season, but our final record of 7-6-1 secured us a spot in the Eastern Playoffs.

On November 11, 1961, we met Ottawa in the Eastern Playoff Semi-Final and behind a world-class performance by Tobin Rote came away with a 43-19 victory. Rote passed for four touchdowns and added two rushing touchdowns. We were now set to meet the Hamilton Tiger-Cats in the Eastern Finals with the winner of the series getting the chance to play for the Grey Cup.

On November 18, again behind Rote's passing, we defeated Hamilton by a score of 25-7, but the next week Hamilton beat us handily by a score of 48-2 and secured their chance to play for the Grey Cup Title with a playoff final total score of 55-27. The Tiger-Cats would meet the Winnipeg Blue Bombers the next weekend for the Grey Cup Title. Winnipeg would prove victorious and would celebrate their 21-14 victory in front of the approximately 33,000 fans that attended the game.

The end of the season seemed like a missed opportunity for the Argonauts because we all felt we had the talent to win the Grey Cup. I had put my personal feelings aside when I had been regulated to only playing defense, but the continued articles portraying me as a possible cause of the team's failed season started to weigh on me. Several articles, all from unnamed sources, talked about how I was allegedly late or unprepared for games and insinuated that this was the cause for our team's failures. I knew the unnamed sources were either Hayman or Agase trying to make me the scapegoat, but as long as they continued to pay my contract, I was going to keep my feeling to myself.

At home things were not going well, as I had distanced myself from Gwen. Looking back I realize that I had become caught up in being "Cookie Gilchrist the star football player," and let the adulation go to my head. The newspaper stories that continued to paint me in a poor light made me obsess over the "Cookie Gilchrist" image and for that period of time I was lost in all of the trappings of being a professional athlete.

The off-season would bring about events in American football that would ultimately affect my future. In the first week of December 1961, both the AFL and NFL held their respective drafts. Ernie Davis, the first black Heisman Trophy winner, was drafted by the Buffalo Bills in the first round of the AFL draft and by the Washington Redskins in the NFL draft.

Redskins owner George Preston Marshall, who had refused to sign black players, only considered doing so after the United States government threatened to revoke the Redskins' 30-year lease on their brand new, publicly funded stadium. In response to the government's threats, Marshall made Davis the team's first-round draft pick in an attempt to satisfy the government.

Davis publicly commented that he would never play for Marshall based on his overt racism and forced a trade of his draft rights to the Cleveland Browns. Davis had played at Syracuse and had become friendly with Browns star and Syracuse alum Jim Brown. Davis chose to play for Cleveland and could not pass the chance to reunite with Jim Brown. This opportunity was too much of an incentive for Davis to pass up and more than the Buffalo Bills could offer him. Sadly, Davis would never play professional football, because shortly after being drafted he was diagnosed with leukemia and passed away on May 18, 1963.

The camp for the 1962 season started uneventfully and our team was touted in the press as having the best backfield in Canadian football. High expectations had been placed on our team for the 1962 season, but behind the scenes there were whispers that coach Agase had lost control of the team. Some blamed him for our uneven performance during stretches of the 1961 season and if we started out flat he would be the first to go.

The night before a preseason game, teammate Boyd Carter and I ran into coach Agase in the lobby of the team hotel at 3:00 a.m. Coach Agase did not say a word to either of us, and for the moment I considered it a non-issue that we were out past curfew. Unknowingly, I had given Agase the opportunity to show the team that he was laying down the law for the coming season. What better way to show that he was in charge than to go after the highest-paid and most high-profile player on the team?

Agase went to Lew Hayman and told him that he wanted to place me on waivers for conduct detrimental to the team. At the end of the previous season, the team had relegated me to defense and still had moderate offensive success. I suspected that Hayman was having some buyer's remorse regarding my large contract, which prompted him to agree to Agase's request. Putting me on waivers would let Agase set the tone that there was a new sheriff in town, and Hayman could try to get out from under the four years remaining on my contract. The kicker was that Boyd Carter only received a minimal fine and was never suspended, while I was placed on waivers.

Any team in the league could pick me up for the paltry waiver fee of $350, but I had two things working against me. Most of the other teams could not afford my large contract, but more importantly word had spread that Hayman had blackballed me and no team was going to cross another organization. When the waiver period expired, I found myself not just without a team, but also without a league.

Prior to my being placed on waivers, the AFL had set up a system on how they would fairly divide talent coming from the NFL and CFL. The Buffalo Bills had the rights to any players discarded from the 49ers and Packers of the NFL and from the Argonauts of the CFL. The Los Angeles Rams of the NFL would be the team that would have the first chance to sign me out of the CFL.

The Rams had Ollie Matson as their leading rusher, but were looking for his eventual replacement. Matson was one of the best players to ever grace the gridiron and would become a member of the Pro Football Hall of Fame, but the Rams suspected that he was coming to the end of his career. The assistant coach of the Rams was former Argonauts coach Hampton Pool, who coached me early on in my tenure with the team. Coach Pool advised the Rams management that I was married to a white woman, and that ended any talk of the team making a play for me. Pool was contacted by the press to gauge the Rams' interest, but he stated that while the team was looking for a fullback, he could not recommend me based on disciplinary issues. This was a cover story because they could not publicly say that their decision was based on my interracial marriage.

The Buffalo Bills needed a running back now that they had wasted their first round pick on Ernie Davis. Working in my favor was the fact that one of my coaches from my days in Kitchener, Harvey Johnson, was now working for the Bills as an assistant coach. Harvey told head coach Lou Saban and Bills owner Ralph Wilson that I might be available and sold them on signing me. The Bills were aware of my marital situation, but were having financial trouble and were unsure if they could survive without a winning product on the field. Badly needing to turn the franchise around, the issue of whom I was married to, became a non-factor. What mattered to the Bills was how well I played football and whether I could help the franchise survive.

Once the Bills decided to investigate signing me, they sent Harvey to meet with me to see what my contract demands would be. Harvey and I agreed in principle on a $20,000 contract with a $5,000 signing bonus. If I had a good season, the Bills would also pay me a year-end incentive bonus of $3,000. Harvey negotiated my immediate release from the

Argonauts and the $5,000 signing bonus from the Bills would be used to repay a $5,000 salary advance the Argonauts had given me earlier that summer. I was happy that the Bills had provided me with an opportunity to continue playing football, but still could not understand how the Argonauts could get away with reneging on the remaining four years of my contract. The whole incident left a bad taste in my mouth, but I had landed on my feet and was going to make the most of this new opportunity.

Cookie had attained a not-so-long-ago unthinkable level of stardom and celebrity status for a black man playing professional football. Fans on both sides of the border would forever argue that their league was the one with the most talented players in football. Now fans of the Buffalo Bills and the AFL would see firsthand what those in Canada already knew, and that was that regardless of where he played, Cookie Gilchrist had become one of the best to ever play the game.

Buffalo, get ready, because...lookie, lookie, lookie, here comes Cookie!

Cookie and the Colonel

Throughout his life Cookie was constantly looking for the next great business opportunity. Once his football career started to take off, many doors that normally would have been closed to a man of color in the 1950s were now suddenly opened. Having a public name to trade upon, Cookie wanted to build a business empire that would sustain him once the cheering on the football field ended.

I was always looking for a way to make extra money. During my life I had a few good business ideas, but had many more misses than hits. Once I had my first few dollars burning a hole in my pocket, I looked for a way to expand my finances. I would be ahead of the curve when it came to imagination, but the day-to-day operations were where I'd get into trouble. Some might say that I would get bored with a particular business and let it flounder because I had already become enthralled with a new exciting venture. Looking back, I now think it had more to do with my lack of formal education and my trusting nature. They were my downfall when it came to running a successful business.

My aspirations of running a thriving business started modestly. The first and possibly most profitable business I ever started was a car washing service back in my hometown of Natrona. I started this endeavor with two of my high school teammates as a way for me to help out financially at home. That was a good source of income until I signed my first football contract.

Playing football brought me the opportunity to cross paths with several titans of the business world. This inspired me to expand my own business horizons. Once I started earning some money playing football I started receiving business proposals from family and friends. The enterprises that I owned at different times included a cleaning service, an electrical supply company, and a lighting supply warehouse. On the side of the lighting company vans, I even put the slogan "Lookie, lookie, lookie, here comes Cookie." I used any angle I could to market my businesses and hoped my name would help to promote each of these projects.

I started the cleaning business to handle the cleaning of office buildings. My plan was to add a residential arm to the business when

I noticed that more and more women were leaving the home for the workplace. Regrettably, the business folded due to poor staff and financial management, prior to the implementation of the residential division.

My vagabond lifestyle in professional football brought me to many different locales. In each new community I looked for an opportunity to open a profitable business. During the December holiday season, Buffalo residents would find me running a Christmas tree lot outside of War Memorial Stadium. The Toronto natives could rent binoculars from my stand at Woodbine Racetrack. Each new location brought a new chance at the Brass Ring.

While playing in Buffalo, I brought many of my business ideas to Bills owner Ralph Wilson. I tried to get him to invest in a Buffalo sporting goods store, which I wanted to name Cookie's Closet. As usual he passed on my business proposal. For a man that risked so much starting the fledgling American Football League, I found him to be financially conservative. Wilson, Lamar Hunt, and the other original AFL team owners even started calling themselves members of the "Foolish Club" for taking on the NFL in what originally appeared to be an unwinnable fight. As history would show, the AFL more than held their own in the tug of war for professional football dominance, which ended in a merger of the two leagues.

The one business I was able to convince Wilson to take a small stake in was a mineral mining company I owned with prospector Bill Richardson. I had met Bill in a Hamilton shoe store, where we struck up an unlikely conversation. During our conversation, I was able to draw comparisons between my life and Bill's prospector lifestyle of feast or famine. Bill's mining operation was one of the first to find uranium deposits in Saskatchewan. When Bill offered me a stake in his mining company, I jumped at the offer. He had a supreme confidence about him. If he told you he would find a mine, you had no doubt he would come through.

Wilson made a profitable return on his investment in the company, but soon soured on being in business with me. The last straw was when, instead of being at a Bills press conference to announce my new $30,000 contract, I was jumping out of a helicopter to plant mining stakes in the copper-rich Texas Gulf Sulphur. The Bills were understandably concerned that I disregarded the press conference, but were even more worried that I would be near deep bodies of water. My swimming skills were so bad that it was once said that the Venus de Milo could beat me in a swimming contest. I told the Bills not to worry, because I only go out as far as I can walk. But they had just placed a large financial investment in my football skills and were not amused when I shook off their concerns regarding my health.

I should have followed Wilson's lead and gotten out of the mining business while I was still ahead. The next big claim never came, and in the end my shares in the business were worthless. The one lesson I did learn was that, like a prospector, I could have a million dollars one day and lose it the next, and it was important to stay the same person despite the rises and falls in my fortune.

The press conference incident wasn't the first time I didn't use tact in conducting business. There was one instance when I approached a newspaper in Canada about using my lighting supply service. The purchasing department manager threw me out in a fit of anger upon hearing my business proposal. It took me a few minutes to figure out why this man was so angry, but then it hit me. I had gone to ask for business from a newspaper that I had, a short time earlier, brought legal action against. I had filed a suit for slander and mental anguish after they printed a completely fabricated story about me. The matter was settled out of court for five thousand dollars, and I had considered the matter water under the bridge. The call for security to escort me from the building let me know that they did not. Always pushing the hard sell, I made one last business offer as I was escorted from the building: "How about I come back next week with a proposal for you guys to use my cleaning service?" They passed on that offer, too.

The poor budgeting of my time and my lack of interpersonal skills may have been seen as the cause for my failings in business. The real cause, though, I'd say, was my tendency to overthink a situation, which would lead me down the wrong path on more than one occasion.

While I lived in Hamilton playing for the Hamilton Tiger-Cats of the CFL, I opened a drive-in restaurant called Uncle Tom's Cabin. The restaurant's name was a reference to the anti-slavery novel written by Harriet Beecher Stowe. I was sure the NAACP would not be happy with my choice of the name, but this was also a way for me to make a political statement so everyone would know I wasn't afraid to confront racism head on. But it may not have been the best way to market a family-friendly restaurant.

The main dishes served at the restaurant were barbecue spareribs and fried chicken, both made from family recipes. I should have known that the business would fail when even the grand opening was a comedy of errors. I had paid for local advertising for the opening of the restaurant. The wrong date was given to the public, and a large crowd showed up a week before the scheduled opening date. I had not even finalized the hiring of a cook or waitstaff. There were so many people gathered at the restaurant that I opened the doors and began cooking for the customers myself. I was so happy that everyone enjoyed my food that I forgot to collect for the meals on the first night.

One day I received a visit to the restaurant from a distinguished gentleman dressed in a white suit and a black string tie. He introduced himself as Harland Sanders, but said that I could use the name that his friends called him by, which was Colonel. The reason for the Colonel's visit was that he was trying to get established restaurants to buy into his Kentucky Fried Chicken franchise.

The Colonel told me his story of starting his fried chicken business by cooking at a service station in Kentucky. He said the business prospered, so he expanded into a larger restaurant adjacent to a tourist motel. But then the road he was located on was re-routed to a new interstate, and he lost the majority of his tourist business. This brought the idea for his new business proposal of franchising his recipes into established restaurants around the United States and Canada. The Colonel said that he originally had a larger menu, but a recent overhaul by a new franchisee named Dave Thomas limited the menu to revolve around his fried chicken recipe.

This new business model of specializing in foods that could be made quickly was becoming the rage. The quick turnaround time gave birth to the term "fast food." Dave Thomas would later sell his shares in the Kentucky Fried Chicken franchise and use the proceeds as start up money for a new chain of fast food hamburger restaurants. He would name the restaurants Wendy's after his daughter's nickname. Both Thomas and the Colonel would later become the spokespersons for their respective franchises, which would become part of the billion-dollar fast food industry.

The Colonel asked if he could whip up some of his special-recipe fried chicken in the kitchen. I agreed, and, as everyone knows, that man could make some great fried chicken. At the time, I was concerned by the fact that the Colonel's first restaurant had gone out of business. Though the product was without a doubt spectacular, I chose, for one of the few times in life, to be financially conservative and passed on what would become one of the most lucrative business models in the world.

Most people are lucky to have one brush with a million- dollar opportunity. I was fortunate to have a second such opportunity when I met Preston "Sandy" Fleet. Sandy was the visionary who put photo-developing kiosks in shopping centers. The company he started in the 1960s was called Fotomat and was known for their fast film developing services.

In the 1970s, the gold-topped pyramid of the Fotomat kiosks became as recognizable to consumers as the golden arches of McDonald's.

Sandy had approached me about investing in the business and emphasized the low overhead. He said the costs would be minimal because the kiosks needed very little operating space and only required one employee to man each location. Once again I passed on a great business opportunity when I incorrectly predicted that the idea was a fad that would quickly fade out. In the end, I can say that I was partially correct. It took forty years, but the Fotomat fad eventually ended when they ceased operating in 2009.

One of my last business ventures was The Cookie Gilchrist Carrot Cake Company. The company produced all types of baked goods, but the signature item was my carrot cake recipe. In marketing the company I publicized the fact that all of the products were made using only all natural ingredients. The company did well in the beginning, and the carrot cake recipe drew the attention of one of the largest food companies in the world, General Mills. General Mills offered me a lucrative buyout of the carrot cake recipe, but the deal was contingent on me staying on as a paid spokesman for the product. I have to admit thoughts of being the carrot cake equivalent of what "Famous Amos" was to chocolate chip cookie intrigued me. This could have been a financial windfall for me and would be very welcomed considering that my main source of income was my NFL pension, which maxed out at six hundred and ten dollars a month.

Right before we signed the contracts, General Mills mentioned that they were going to change a few of the ingredients to lessen production costs. These changes included several processed food items, and I could not in good conscience promote the product as all-natural. I was a devout vegetarian and proponent of a diet that included all natural foods. General Mills' insistence on those changes forced me to walk away from the deal. Although I could have used the income from the deal, I felt there was no sum of money that would be worth going against my beliefs.

Without the financing and marketing that the General Mills' deal offered, The Cookie Gilchrist Carrot Cake Company folded. Those around me called me foolish for not taking the deal with General Mills. They said that now that the company had folded I was left with nothing to show for my efforts. Although I wished it had worked out, I was comfortable with my decision and brushed off the criticism. I had received similar criticisms during my life for standing up for my beliefs regarding race, religion, and player's rights, and learned early on that the only person that I needed to answer to was myself. I lived by the rule that I had to do what I felt was right, even if it was not in my own best interest. Unfortunately, not everyone followed that same rule, and most would just go along to get along. This would be my Achilles heel not just in business, but also in all facets of my life.

Time after time, Cookie failed in the world of big business, although it was not from lack of trying. Poor decisions and bad timing led to his downfall as a would-be titan of industry. Those close to Cookie, including his longtime friend and former teammate Booker Edgerson, said that he could have become a very wealthy man just by doing promotional appearances and autograph shows in and around Buffalo. Cookie refused to do "the circuit," as he called it, because he felt that during his football career others had traded upon and profited greatly from using his name and he refused to continue this practice. Often athletes would only make a small fraction of the money that their appearances generated. Cookie felt that if anyone were going to benefit financially from his name and image, it should be him. For most people, being a revered athlete earning money for signing a few autographs would be enough, but he felt that by doing these appearances he was selling out and allowing himself once again to be used. Still, this created an internal struggle because he realized that football and the opportunities associated with the sport would be his best chance at a sustainable income.

Cookie was well aware that he had been blessed with more than one chance at being extremely wealthy. He unknowingly passed on what would become some of the greatest business opportunities of his generation. Yet, until the day he died, Cookie refused to play the game of "What If?" regarding his decisions and he persistently held out hope that the next great opportunity would be just around the corner.

Welcome to the American Football League

Now, for the first time in his professional career, Cookie would finally have his chance to play in the United States. After being forced out of the Canadian Football League, he was going to make the most of this new opportunity playing for the Buffalo Bills in the American Football League. He was on a mission to prove to those in the CFL who so quickly cast him off, as well as to the fans of the AFL, that he was still a force to be reckoned with on the football field.

When I first arrived for Bills training camp in 1962, I took coach Saban by surprise. Coach Saban was new to Buffalo as well, and was doing his best to turn the team into a winning franchise. Despite my negative reputation, which had always preceded me, he agreed to sign me, hoping that my ability to run the ball would give the Bills a potent rushing attack. He planned on pairing me with Wray Carlton in the Bills backfield and would lean on us to provide the majority of the team's offensive output, while he continued to search for a starting-caliber quarterback to lead the team.

I arrived literally at the last minute for training camp. Coach Saban told me he thought I wasn't going to show and had planned on voiding my contract. He said he'd heard stories of me being continually late or not even showing up for practices and told me he wouldn't stand for that type of behavior. This was the first time that I had met the coach, and he wanted to instill in me what he expected from his players. At that first meeting, he also advised me that in addition to playing fullback, I was also going to handle the duties of placekicker as well.

The first game I would play in a Buffalo Bills uniform would be a preseason game against the New York Titans, who would later be renamed the Jets. The game was held at Bowens Field in New Haven, Connecticut. Prior to leaving our training camp facility I drew the wrath of coach Saban for my chosen attire for the trip. I had dressed rather casually in a nice pair of shorts and a collared short sleeve shirt, but was informed by the coach that he required players to wear shirts and ties. My free-spirit type of lifestyle now needed curtailing if I wanted to make the most of the opportunity the Bills had given me. Once I changed into the attire required by coach Saban, we left for New Haven.

In the locker room before the start of the game I was trying to get everyone going. I was telling my new teammates that despite it being a preseason game we needed to set the tone for the season. The crazy looks I was getting from my new teammates told me that they could care less about what I had to say and it was then that I realized that I needed to lead by example. I made my point when I kicked off to start the game and proceeded to run down the field, knocking down three defenders before making the solo tackle. After that I gained my teammates' attention; they knew I could back up my brash and bold comments.

To be honest, I had not yet learned many of the plays in the playbook and relied on a play called 34-slide/35-slide. This was a straight hand-off to me where I looked for running room between the guard and tackle. Every time we entered the huddle I would ask to run that play again because if we called something else I might be out of position due to my unfamiliarity with the playbook.

At halftime I put the scare of his life into coach Saban and took my teammates off guard as well. When we entered the locker room for the half I stripped down naked to take a shower. My teammates were unsure why I was walking around the locker room in my birthday suit and ran to tell the coach. In a panic coach Saban came running into the shower and said, *"Cookie, I don't know what they do in Canada, but here in America we play two halves of football."*

But this was a ritual I had maintained throughout my career because I hated being sweaty and dirty and would change into clean clothes between the halves. Something told me it would take some time for coach Saban and I to get accustomed to each other, if at all. We won the game by a final score of 20-10 over the Titans, but the game would forever be remembered by my new teammates for my unexpected striptease.

During the preseason we had a game scheduled against the Houston Oilers in Mobile, Alabama. This would be my first time south of the Mason-Dixon Line and I felt very uneasy about the trip. When the team arrived in Mobile, the white players were dropped off at one hotel and the other Negro players and I were then taken to a colored hotel.

Coach Saban had spoken with rookie defensive back Booker Edgerson regarding the segregation issue. Even though Booker was a rookie, he had been recruited and coached by Saban at Western Illinois and they seemed to have a father-son type of relationship. Booker said that coach Saban relayed the fact that he had no problem if we refused to play due to the way we were being treated, but that we all needed to stick together. This was an all-or-nothing proposition to protect individual players from retaliation. If one person voted to play, then we all needed to play. One of the other players did vote to play, fearing that he would be cut from the team if he were part of an insurrection, forcing the rest of us to play the game as scheduled.

While we waited at our hotel for Eddie Abramoski, the team trainer, to arrive in order to prepare us for the game, we stood around discussing how unfair we felt the situation was. When Eddie arrived, Tom Day yelled out "Get Whitey" sarcastically. Eddie turned pale as a ghost. I approached him and told him not to worry, they wouldn't bother him. Tom later told Eddie that he would not have let anything happen to him, but looking back, there were other Negroes staying at the hotel who could have taken Tom's sarcastic battle cry seriously.

We won the game by a final score of 21-14 behind a two-touchdown performance by quarterback Warren Rabb. The win was overshadowed by the open discrimination that was still going on in the south. I didn't see one face of color in the sideline stands. The Negroes were only allowed to view the game from behind the end zones while the white fans lined the prime sideline seats.

We finished the preseason with a record of 3-1 after a win in our final preseason contest against the Boston Patriots. It appeared that coach Saban had the team moving in the right direction, but the quarterback position was still an area in question. The team had recently acquired Al Dorow to compete with Warren Rabb for the starting quarterback position, but neither appeared to be the long-term solution. We would have to rely on our ground attack to provide offense and on our-up-and coming defense to keep the games within reach.

After training camp broke, I made arrangements to share a three-bedroom apartment with teammates Booker Edgerson and Monte Crocket. I purchased all the furniture for the apartment, except for their bedroom sets. For the time being, Gwen and the boys were staying in Toronto and I was commuting back and forth to see them. My roommates often joked that they reaped the benefits of my lavish tastes in decorating because I spent more time in Toronto than in my new Buffalo apartment. Things had not been going well at home due to my constant nights out and my being wrapped up in the celebrity that playing professional football afforded me. Living on my own and continually roaming the Buffalo nightlife did not improve the situation between Gwen and me.

The Bills opened the regular season on September 9, 1962, at home against the two-time AFL Champion Houston Oilers. The Oilers were known for their high-powered offense, which was led by quarterback

George Blanda, receiver Charlie Hennigan, and running back Billy Cannon. Al Dorow started at quarterback for the Bills and was quickly replaced by Warren Rabb after he threw three interceptions. This would be the start of a quarterback carousel for the Bills that lasted throughout the 1962 season.

The Oilers offense led by Hennigan's 145-yards receiving and two touchdowns proved too much to handle. I scored my first points as a Buffalo Bill by kicking a 40-yard field goal in the first quarter, but the Oilers left War Memorial stadium with a 28-23 victory.

The following week we had another home game against the Western Division Denver Broncos. I had not made my presence felt during the Oilers game and wanted to set the tone early against the Broncos. In the first quarter we ran a sweep play and I was able to break several tackles before rumbling in for a 42-yard touchdown. Gene Mingo of the Broncos kicked a 29-yard field goal in the first quarter to put Denver on the scoreboard. Gene and I were the only black placekickers in the league, which was a position that historically few Negroes played.

This game was a tale of two halves. The Bills dominated the first half and entered the locker room with a 20-3 lead. In addition to my rushing touchdown I added an 18-yard receiving touchdown thrown by Al Dorow. The Broncos defense came out in the second half and shut us out on offense. My former Saskatchewan teammate Frank Tripuka led the Broncos offense at quarterback and had a dazzling two-touchdown performance in the second half, including a 96-yard pass to receiver Al Frazier. The Broncos put up 20 unanswered points in the second half and left Buffalo with a 23-20 victory, dropping the Bills to 0-2 on the season. I had rushed for 131 yards in the game and set the Bills single-game rushing record, which I would break several times during my career in Buffalo.

We fared no better in the third game of the season against the New York Titans, who beat us by a final score of 17-6. The fans of Buffalo were in an uproar over the team being 0-3. They were quickly growing impatient with coach Saban's plan to turn the franchise around. Al Dorow had another less than stellar performance in the game, but we would soon find our quarterback of the future.

Jack Kemp, who was the San Diego Chargers starting quarterback, had dislocated the middle finger in his throwing hand during a September 16 game against the Titans. Kemp finished the game fearing that if he left the field he might lose his starting position to his back-up John Hadl. Once the game was over Kemp's hand required medical treatment and it was determined that he would be sidelined for several weeks.

When he had his finger set by the team physician, he brought along a football so the finger could be set in the position needed to properly grip the ball. For the rest of his life Kemp could remember his playing days just by looking at his finger, which became fused at the knuckle.

The Chargers coach Sid Gillman tried to pull a fast one on the rest of the league and placed Kemp on the waiver list on Friday September 21, in order to activate another player for the Chargers game the next day. Gillman hoped no other team would realize that Kemp was available, allowing Gillman to recall him from the waiver list following the September 22 game. Gillman either forgot the rules or thought no one would notice, because there was a rule that a team couldn't put someone on waivers the night prior to a game and then recall him: it was considered manipulating the schedule. The Bills by virtue of our 0-3 record were awarded Kemp's services for the waiver fee of one hundred dollars and we had now secured our quarterback of the future.

The fourth game of the season was our first game on the road and brought us to the Cotton Bowl to face the Dallas Texans. The Texans were owned by Lamar Hunt, who would soon move the franchise to Kansas City and rename them the Chiefs. The game was a Texans blowout led by running back Abner Haynes, who rushed for 164 yards and added touchdown scores of 71 and 13 yards. I added a short six-yard rushing score early in the fourth quarter, but the final score of Texans 41 and the Bills 21 was an embarrassment to coach Saban and the entire Bills organization. The day following the game, coach Saban traded or let go several players in an effort to shake things up. The Bills quarterback combination of Dorow and Rabb accounted for only one touchdown and three interceptions. As far as the team was concerned, Kemp couldn't heal fast enough.

We continued our road trip and for the second time that season faced the Houston Oilers, but this time we played on their home field, Jeppesen Stadium. In that game we dominated the Oilers for a majority of the game, but as time was running down, a rushing touchdown I scored was waived off. This was because the official alleged that our quarterback never got the play off before the play clock had expired.

After the game the officials would acknowledge their mistake, but it didn't change the outcome of an Oiler victory by a score of 17-14. We were now 0-5 and licking our wounds on the long trip back to Buffalo.

On October 13, 1962, we played a home game against the San Diego Chargers. I was sure that Sid Gillman was still upset over losing Jack Kemp and would have loved nothing better than to stick it to us. Probably sensing that Kemp was waiting in the wings, Warren Rabb had his best game playing quarterback for the Bills passing for 144 yards and scores of 19, 76, and seven yards. Wayne Crow and I each rushed for over 100 yards and a score, while I also accounted for a receiving touchdown as well. Our offense exploded that day and carried us to a 35-10 victory over the Chargers for our first win of the season.

The next week we improved to 2-5 with a 14-6 victory at War Memorial over the Oakland Raiders. I led the Bills offense that day with 143 yards rushing and a seven-yard rushing touchdown. My teammates and I were now starting to click on offense and the results could clearly be seen on the field. The Bills were becoming a team that demanded respect.

We now flew to Denver to play the Broncos in what was an offensive shoot-out. Quarterback Frank Tripuka paced the Broncos with five touchdown passes, but I countered with 165 yards from scrimmage. I also added two rushing touchdowns and a 33-yard field goal. The Bills won by a score of 45-38 and now had a three-game winning streak.

I will forever remember this western road trip for an incident that happened in Denver when we received our payroll checks. Although no one on the team ever had trouble with payroll checks issued by the Bills, there were stories of other franchises bouncing their employees' paychecks. Just to be safe, as soon as we received our checks we decided to head over to a local bank in Denver to cash them. I went over to the bank with Booker and some of my other teammates and we approached the bank manager about cashing the checks. The manager agreed to cash all the checks except mine because the amount of my check was too much for the bank to risk in case the check bounced.

Once I learned they wouldn't cash my check, I told Booker that the drinks were on him. This was the only time Booker let me get away with crying poverty.

On November 3, 1962, we played the Boston Patriots at War Memorial Stadium, which eventually ended in a 28-28 tie. We started the scoring early in the first quarter when I rushed for a two-yard touchdown, which I also kicked the extra point for. The game was a back-and-forth struggle throughout, and I finished the afternoon with another 100-yard rushing performance and added two more touchdowns to my season total.

We were now embarking on a three-game road trip that would take us to San Diego, Oakland, and Boston. In San Diego we came away with a 40-20 victory over the Chargers behind the play of Wray Carlton and Warren Rabb. Wray had 90 yards rushing and two touchdowns, and Rabb added touchdown passes of 68 and 12 yards. I added a rushing touchdown and two field goals to round out the scoring.

In Oakland Jack Kemp finally made his first appearance as a Buffalo Bill. He came into the game in the third quarter in relief of Rabb. Kemp threw a six-yard touchdown pass to Wayne Crow and immediately made his presence felt. The Bills won the game 10-6 and I finished with 103 yards rushing for my fourth 100-yard rushing game of the season.

Entering the twelfth game of the season against the Patriots, we had a record of 5-5-1 and had finally reached the .500 mark. Kemp started his first game for the Bills and accounted for the only Bills touchdown of the day when he rushed in for a six-yard score. I sprained my ankle early in the game and was unable to continue, which severely hindered our rushing attack. The Patriots were led to a 21-10 victory by their back-up quarterback Tom Yewcic, who accounted for 231 yards passing and three touchdowns. The defeat dropped us to 5-6-1 and removed us from any chance at making the playoffs.

December 2, 1962, would be Kemp's first home game as the Bills' starting quarterback. We were facing the Dallas Texans, and were looking to avenge the embarrassing loss we suffered against them earlier in the season. Kemp did not disappoint the War Memorial crowd, passing for 248 yards and throwing two touchdown passes. I added 132 yards from scrimmage, rushing for one touchdown and kicking a 37-yard field goal. We handed the Texans a 23-14 loss and were now back at .500.

Entering the last game of the season against the New York Titans at the Polo Grounds, we had a chance to finish the season with a winning record. Prior to the game I made it known to my teammates that I fiercely wanted to win this one and set the tone for next season. Throughout the game I was trying to fire everyone up on the sideline and did my best to lead on the field. I finished the day with 143 yards rushing and two rushing touchdowns of 42 and 30 yards. I also added field goals of 42 and 27 yards. We dominated the Titans and finished the game with a 20-3 win and a final season record of 7-6-1.

The Buffalo Bills had finished the season with a winning record, but more importantly, we had come together as a team. Better days were ahead for us.

Following the game, I was informed that I had won the league rushing title with 1096 yards rushing, and I was the first player in league history to eclipse 1000 yards in a season. I led the league in several statistical categories including rushing touchdowns (13), and rushing yards per game, with a 78.3-yard per game average. Gino Cappelletti of the Boston Patriots and I tied for second place in the league in total points with 128 each.

The Associated Press and United Press International both named me player of the year, and I was also honored as an Eastern Division All-Star.

I knew something special was happening in Buffalo and was glad I was a part of it. We now had a powerful core of players and hoped that the 1963 season would bring the franchise's first playoff appearance.

My bond with my teammates had become strong during the 1962 season, and the friendships I started with Booker and Kemp would last the rest of our lives.

Cookie hit the ground running when he joined the American Football League and continued his dominance on the gridiron without skipping a beat. He had become a box-office draw for the Buffalo Bills and the first marquee star of the AFL. The Bills were now on their way to becoming one of the most dominant franchises in the AFL, but an alleged traffic infraction in the off-season would soon jeopardize all that Cookie and the team had worked for.

The People of the State of New York v. Cookie Gilchrist

The evening of May 14, 1963, started for Cookie like any other in Buffalo, but the events that would unfold that night, and the media coverage that followed, would change Cookie more than he ever could have imagined. Never one to shy away from addressing racism, May 14 became the night he decided enough was enough. He was going to use his celebrity status to make a change.

Cookie at first had a hard time understanding why other people of color did not stand up and assert themselves in the fight for equal rights. But as he grew older, he came to understand that his celebrity status had afforded him better treatment compared to that of others of color. The night in question, however, showed him that being a celebrity also brought a downside. Certain segments of the population weren't ready for the social change that was sweeping through America, and they were about to make Cookie their example of why that change should be stopped in its tracks.

On the evening of May 14, 1963, I had been at the home of Dr. Walsh, a University of Buffalo Professor, along with my friend Samuel Green, who would later became a New York State Judge in Buffalo. The evening was spent discussing the plight of the Negro race in the United States and comparing how Negroes were treated in Europe and Canada. I had lived in Canada for several years playing football and shared that I felt that the treatment for people of color was far better on the Canadian side of the border. Our discourse lasted late into the evening and when we decided to call it a night, I drove Sam home before heading home myself.

I got out of my car and was approaching my residence when I noticed that two police officers had pulled up behind my vehicle in a marked police car. They exited the car and were approaching me, slapping their nightsticks against their palms.

The first thing out of their mouths was a stream of racial slurs. They asked me how a nigger could drive such a nice car.

I remember thinking to myself, how can police officers from a northern city still get away with conduct like this? I advised the officers that this was not the way to handle the situation and asked why I was being stopped.

One of the officers said that I had passed through a stop sign without stopping three blocks back. I knew that was bullshit. I didn't go through a stop sign, and if I had, why had I not been pulled over earlier, with lights and sirens?

When I questioned the officers' account, one of the officers came up behind me. He put his nightstick across my neck, and shoved his knee into my back in an attempt to choke me.

Several other officers then arrived at the scene. They roughed me up for awhile, before finally pushing me into the back of a police car. In the arrest paperwork, they claimed it took seven of them to take me down and that I struck one of the officers, causing him severe injuries. Both were lies. In addition to the criminal charges I was now facing, a threatened lawsuit from the allegedly injured officer also became a serious concern.

I was transported to the sixth precinct in Buffalo for arrest processing, and the arresting officers initially wanted to charge me with eight different violations, including drunk driving and assault on a police officer, which was a felony. Once the officers realized I had been with Dr. Walsh and Samuel Green before the confrontation, they withdrew the drunk driving charge. This was because Dr. Walsh and Sam were considered respected members of the community, and they would be witnesses who could corroborate that I hadn't consumed any alcohol that evening.

While I waited in the station's holding cell, several officers walked past me spewing different racial slurs. "We should have checked that black bastard for needle marks," I remember hearing. "He's probably been shooting heroin like Big Daddy Lipscomb. Give a nigger a little money and he thinks he owns the world. He runs a few touchdowns for the Bills and he thinks he's a big shot, but we'll put him in his place."

He was referring to Eugene Big Daddy Lipscomb, the six foot, six inch, defensive lineman for the Pittsburgh Steelers and professional wrestler. Big Daddy had just passed away on May 10, due to a heroin overdose, and the officer was suggesting that I might be a heroin user, too.

It amazed me how low people would go just to spew their closed-minded opinions, not to mention that these comments were coming from those sworn to protect the community. Big Daddy had been a friend of mine. I had made plans to attend his funeral, but this new situation would derail those plans.

The next morning I was transported to the courthouse to face seven charges, the most serious one the felony assault on a police officer. I had the indignity of being transported to court in, of all things, a K-9 police vehicle, and I was made to sit in the area meant for the dogs.

My attorney received a full list of the charges against me as well as the arresting officer's alleged version of the previous evening's events. Before the judge, the officer swore out a complaint that stated that I refused to produce an operator's license and car ownership certificate. He further stated that I became disorderly, resisted arrest, and used abusive and profane language. As far as I was concerned, this was all a cover story to hide the improper and illegal stop they conducted.

The judge asked me if I had any words for the court regarding the allegations leveled against me. Against my attorney's advice, I told the judge my defense was that if I had punched the officer as alleged, he wouldn't be here to swear out a statement against me because he would still be in the hospital. Needless to say, my statement did not go over well with the court.

The arraignment was short, and I was released on my own recognizance, which infuriated the Police Chief and the rank and file of the department.

Several court appearances followed, and numerous judges recused themselves from the case for reasons ranging from health problems to conflicts of interest owing to their being Buffalo Bills Season ticket holders. The real reason for the turnover was that the Fraternal Order of Police had threatened each judge with the loss of their support during the upcoming elections if I were found innocent.

I was eventually fined ten dollars for failing to stop at a stop sign and an additional fifty dollars for refusing to obey a lawful request of a police officer. All of the other charges were dropped except the felony count of assault on a police officer, which was held over for a grand jury.

The officers thought they would send me a message, and that things would play out as usual when a Negro was accused of a crime: They expected me to roll over and take it. So they couldn't have expected the case to become a hot-button political issue.

The incident snowballed in the media and became a hot potato for all involved in the Buffalo political landscape. In response, the Police Department decided to apply more pressure so I would take a plea bargain and go away.

While awaiting the grand jury decision, marked and unmarked police vehicles followed me wherever I went. Most of the time, they were bold and parked right behind my vehicle, just to let me know they were watching. Checkpoints and radar-equipped vehicles were set up in the area around my home in the hope of catching me in a situation where they could file additional charges. Then the Fraternal Order of Police could campaign that I was a public threat, and that I should be locked up with the key thrown away.

It was so bad that one night a friend I'd lent my car to also felt the wrath of the police. Two officers pulled over my car, thinking they'd caught me speeding. When they realized that I wasn't in the vehicle, they were so disappointed that they couldn't contain their anger. The officers even threatened to charge my friend with vehicle theft because they were so frustrated that I wasn't the one driving.

A Negro photographer happened to get photos of the incident that clearly showed my friend being detained and the officers' frustration. Once the officers noticed him, they confiscated his film saying they needed it as evidence and threatened arrest if he complained.

I wondered to myself, could part of this be because I was in an interracial marriage? The escalation of the situation made me concerned for my family's safety. Interracial marriage was not commonplace at the time and was hardly accepted in the United States. Some States still had it on their books as being illegal. Our interracial union was one of the first if not the first in professional football, and it was one of the reasons that I never played in the NFL.

(It took several more years and the strong personality of coach Vince Lombardi to bring the NFL around on the issue of interracial marriage. In 1965, Lionel Aldridge, the Green Bay Packers defensive end, became engaged to a white woman. Worried he would be blackballed and thrown out of the NFL, he went to coach Lombardi with his concerns and asked permission before he married. To his credit, Coach Lombardi said, "I don't care who you marry as long as you keep your nose clean and play good football." Even when the Commissioner of the NFL, Pete Rozelle, traveled to Green Bay to stop the wedding, saying an interracial marriage would be a public relations nightmare for the league, Lombardi stood his ground. Aldridge and his bride married, giving the NFL its first interracial union).

Fearing for my family, I approached my attorney, Mr. Messina, and asked him to send the Buffalo Bills a formal request for a trade. A hastily completed trade request was sent to Dick Gallagher, the Buffalo Bills general manager. I made the request not because I did not love my Buffalo teammates or fans, but out of legitimate concern for the safety of my family. While I had no problem standing up for what I felt was right, I did not want to put my wife and children in the crosshairs of this battle.

On July 22, 1963, the Bills owner, Ralph Wilson, sent my attorney a written response to my trade request:

Dear Mr. Messina,

This will acknowledge your letter of July 18, 1963 to Mr. Gallagher relative to Cookie's desire to be traded.

We can understand how Cookie feels at the moment with a pending indictment and the consequent effect on his personal life. However, we think it would be a mistake to trade him now for the following reasons:

1. *In spite of his problems with the police and in his business relations, we are sure the people of Buffalo and especially the Bills fans are almost 100% behind him.*
2. *I personally and the Buffalo Bills, including the staff and the players, are 100% behind him.*
3. *I think from Cookie's point of view it would be very bad for him to quit under fire and move to another town. People admire a man for facing up to his problems and making a fight for his rights.*
4. *From the club's point of view, regardless of Cookie's wishes, if we traded Cookie now, sports fans everywhere would think we had run out on him when he was in trouble.*
5. *An indictment is not a conviction and Cookie is presumed innocent until he is convicted. We intend to take this position with everybody. Lots of things can happen between an indictment and a trial. Even if a trial is necessary, it may not take place until the season is over and the present publicity and harassment has subsided, as we are sure it will.*

I want Cookie to play for the Bills this fall and the people of Buffalo and his teammates want the same thing. When he appears on the field the night of August 16th in our game against the New York Jets, we are sure the ovation he will receive will convince him that he should not go anywhere else.

Sincerely,
Ralph C. Wilson, Jr.
Western New York Football Club

The letter from Mr. Wilson made me reconsider my stance on leaving Buffalo. I noticed during my earlier court appearances that few Negroes attended. I had expected a large turnout of people of color to support me, but only a few close friends attended the proceedings.

This spurred me on to rally the Negroes and other people of color in Buffalo to stand up for their rights. I started by addressing different groups as a speaker on civil rights. I described my treatment and said if this could happen to me, it could easily happen to them, but that if we all stood together, we would be heard as a community.

The press was my weapon against the injustice of what was transpiring, so I publicly asked, in the court of public opinion, wouldn't taxpayer money be put to better use on education or other public services rather than for a "witch hunt" to get Cookie Gilchrist?

The Appellate Division of the State Supreme Court eventually dismissed the final charge of felony assault. My attorney had successfully petitioned the Appellate Court stating that my earlier guilty plea to resisting arrest and the subsequent fifty dollar fine protected me from double jeopardy. The court sent down a decision that the resisting arrest plea also covered the alleged police officer assault; therefore I could not be tried for the same crime twice under the double jeopardy legal statute. The media attention from the case put a spotlight firmly on the police and their Gestapo tactics, and helped to spur change within the Buffalo Police Department.

I eventually decided to stay in Buffalo. The night of May 14, 1963, convinced me that football had given me a platform for change and that now was the time to start using it.

Cookie's vigorous defense of the charges and the publicity that the case garnered brought needed attention to race relations in Buffalo. The relationship between the Buffalo Police Department and people of color needed to be changed and Cookie used his experience to highlight the issue. Cookie also took Ralph Wilson's letter to heart and decided to stick it out in Buffalo. This respite would be short-lived, as Cookie's role in the golden age of Buffalo Bills football would far too soon find its expiration date.

Buffalo Bills Reborn

Cookie spent the off-season dealing with the legal issues that arose from his May 14 arrest, and was now ready to focus on getting back to the business of playing football. He withdrew his trade request, after receiving Ralph Wilson's heartfelt letter of support. At the start of the 1963 season's training camp, Cookie reported to the Camelot Motor Inn looking to build on the team chemistry that the Bills had displayed toward the close of the previous season. Expectations were high for the Bills, and simply finishing the season with a winning record would not suffice. It was playoffs or bust for the 1963 Buffalo Bills.

When I arrived at training camp for the 1963 season I couldn't wait to suit up and play football. My legal troubles had been a constant cause of worry and distraction, but football would now give me focus and a way to release my anger and frustration. Even in practices, my teammates would argue that they didn't want to face me, fearing they'd be injured. They felt I didn't know how to play at half-speed.

I approached coach Saban about playing "Ironman" football again. The 1962 season was the first in which I didn't play both offense and defense. When I only played offense, I got bored sitting on the bench. I wanted to play linebacker and fullback for the 1963 season and felt playing the full sixty minutes of the game made me a better player. Coach Saban did consider my suggestion, but ultimately decided against it, probably because I also asked for an additional salary to play a second position.

During the offseason my legal troubles, on top of my late nights out, had put too much of a strain on my marriage to Gwen. We both saw the end coming, and the blame could be squarely placed at my feet. Hindsight now gives me the perspective to see that it would have been difficult for anyone to deal with the situation I had created. My ego was too inflated by the adulation I received from being a football star. The force inside me that drove me toward becoming one of the best that had ever played the game also created a void between me and anyone with whom I was close. I was too concerned with what sports writers were saying about me to show concern for anyone else. I soon would realize the error of my ways, and the failure of my personal life would, in retirement, compel me to counsel other athletes facing similar challenges.

Throughout the years, no matter how many other relationships I had and despite our troubles, Gwen was always there if I needed her. My lifestyle had in effect made her a single parent to two young boys who were the product of an interracial marriage, a relationship still frowned upon by many. She did the job of both parents and raised two remarkable young men, and for that I will be eternally grateful. Gwen will always be the true love of my life and it was unfortunate that I lost sight of what should have come first, which was Gwen and the boys.

After losing the preseason opener to the Chiefs in Kansas City by a score of 17-13, we returned home to face the New York Jets. This was my first appearance in a game before the Buffalo fans since my arrest, and I was uneasy about the type of reaction I might receive. More than 19,000 fans came to the preseason game and cheered me when I stepped onto the field. My fears of having alienated the Bills fans were quickly dismissed, and I went out on the field to give them the show they came for. In limited action I rushed for 63 yards on nine carries and scored a two-yard touchdown, helping to secure the 23-8 win over the Jets. The fans' response touched me with emotion and confirmed that I had made the right choice by staying in Buffalo.

Jack Kemp was clearly the number one quarterback entering the season, but a rookie quarterback drafted out of Notre Dame was creating a buzz in camp. Daryle Lamonica had chosen to play for the Bills over the Green Bay Packers and quickly secured the back-up quarterback position on the team. Lamonica's superb play put an end to quarterback Warren Rabb's career as a Buffalo Bill, and he was released following the Jets game.

After another home preseason win against the Boston Patriots, we traveled to North Carolina to play the Denver Broncos in our last preseason contest of the year. While we won the game 21-14, I tore the cartilage in my ribs and suffered a sprained ankle, putting in doubt my ability to start the season opener.

Following the game my teammate and friend Booker Edgerson asked me why I always chose to run over people instead of trying to run around them. He felt that my injury could have been prevented if I had only attempted to be more elusive on the field. That's when I explained to Booker that although I knew I could easily avoid many would-be tacklers, I ran directly at them with all the force I could generate to teach them a lesson I did not want them to forget. I hoped the punishment I dished out would become a deterrent for other players who would consider trying to tackle me. For the most part, this strategy had worked.

The Bills opened the regular season on September 8, 1963, in San Diego against the Chargers. I was still hampered by my injuries and limited to two carries during the first series of the game. George Saimes, originally slated to play safety on defense, took over rushing duties. Kemp threw three interceptions in his San Diego homecoming, and we lost to the Chargers 14-10. This was the fourth season opening loss in the franchise's four-year history. Our 3-1 preseason record had given us hope that this would be a playoff season for the Bills, but losing the first game did allow some doubt to creep in.

The second week of the season we faced the Raiders at Frank Youell Field in Oakland. I was able to play, but nowhere near full strength. This game was played through the air with Kemp and Raiders' quarterback Cotton Davidson trying to outplay each other. The star of the game, though, was the Raiders Clem Daniels who accounted for 172 yards receiving and 76 yards rushing with a 73-yard touchdown reception. The passing combination of Davidson to Daniels gave the Raiders a 35-17 win, and now we were 0-2 to start the season.

We returned home for the third game of the season against the Kansas City Chiefs and hoped our fortunes would change with the backing of the War Memorial faithful. At this point I still felt pain with every breath, but my ankle was starting to heal. Although not at one hundred percent, I was the team's number one option to run the ball. Kemp was aware that I was still limited and took to using his legs to extend plays and for some goal line scores. Despite a 20-10 lead we held at the half, the Chiefs tied the game with less than a minute to go in the game. The final score was 27-27; although not a loss, 0-2-1 was not an encouraging record for a team with playoff aspirations.

Coach Saban tried everything to turn the team around. Extra practices that were more intensive than usual became customary. Still, on September 28, 1963, we suffered our third loss of the year. The Houston Oilers came to War Memorial and defeated us 31-20. The Oilers' star receiver Charlie Hennigan accounted for 123 yards and three touchdown receptions from quarterback George Blanda. The passing attack that the Oilers displayed that day reminded us why the Oilers had won the first two AFL Championships.

On October 5, 1963, we won our first game of the season at home against the Oakland Raiders. It wasn't a pretty game by any stretch of the imagination, with the only touchdown of the game being scored on a pass from Kemp to Bill Miller. The final score of the game was 12-0, and we had finally secured our elusive first win of the season.

During the flight to meet our next opponent, the Kansas City Chiefs, the team seemed uneasy. We had just secured our first win of the season, but still doubted whether we were back on track for a winning season. While I was healing, rookie Roger Kochman had started handling the bulk of the rushing carries. Wray Carlton had a nagging groin injury, and I was still nursing my wounds, opening an opportunity for the promising rookie. The plan entering the game was to let Kochman get us inside the red zone, where I would be asked to take the goal line carries. Kochman had a great game against the Chiefs, accounting for 166 all-purpose yards and a receiving touchdown. I scored two one-yard touchdowns and we left Municipal Stadium with a 35-26 win over the Chiefs. We now had a run of two consecutive victories.

For the next game we stayed out west and made our annual trip to Jeppesen Stadium to play the Oilers. Unfortunately, George Blanda had his way with us again, passing for 233 yards and three touchdowns, leading the Oilers to a 28-14 victory. The loss was bad, but what was more upsetting was the severe injury that Kochman suffered to his leg. During the game his leg got pinned and twisted completely around in a disfigured position. After several operations doctors were able to save his leg, but he lost all of the toes and part of the foot due to gangrene. Kochman had been a rookie on the rise, and he was cut down in an instant. This was another reminder of how quickly your career could end and how deadly the game of football could be.

On October 26, 1963, we played a home game against the Boston Patriots, who were tied with the Houston Oilers for first place in the Eastern Division with identical records of 4-3. Kemp urged us to rally together as a team, and he went out and led in an impressive fashion. He threw for 317 yards and one touchdown, but also rushed for three additional touchdowns. We won by a score of 28-21, and by defeating the first-place Patriots, we gained the confidence that we had sorely lacked for most of the season.

Next we traveled to Denver, where I would have my first big game of the season facing the Broncos at Bears Stadium. I rushed for 125 yards, scoring both a rushing and a receiving touchdown. This was a complete game by our offense, which was needed to squeak out a 30-28 win over the Broncos. Denver rookie quarterback Don Breaux threw four touchdowns to pace the Broncos, but our quarterback combination of Kemp and Lamonica secured the victory.

The next three weeks of the season were up and down with another win against the Broncos and consecutive losses against the Chargers and Patriots.

It was during this season that some of the friction between Bills owner Ralph Wilson and I began. I was always trying to earn money off the field, and Mr. Wilson felt that I was sometimes more preoccupied with my business interests than I was focused on playing football. I even tried to get Mr. Wilson to invest in several of my business ventures, which he usually declined. When I negotiated my contracts with the Bills, there were no agents or middleman, and I fought directly with management for every penny I thought I was worth, even knowing I was pushing my luck sometimes by asking for too much.

Today it's easier to make an agent the bad guy who's asking for too much, but the face-to-face negotiations that players of my era had to handle often created bad blood between players and management. If you took a team's offer without complaining, you were a good soldier, but if you dared to speak up, you were branded a troublemaker. Mr. Wilson once said that he often thought of getting rid of me, but when he watched me run the ball he forgot why he was upset in the first place. The next game of the season would help him forget for a while.

December 8, 1963, would see the best game of my professional career. Coach Saban decided to start Lamonica at quarterback over Kemp, who had had a difficult outing the previous week against the Patriots. We were playing at War Memorial against the New York Jets, and we needed to win to keep any chances at the playoffs alive. Lamonica consistently handed me the ball and, finally feeling one hundred percent physically, I made the most of the opportunity. On that day, I carried the ball thirty-six times for a new AFL and NFL record of 243 yards, which topped Jim Brown's previous record - set in '57 and equaled again in '61 - by six yards. Two holding calls against Bills receiver Glenn Bass actually negated 50 additional rushing yards I had gained, which would have put me close to 300 yards for the day. I also set a record with the five rushing touchdowns I scored, leading the Bills offense to a 45-14 win over the Jets. Once I broke Jim Brown's rushing record the comparisons between him and me started, and the question of who was better became a bone of contention among fans of the game. On a personal level, I was proud of what I had accomplished on the field against the Jets, but I was happier that we remained in contention for a chance at the playoffs.

Entering the last game of the season we had a 6-6-1 record and would need a win, coupled with losses by the teams at the top of the division, in order for us to make the playoffs. We traveled to the Polo Grounds to face the Jets for the second week in a row. In the first half, the Jets led by a score of 10-3 behind a Don Maynard 73-yard touchdown reception from

Galen Hall. We came out in the second half and scored 16 unanswered points leading to a 19-10 Bills win. I rushed for 114 yards including a two-yard touchdown run in the victory, and we finished the season with a record of 7-6-1.

That day luck also played a role in our playoff fate, because the Patriots lost to the Chiefs and dropped to an identical record of 7-6-1. The following day the Oilers had the opportunity to win the division, but they lost to the Chargers, leaving the Patriots and the Bills tied for first place. We had now secured our first appearance in the playoffs and would have to go through the Patriots for a chance to meet the San Diego Chargers for the AFL Championship.

The Bills' first playoff game was held on December 28, 1963, at War Memorial Stadium, under frigid weather conditions. This game was personal for coach Saban. He addressed the team before the game and said he would appreciate a win against the Patriots, whom he'd coached prior to his arrival in Buffalo. A player or coach can spin it however they want, but when you face a former team you always want to beat them.

The weather was below freezing, and the field was a sheet of ice. I was unable to get going and had only seven yards rushing on eight attempts. Kemp and Lamonica split time at quarterback, but between them accounted for only one touchdown and four interceptions. The Patriots handily defeated us in front of our home crowd by a score of 26-8. The Patriots moved on to face the Chargers and lost by a lopsided score of 51-10, behind the Chargers' Keith Lincoln's 329 all-purpose yards and the leadership and passing ability of my former Toronto Argonauts teammate Tobin Rote.

Following the loss to the Patriots, Kemp and I talked about our disappointment over losing the big game in front of our home crowd. We made a pact that we wouldn't let another opportunity like this slip through our fingers, nor let luck be the deciding factor in our making the playoffs. We wanted to hit the ground running for the 1964 season and be the masters of our fate from now on.

At the end of the season, I was named an Eastern All-Star and finished third in the league in rushing despite the nagging injuries, which limited my production during the early part of the season. I led the league in rushing touchdowns with 12, and rushing attempts with 232, while also placing fourth in league scoring. All personal accolades aside, I knew that the Bills had enough talent to win a championship and I would now focus on making that dream a reality. At every level of football from high school through the CFL, I had won a championship and I would not be satisfied until I could call myself an AFL Champion as well.

The Bills had now finished two seasons in a row with a winning record and had made their first playoff appearance. Despite being hampered early on by injuries, Cookie was still a force in the league and showed how dominant he could be with his record-setting performance against the Jets. His personal life was now damaged beyond repair, and he sought refuge and distraction within his personal goal of becoming an AFL Champion. There was an unwavering and driving force within him to become one of the best who ever played the game, but this same drive would eventually cost him everyone close to him. Cookie couldn't wait for the start of the 1964 season and the next step in his quest for an AFL Championship. Unfortunately, he would discover that there was no football accolade or title that would ever fill the void he had created within himself.

The Poem and the Apology

The 1964 Bills were on a roll, and won their first nine games of the season. The tenth game, scheduled for November 15, against the Boston Patriots would be a turning point for the Bills that required Cookie to evaluate himself as a player and, more importantly, as a person.

We were entering the game against Boston with an undefeated record of 9-0, and I was well on my way to a second AFL rushing title. The game was held before a sold-out crowd at the "Old Rockpile," a.k.a. War Memorial Stadium.

From the opening kickoff, the Patriots were bringing the blitz. This threw off the timing of our starting quarterback, Jack Kemp. Kemp had the latitude with coach Saban to call his own plays from the huddle and was now desperately looking for a way to beat the Patriots' defensive scheme. As the game progressed, the option to run the ball fell by the wayside. Kemp wanted to attack using a pass-first option in the hope that this would make the Patriots' defense abandon the blitz and force them to drop their defensive backs into pass coverage. In the huddle I asked Kemp to call a running play because I felt I could break through the Patriots' defensive line and put some points on the board. Despite my suggestion, Kemp continued to sling the ball whenever he wasn't crushed under a pile of Patriots defenders.

Right before the end of the first half, I became frustrated with the play calling and walked off the field in protest. I sent in my back-up, Willie Ross, to replace me on the field. Coach Saban was not pleased, to say the least, and was not shy about letting me know how he felt. While I was walking off the field, he defended the play calling and said he was doing what was in the best interest of the team.

The locker room at halftime was tense and filled with anger toward me and my one-man boycott. I didn't like to lose, but more than that, I didn't like it when I felt I was being taken advantage of. Many people were unaware that I had incentives within my contract tied to carries, yardage and touchdowns. I was leading the league in rushing and those incentives were starting to look more like a formality than an unattainable goal. A few weeks prior to the Patriots game, I'd spoken privately with Kemp about how I felt he sometimes abandoned the running game too quickly, and told him I felt a balanced attack would be the key to winning the championship. Kemp agreed to be mindful of balancing the offense during the games, but despite our heart-to-heart talk, he'd started to call my plays less than he had in the past. The thought that he was being told by team management to keep my statistics down, in an effort to avoid paying my bonus, did cross my mind. That said, my overall concern was winning the game, and I felt that we needed to run the ball to beat the Patriots.

Kemp was ultimately pulled from the game for Daryle Lamonica, our other star quarterback. Lamonica would later become known by the nickname the Mad Bomber for his love of the deep pass, but he was unable to change our fortunes against the Patriots. This would be the Bills first loss of the season, with a final score of 36-28. The quarterbacks combined for 53 passing attempts with only 20 completions.
In comparison, I had only 11 rushing attempts for a season low 33 yards. The news reports following the game were not kind to me and I was even accused of letting the Patriots' defenders get past me for a clean shot at hitting Kemp.

I now became the media's focal point for the Bills' first loss of the season. This loss was magnified because it ended our chance for an undefeated season, which at 9-0 had appeared within our reach. After the game I went back to my apartment thinking that everything would blow over. The next day I read a news article where coach Saban was interviewed about the incident, and he made a very telling statement: "His only concern is himself and how much yardage he can gain."

This was a clear shot at me. Coach Saban's quote was referring to the performance incentives in my contract and implied that I was more concerned with personal statistics than winning football games. Once I read it I knew my time in Buffalo could be coming to an end.

On November 17, 1963, I received word that coach Saban had convinced Buffalo Bills Owner Ralph Wilson to put me on waivers. The Bills released a statement that the waiver process was necessary due to what they deemed conduct that was detrimental to the team. The waiver process allowed other teams in the league to pick me up for the waiver fee of $100 plus the cost of my remaining contract. The Raiders, Jets, and our last opponent the Patriots filed for my rights. By holding the worst record of the three, the Raiders would have the first shot at my services.

Once the Raiders knew they would be first in line to secure my services, I received a phone call from the team to gauge my interest. The call came from Art Powell, who was the Raiders star receiver under coach Al Davis.

Art and I had been friendly, and he was well aware that I preferred the East Coast lifestyle. The purpose of Art's call was to talk up the Raider organization and the benefits of living on the West Coast. This was the Raiders' effort to keep me from refusing to report to the team and making a behind-the-scenes maneuver to play for the East Coast-based New York Jets. Despite Art's call, the thought of playing for the Jets did intrigue me because New York City provided the grandest stage in sports. It was also the advertising and media capital of the world and could be a potential springboard for endorsement deals and other opportunities after football.

The previous summer when I had asked for a raise in my Buffalo contract, there was some discussion of my being traded to the Jets. Sonny Werblin, the new owner of the Jets, was an entertainment impresario who wanted a marquee name for his New York-based team. Werblin was determined to cut into the large NY Giants fan base that owned the hearts of many New York football fans. The trade talks between Ralph Wilson and Werblin hadn't panned out, and Werblin finally found his star in 1964 when he signed quarterback Joe Namath out of the University of Alabama, for a then-record $400,000 contract.

While I was home trying to figure out my next career move and preparing to wear a new team's jersey, my teammates were still discussing a possible future for me in Buffalo. The Bills players were meeting to discuss the possibility of approaching coach Saban about pulling the waiver claim.

There were differing opinions regarding my place with the Bills. Some players wanted me back because they enjoyed me as a teammate, while others felt I was a malcontent and a distraction. The sentiment that won out was that they felt they had a better chance to win the league championship with me than without me.

Being two of the team's leaders, Jack Kemp and Billy Shaw took the final decision to coach Saban, which was that the team wanted me to come back. Coach Saban said that he would consider pulling the waiver claim, but that the air needed to be cleared. He would require an apology to the organization, the team, and the fans before I could return.

Kemp came to my home to discuss what the team had proposed and asked me to come back. He started the conversation by giving me a personal apology for his play calling during the game. Kemp and I also discussed the accusations in the newspapers that alleged that I allowed the Patriots to repeatedly hit him during the game. I let Kemp know in no uncertain terms that I was unhappy with the play calling, but that I would never do anything to jeopardize his safety.

After speaking with Kemp for several hours, I realized that I had been wrong for the way I handled the matter. I still felt I had a right to be upset with the play calling, but the matter should have been handled in-house and out of the public eye. Kemp also brought up the fact that we now had a chance to do something special in Buffalo: if we stayed together, the league championship would be ours. The thoughts of a big payday with Al Davis' Oakland Raiders or Sonny Werblin's New York Jets quickly faded, and I realized that I had to put our team first.

That was when Kemp brought up coach Saban's condition of an apology. Kemp suggested that I prepare a written apology and chalk the matter up to being caught up in the heat of the game. I knew that a carefully worded statement would not be enough for this transgression. This apology needed to come from my heart.

I was fully aware that I had to do what was right for the team. The loss to the Patriots had been unfairly placed on my shoulders alone, but I knew that if we didn't win the AFL Championship, it would be my fault. Kemp left for the evening and I spent the rest of the night collecting my thoughts. The next day would be difficult, but necessary.

While I tried to organize my thoughts about men working together on a football team, I composed a poem. The poem was titled "U Are 'A' Superstar," and it discussed how football was a metaphor for life. This outpouring of emotion while thinking about my team gave me the emotional lift that I needed to undertake the difficult day ahead of me.

The original version of the poem spoke about the Championship of life, but I later changed it to the Super Bowl of life when that became the moniker for the football championship game.

U Are "A" Superstar!

Life is like a game of football and you play it every day.
It isn't just the breaks you get, but how well do you play?
Stop and look the whole team over, you've some pretty rugged men.
If you work them all together, there's no goal you can't defend.
Your fullback's name is courage, you need him in this game.
For truth and faith your halfbacks, there'll be many yards to gain.
Your quarterback is very fast though small and hard to see.
So watch, Sons and Daughters when he gets the ball, he's opportunity.
At right end there's religion, he's stood the test of time.
At left end there is brotherhood, he's in there always trying.
Your right tackle is ambition, don't ever let him shirk.
Left tackle is a husky man, you'll find his name is work.
Your left guard's name is humor, he's important to the team.

While honor's playing right guard, your game is always clean.
If love plays at the center spot and does his and her very best.
Then you shall have a winning team and really know success.
The other team is strong, my Sons and Daughters, greed, envy, hatred and defeat.
Are four strong backs you'll have to buck to make your game complete.
Discouragement and falsehood are the big boys on the end.
You'll have to tackle hard, Sons and Daughters, when you meet up with these men.
Selfishness and jealousy, you'll find them playing guard.
While carelessness and a man called waste are tackles you can't disregard.
There's one more man you'll have to watch all through the game, my dear.
He's playing center for this team, I'm told his name is fear.
This game will not be easy, there'll be struggle, there'll be strife.
To make the winning touchdown, for it's played in the Super Bowl of life.
So stand behind your team, Sons and Daughters, there'll be many who'll applaud.
Just remember you're the captain and the referee is God.

The next day I headed to the stadium to make amends with my teammates. The team was out on the field practicing while I awaited their return in the locker room. As I paced through the locker room, I saw that my nameplate had already been removed from my locker. The name Ray Collins was now affixed to my locker, and all of my gear had been put in a box on the floor. This was a clear reminder from coach Saban that everyone was replaceable.

When the team returned to the locker room, I told them that I was wrong for the way I handled things and that I wanted to continue as a member of the Bills, if they would have me. By this time I was well-traveled and had not yet cemented myself with a home base. I felt Buffalo was the perfect team and location to set permanent roots. I wanted to finally stop the vagabond lifestyle I had been living.

After I addressed the team, there wasn't a sound in the room. I think the team realized it was difficult for me to acknowledge my mistake in an open forum. They realized the effort it took and that I did it to put the team before my own feelings. They knew that the matter had humbled me and that I could have left Buffalo without saying a word, possibly even scoring a larger contract from a new team.

After I said my piece, Billy Shaw went in to get coach Saban, who was inside his office. I then repeated to coach Saban what I had told Shaw, Kemp, and the rest of the team. Coach Saban agreed to pull the waiver claim, but said that I needed to apologize publicly. The team called a hastily organized news conference where I was now expected to make a public statement regarding the events of the past week.

The apology to my teammates and coach was a necessary and humbling experience. In my life I've always felt that I needed to fight tooth and nail to protect my livelihood and myself.

For the public news conference, I was supplied with a written statement that was composed by coach Saban. This statement wasn't the same as my heartfelt plea to my teammates; it was a well-worded statement designed to soothe the egos of both coach Saban and Bills owner Ralph Wilson. I knew I'd crossed the line by walking off the field twenty-four seconds before the end of the first half, but I felt that the press conference was now just about protecting Saban's reputation. The coach just wanted this public display to show he was still the team's "alpha dog."

At the press conference, which was attended by television and print media, I read the statement Saban supplied me: *"I am here to publicly apologize to my teammates, coaching staff and the fans of Buffalo. In the past, I have said and done things for which I am truly ashamed. I have criticized my teammates and my coaching staff unjustly. For this I am sorry."*

Making this statement did not come easy for me. I did not agree with the message because I felt that it portrayed me as giving a "mea culpa" for my entire life. I had already apologized to my teammates for not handling the Patriots incident correctly, but this statement was a way for Saban to put the screws to me. I had gained a reputation during my career and had been pegged as "uppity," which was a term given to Negroes who stood up for their rights. Regardless of race, if I saw or experienced something that I felt was unjust, I opened my mouth and said my piece. I was blessed with many physical gifts such as size and strength, which helped make me a great football player. The one thing I was born without was a filter, which at that time was a detriment to being a Negro in America.

While happy that our team was back together and on our way towards the league championship, I was having a hard time swallowing the fact that I'd given in and made management's self-serving public statement. I wished that I hadn't agreed to read Saban's statement and instead spoke to the public from the heart, which would have allowed me to explain the entire situation.

In the days following my public apology, the media ran stories claiming the whole incident was portrayed as a public relations stunt. Coach Al Davis of the Raiders was interviewed and did not hold back his anger toward the Buffalo Bills. He complained that the Raiders should have been awarded my contract once the Bills placed me on waivers. Davis felt that the Bills were not abiding by the unwritten gentlemen's agreement set by the AFL owners that once you place a player on waivers, you don't pull him back. Saban claimed that my public apology was considered an extraordinary circumstance, which he and the Bills could not have foreseen, and he publicly apologized for upsetting Davis and the Raiders organization.

I called coach Davis right before the Bills pulled me off waivers, to thank him for his interest in me as a player and added that I would have been honored to play for him. Davis was known for being a progressive coach on the field and for how well he treated his players. He was one of the first coaches that I could remember who didn't care what color you were as long as you played good football. The Raiders are now known for setting several league firsts when it came to race. They had the first Latino quarterback and later head coach in Mexican-American Tom Flores. Later Davis hired former Raiders offensive lineman Art Shell as the first modern-day Negro NFL head coach. Later in life, when I reflected back on my career, I wished that at some point I had gotten an opportunity to play for a football visionary like Al Davis.

Within a few days, the news stories on our first loss and subsequent team schism died down as our next opponent became the sports news of the day. Our team was now stronger with a unified goal of bringing a championship to Buffalo. Next up on the road to the championship, the San Diego Chargers.

With the apology incident behind him, Cookie was now determined to play his part in bringing a title to Buffalo. Cookie found the incident to be a learning experience on many levels. He grew as a person and learned that he could not always let his temper get the better of him. Though he still believed that the consistent calling of pass plays was a way to deter him from gaining the yardage needed for his contract incentives, he realized now that he needed to voice his displeasure in the privacy of the locker room.

In that same vein, Cookie learned that he still needed to be guarded whenever dealing with management. While he didn't agree with the scripted words in the public apology the Bills required for his return, he read them nonetheless. He made the apology in order to stay with the Bills so they could build a football dynasty in Buffalo together.

This was Cookie's chance to repair his bad-boy image and set permanent roots in Buffalo. However, even though he checked his ego at the door in order for the team to move on, his days in Buffalo were now numbered. Cookie's public apology and his continued great play on the field during the remainder of the season would increase his trade value to the Bills. This would make it possible for the team to trade him in the offseason for equal value instead of losing him for no appreciable return as a waiver wire cast-off. Cookie did what was right for the team, but so did they.

The Road to the Championship and the Hits Keep Coming

The Buffalo Bills and Cookie had for the moment settled their differences, and the task of bringing a championship to Buffalo was now a burden felt by all. Cookie was determined to use his athletic gifts as well as his personal brand of motivational skills to further this bid for football glory. Now unified, the Bills were on their way to bringing a football championship to Western New York.

Our first test following the Patriots loss was the San Diego Chargers and their passing combination of quarterback John Hadl to receiver Lance Alworth. The game was held in the sunny confines of the Chargers' home field, Balboa Stadium. The Chargers controlled the first half until Gene Sykes intercepted Hadl and ran the ball back to just inside the Chargers' one-yard line. We were now back on offense and deep in the red zone. Jack Kemp called the quarterback sneak and ran in for the one-yard touchdown. This gave us a 14-10 lead after Pete Gogolak's extra point kick.

During half time and throughout the rest of the game, I tried to motivate the team by telling everyone that we were going to win if we went all out and left it all on the field. I said that if we played a complete game, no one could beat us.

In the second half, both teams went scoreless until the Chargers went on a run with a late-third-quarter touchdown on a Hadl pass to Don Norton. The Chargers added another quick score in the opening seconds of the fourth quarter, and that's when our team took over. The Bills team was known for its offense behind Kemp and me, but we were truly ferocious on defense with players like Butch Byrd, Booker Edgerson, and Mike Stratton. Our team came to life when Stratton sacked Hadl in the end zone for a safety. That defensive play gave the team the spark it had lacked for a good part of the game. Daryle Lamonica came in at quarterback, spelling Kemp and capped off our next possession with a one-yard touchdown run. He added another score when he ran in the two-point conversion. I had to give Lamonica a little love tap, as I liked to put it, so he could get that extra push over the goal line during the two-point conversion.

We had tied the score at 24-24 and felt the win was within reach. The Chargers put themselves into good field position on the following kickoff, but our defense once again came to life with Stratton jumping up and intercepting Hadl as he attempted a pass. My number was called three times by Lamonica, and I was able to get the ball down to the 26-yard line. Gogolak was called in and split the uprights with a 33-yard field goal, and we left the field with a 27-24 win. We now had a season record of 10-1 and the confidence that we could beat anyone in the league.

The following week brought us to Oakland to face our next opponent; Al Davis and his Raiders. This was a low-scoring game, which ended in a Raiders victory and a final score of 16-13. Late in the game we were leading 13-10. Just as time was about to run out, Davis had to decide whether to go for the tie with a field goal or to take one shot at the end zone for the win. Being the Maverick that he was, Davis took his shot at the end zone, and the Raiders won the game on Art Powell's touchdown reception from Tom Flores.

I was sure that Davis wanted the win to show his scorn for Saban and the Bills following the waiver wire fiasco. I'd learned from those around the Raiders that if you were loyal to Davis, he would treat you like family - but don't ever cross him. Apparently, other than a woman scorned, no one had a longer memory.

During this era in football, the league owners found it easier to schedule the West Coast games for consecutive weeks to save on travel time and expenses. As air travel became less expensive and time-consuming, the consecutive week road trips became a thing of the past.

I was not a fan of air travel and despised the longer flights. You could call me a nervous Nellie, worrywart, or something to that effect. I had no problem going toe to toe with Ernie Ladd or any of the other defensive giants on the football field, but at the thought of spending time in an airplane, I froze. I even took to waiting for the pilot to leave the cockpit and applauded him after every flight for a job well done.

The previous year, in a bid to get over my fear of flying, I took flying lessons and bought a Piper Cub prop airplane. I thought that I could use the plane to travel between Toronto and Buffalo, making it easier to visit my family and saving me extensive travel time. During my lessons I met a nice guy, whose name eludes me, who was also taking lessons at the airfield. We agreed to split the purchase cost and maintenance of the plane, and it seemed like a good business arrangement. As soon as we signed the title to the plane, the other guy wanted to take the plane out for a test run because he'd heard something rattling in the engine.

The plane was a beautiful sight as I watched it take off and fly into the sunset. That image had to last with me; because that was the last time I ever saw him or the plane. Needless to say, after that incident I became more of a boat person and less trusting in my business relationships.

Many players passed the time on these West Coast plane trips by playing cards, and this was one way I tried to keep myself from obsessing about my fear of flying. The only problem was that I was by far the worst card player on the team. I think my poor card playing even supplemented the income of many of my teammates and the coaching staff. There were a few who I was sure made more money playing cards against me than they did from their paychecks from the Bills.

The last game on our three-game West Coast trip was scheduled for December 13, 1964, against the Denver Broncos. The Broncos played their home games in Bears Stadium, usually to less than stellar attendance. We defeated the Broncos by a final score of 30-19. Quarterback Daryle Lamonica, who started in place of Jack Kemp, led the win. Receiver Ed Rutkowski and running back Wray Carlton were also, surprisingly, given starting nods this week. Coach Saban was worried about shuffling the starting lineup because he didn't want to disrupt the team chemistry, but he rolled the dice and won.

Carlton had been injured during the preseason, and this was his first game action of the regular season, while Ed Rutkowski was chosen to start over sure-handed receiver Glenn Bass. All three responded by leading the team's offense and securing the win over the Broncos. Rutkowski led the Bills' receivers with 69 yards and a receiving touchdown. Carlton added 74 all-purpose yards and a touchdown to the box score, while Lamonica accounted for one rushing and one passing touchdown.

During this three-game western swing I didn't have any eye-popping statistics. I spent most of the games pass blocking or gaining the yardage needed to set up the field goal unit. The entire team put their personal statistics aside in favor of team wins. We were now 11-2 heading into the final regular season game against the Boston Patriots, who were only a half game behind us in the league standings. The Patriots had amassed a 10-2-1 record and would need a win or a tie against us to secure the Eastern Division crown. Both teams knew what would be at stake once we stepped onto the field at Fenway Park. It was time to let it all fly.

The last time we'd played the Patriots, we suffered our first loss of the season. That was also the game where I pulled myself off the field in protest. This time I wanted to make my presence felt by the Patriots and wanted them to know that I was determined to leave Boston a winner.

The start of the game was delayed due to snowfall, while the Boston grounds crew cleared the field for kickoff. As we waited in the locker room, I could barely sit still. I wanted to set the tone of the game early, and when we finally hit the field, the Patriots felt it. On the first play from scrimmage, I broke off a nine-yard run and hit Patriots defensive back Chuck Shonta with all I had. I didn't try to go around him because I wanted the Patriots to know we were going to run right through them.

Shonta lay on the floor, knocked unconscious by my blow. While the rest of the Patriots defense huddled around their unconscious teammate, I stood nearby taunting them. I made sure they heard me when I said, *"Which one of you motherfuckers is next?"*

Needless to say, there were no takers. We had gotten inside their heads, and in football, sometimes that's where the game is won or lost. Shonta came back into the game a few plays later, though he still looked wobbly from the hit. Jack Kemp seeing that Shonta was off his game decided to attack his side of the Patriots' defense. This strategy started with Kemp throwing a 57-yard touchdown pass to Elbert Dubenion. The Patriots kept pace with a tying touchdown pass from Patriots quarterback Babe Parilli to Tony Romeo.

Unlike the previous meeting between the two teams, I made sure nobody touched Kemp. He stayed upright and accounted for 286 passing yards, one passing touchdown, and two rushing touchdowns. While my statistics were not the highlight of the box score, I had made my presence felt that day. The final score was Buffalo Bills, 24, and the Boston Patriots, 14.

Cookie Barrels over the Patriots Chuck Shonta for a nine yard run during the Bills' 24-14 win at Fenway Park.

Courtesy of the Buffalo State College Archive-E.H. Butler Library.

In the locker room following the game, I overheard Kemp being interviewed by the press. Instead of talking about himself and his great performance, he applauded my effort on the field. *"Cookie had a great game,"* he said, *"and he set the tone for the entire team. He scared the heck out of the Patriots."*

During our first game against the Patriots that season, I had done a great deal of damage to my reputation with my teammates. This game made me see that I was beginning to repair the rift I had created. It was one thing for the team to accept my apology because they felt I could help them win. Now I was starting to feel like they genuinely wanted me in the locker room. I wasn't seen as just a good player anymore; I had become a good teammate. This was the first time I felt like I was just one of the guys and part of something bigger than myself.

We were now Eastern Division Champions and on our way to face the San Diego Chargers in the AFL Title Game. By virtue of our better regular season record, the game would be held in Buffalo at our home stadium. Though the Rockpile was not a thing of splendor by any stretch of the imagination, our home crowd's support made it the place where we most loved to play. The support of Bills fans along with the harsh winter weather of Buffalo would be our advantage against the surfer boys of the San Diego Chargers.

The game was scheduled for December 26, 1964, and a standing-room-only crowd was expected. I actually thought the game might also lead to a profitable business opportunity: the winter weather in Buffalo was known to be severe, and I thought that selling Cookie Gilchrist signature earmuffs outside the stadium prior to the game would be a great way to supplement my income. I even brought my proposal to Bills owner Ralph Wilson to see if he wanted to invest in the idea. Mr. Wilson passed, and, as I learned the hard way, I should have, too. Buffalo had an unusually warm day in the mid-fifty degree range, and I took a bath on my earmuffs idea. When it came to business I only had one type of luck - bad!

We knew the Chargers were formidable on the field, but our meeting a few weeks earlier showed they were beatable. The Chargers had been picked as the early favorite by sports prognosticators - they were loaded with star talent. Lance Alworth, Paul Lowe, Ron Mix, Keith Lincoln, and Tobin Rote were just a few of the great players that lined their bench on offense. On defense, the Chargers were led by six foot nine Ernie Ladd and six foot five Earl Faison.

Prior to the game the Chargers were so confident that Faison walked over to our sideline huddle and said we better play all out because he just might kill someone today. But before the kickoff we learned we had gained an advantage when Lance Alworth was announced as inactive for the game due to a leg injury. Alworth's absence would increase the role of the Chargers' "Jack of All Trades," Keith Lincoln, who would become the focal point for the San Diego offense.

The Chargers started off the game by winning the coin toss, but that would be the end of their luck. An opening possession touchdown pass from Tobin Rote to Dave Kocourek was the Chargers' only lead of the game. On their second possession, our defense set the tone for the game. Linebacker Mike Stratton, recognizing the Chargers' offensive formation, anticipated the play and hit Keith Lincoln so ferociously he broke Lincoln's ribs. It looked like Stratton and the pass from Tobin Rote to Lincoln actually arrived at the same time, ending in the violent collision. It was one of the most devastating hits I ever saw on a football field and, some would say, one of the most famous in AFL history. After Lincoln was carried off the field, the momentum clearly swung our way. We were down 7-0, but we felt completely in control.

"The Hit Heard 'round the World." Mike Stratton's ferocious hit on the Chargers Keith Lincoln set the tone for the AFL championship game, which the Bills won 20-7. Photo by ©Robert L. Smith Orchard Park N.Y.

In the first half, we scored two field goals on Pete Gogolak's kicks of 12 and 17 yards. Wray Carlton scored the lone touchdown on a four-yard run. At halftime, we led the Chargers by a score of 13-7.

In the locker room, I decided to make an announcement to keep the team motivated. An All-Star team like the Chargers was more than capable of coming back if we let down our guard. Coach Saban and the other coaches were inside Saban's office trying to determine the game plan for the second half. I stood up and told everyone in the locker room that we had a chance to make history and that I would kick the ass of anyone who did not pull their weight.

Just as I finished my speech, coach Saban entered the locker room. I turned to him and said, *"I'll start with you first, Coach."*

From my point of view, I was only making sure that everyone on the team knew that I was amped up and ready for action. I later read an interview with Bills teammate Paul McGuire that described his recollection of the game. Speaking of my locker room speech, he recounted that I threatened to summarily kick everyone's butt in language that was not fit to print. "I was so far back up in my locker the only thing sticking out of my locker were the tips of my shoes. If I could have gotten them up farther I would have because I knew he meant it. That was the way Cookie was. His spirit is what Buffalo needed."

The second half brought only one score for either side. A one-yard touchdown run by Kemp secured a Buffalo win by a final score of 20-7.

We were now the AFL Champions, and it felt great.

Although I didn't see the inside of the end zone that day, I contributed 144 all-purpose yards and did my part in the win. The win was a total team effort and the highlight of my time in Buffalo. After the clock ran out, I found Kemp on the field. In the melée of fan excitement we hugged and shouted out in joy: *"We did it!"*

A photographer for the local newspaper captured the moment. It's still my favorite photo taken during my career. Kemp even used it in campaign promotions during his post-football political career. I thought the image was appropriate for what was going on in America at the time. The Civil Rights act had just passed and this photo depicted two friends, of different colors and backgrounds, working together for a common goal. We had come together as a team, and now the AFL Championship resided in Buffalo.

Cookie had found redemption with his teammates and won an AFL Championship in the process. During this period of team success, he also received personal acclaim when he won his second AFL rushing title. Cookie led the league with 981 rushing yards and tied Sid Blanks of the Houston Oilers for the league lead in rushing touchdowns with six.

A championship now in hand, all seemed forgiven and Cookie made plans to participate in the upcoming All-Star Game. For the first time ever, the game was being played in the city of New Orleans. It would be a trip that Cookie and the Crescent City would never forget.

The Boycott of 1965
or No Service Allowed

The annual All-Star Game was usually a fun time for the stars of the AFL, where they could get together and relax while putting on an exhibition for the fans. Following the Bills' AFL Championship win against the Chargers, Cookie, Jack Kemp, Billy Shaw, Ernie Warlick and Butch Byrd all headed to New Orleans to participate in that year's game, which was being held on January 12, 1965. This was the first time the game was held in New Orleans, and it acted as the city's audition for a professional football franchise.

The Fact that the game was being held in the Deep South was a concern for many of the black athletes. Many southern cities had chosen to ignore the Civil Rights Act of 1964 and continued to do business as usual. Joe Foss, the AFL Commissioner, had gotten a guarantee from Dave Dixon, the games promoter, that New Orleans would accept all athletes with open arms, regardless of color. But what happened in the city of New Orleans that January might be described with the famous quote from poet Robert Burns: "The best laid plans of mice and men often go awry."

On Sunday January 10, 1965, at approximately 4:30 p.m., I arrived at the New Orleans Airport along with my Buffalo Bills teammates Jack Kemp and Ernie Warlick, as well as Oakland Raiders receiver Art Powell. Art had met us in Chicago, where we all took the same connecting flight out of O'Hare Airport. We were some of the first players to arrive in New Orleans for the All-Star Game, which was being held for the first time in the Crescent City. New Orleans was campaigning heavily for a professional football franchise and thought this was a way for the city to showcase how football could thrive in the Big Easy.

I had snagged my new, one-hundred-and-fifty-dollar suit on a screw protruding from my seat on the airplane, so I went to speak with the Delta Customer Service Department while Jack, Ernie, and Art collected our luggage. The woman at the Delta office offered to patch my suit, but I felt the suit would look horrible with a patch. I explained that I'd just purchased the suit and asked them to replace it with something comparable. The Delta officials asked me to complete a claim form and said they would speak with their supervisor.

When the Delta service agent reviewed my completed claim form and read my name, she asked, *"You're not going to give us any trouble, are you Cookie?"*

Unfortunately, my public reputation as a troublemaker had preceded me once again. This was my first trip to New Orleans and I hoped to enjoy myself. This was the first indication that I would not be welcomed here.

After my uncomfortable interaction with the Delta employees, I searched the terminal for my teammates. They were still collecting the luggage, so I volunteered to go hail a taxi for our ride to the hotel. Jack, Ernie and I, as members of the East Team, were staying at the Fontainebleau Hotel, while Art was staying at the Roosevelt Hotel with the West All-Stars.

None of the taxis parked along the terminal curb would approach the area where I was standing. I walked over to the line of parked taxi cabs and leaned into the window of one of the taxis to talk to the driver, who seemed almost disinterested in my presence. I said to the driver, "Can't you see me calling for a taxi?" At six-foot three and two hundred and sixty pounds I am kind of hard to miss.

The driver replied, *"You needed a colored taxi."*

"I don't care what color the taxi is," I said. *"I just want to get to my hotel."* I knew the driver was talking about a segregated taxi, but I was trying to defuse the situation with humor. The driver then saw Jack, Ernie, and Art exit the terminal and wave for me to come over. The driver asked if the white gentleman was in my party. I said yes, we both needed to get to the Fontainebleau Hotel. The driver said if Jack allowed me to ride with him, then he could take the fare.

In a mock step-and-fetch-it shuffle, I walked over to Jack and said, *"Mr. Kemp, the nice white taxi man said that I could ride in his taxi if you allow it, Sir."*

"Quit kidding, Cookie," Jack said.

I told Jack what the driver had told me. Jack settled the matter, and the driver dropped off Art at the Roosevelt before driving the rest of us to the Fontainebleau. Still determined to enjoy my time in New Orleans, I retired to my room for a nap before looking to take in the nightlife.

The city was buzzing over finally hosting a professional football game. Pro sports were just starting to make their way into the Deep South. The NFL's Atlanta Falcons were about to begin play in 1965, and the Dolphins would call Miami home starting in 1966. There were rumors that the Boston Patriots might even be moving to Birmingham, Alabama. In baseball, the Braves were getting ready to abandon Milwaukee for Atlanta, with the lure of virgin radio and television territory.

New Orleans was hoping for an expansion or relocation team. The 1960 U.S. Census had ranked it as the seventeenth largest city in the nation, and this helped justify their claim that the city's population would support a professional football team.

The main attraction of any visit to New Orleans is the French Quarter, the section of about twelve square blocks known for its conglomeration of restaurants, taverns, jazz clubs, and strip joints, with Bourbon Street serving as the center of gravity.

That evening, Art Powell called my hotel room and invited me to meet him and several other players at the Dew Drop Inn. The Dew Drop Inn was a colored nightclub, and had been suggested to Art and some of the other athletes by their hotel's Negro employees. I told Art I'd meet up with him and caught a colored taxi to the Dew Drop Inn. The driver struck up a conversation with me and, before I exited the taxi, warned, *"Be careful in this town."*

We stayed at the Dew Drop Inn for several hours having drinks and catching up before a group of us decided to take a tour of the city. Among other things, we had discussed the discrimination we encountered when we first entered the city, but chalked it up to a few bad apples. We decided to put it aside and enjoy our night.

Abner Haynes, Butch Byrd, Bobby Bell, Houston Antwine, and I caught a colored taxi in an effort to tour New Orleans. We asked the driver to show us some of the good clubs in town. The driver said, *"You boys look like football players. You know that Abner Haynes is really something special."*

Playing around, I said, *"No, he's terrible, but that Cookie Gilchrist is really great."*

He said, *"You know, you're right, Sir. If I had him in my cab I would drive him around all night for free."*

Well, I guess it's my lucky day!" I said, and introduced myself properly.

The driver was a great tour guide, and when we decided to call it a night, he refused payment for his services. We graciously declined his offer and made sure to give him a nice tip for showing us around the beautiful city.

We turned in for the night, and I hoped that the taxi incident at the airport, as well as some of the other incidents my companions mentioned were just an aberration and not the norm for the city.

The next morning I received a call from Art Powell, who told me that some of the guys had trouble during the night and that I needed to come over to the Roosevelt Hotel.

I called Ernie Warlick's room to let him know what was going on. Ernie told me he'd seen firsthand how inhospitable New Orleans could be. Jack Kemp and Mike Stratton had invited Ernie out to dinner the previous evening. Jack suggested they dine in the French Quarter. Jack and Mike went into the restaurant first, and when Ernie entered, he was quickly turned away by the hostess, who said, *"We don't serve your kind here."*

Jack said they'd go somewhere else.

They searched for a new place to dine. At the second restaurant, Jack entered alone and spoke with the Maitre d'. The Maitre d' pointed at Ernie, who was standing by the front door of the restaurant. Jack came back and said they'd have to find somewhere else to eat.

Ernie said he finally became so frustrated that he caught a colored taxi back to the hotel and went to sleep.

The other Negro East All-Stars and I traveled over to the Roosevelt Hotel to have a meeting with the Negro contingent from the West All-Stars. Once together we described in great detail the discrimination that we had seen or experienced since arriving in New Orleans. I opened up the discussion by speaking about the taxi problem. Abner Haynes then talked about how he was purposely dropped off at the wrong hotel by a taxi driver. Ernie Ladd, Dick Westmoreland, and Earl Faison talked about having their coats thrown on the floor by white patrons at a local restaurant. No matter how many times they hung up their coats, they would continually get thrown back on the floor. This was a not-so-subtle hint that blacks were not welcomed there. Later that evening, Ernie, Earl and Dick tried to enter a jazz club and were again turned away. When Ernie and Earl protested, the doorman threatened the use of a handgun if they refused to leave.

Bobby Bell said he'd had reservations about coming back to New Orleans because he'd been there before to judge the Black America Beauty Pageant. That was only a few months earlier, and Bobby had had to stay in a segregated hotel on the other side of town. He'd been told prior to the All-Star game that things would be different this time, but apparently they were still the same.

I said to my fellow players that we were invited here as guests to play in the All-Star Game; however, no one cared enough to inform us that we would not be treated as equals. The citizens of New Orleans felt they could still keep whites and blacks segregated, despite the passage of the 1964 Civil Rights Act.

I then called for a vote to boycott the game. The last thing I said before the vote was, "*You all know I will kick the ass of whoever votes to stay and play.*" The vote was unanimous, 21-0 to leave New Orleans.

I suggested that we appoint a spokesperson for our group and nominated Ernie. He was a respected player, and wasn't considered a troublemaker like me. If I had acted as spokesperson, the cause would not have seemed just, because people would just say, *"Oh, that's Cookie being an instigator as usual."*

We all left the room before Ernie could decline the position. And he did us all proud when he gave the following statement to the press who had gathered outside the room where we held the meeting:

> The American Football League is progressing in great strides and the Negro football players find they are playing a vital role in the league's progression and have been treated fairly in all cities throughout the league. However, because of the adverse conditions and discrimination practices experienced by the Negro players while here in New Orleans, the players feel they cannot perform 100 percent as expected in the All-Star Game and be treated differently outside. With the exception of the hotels where the squads have been quartered (the West in the Roosevelt, the East in the Fontainebleau), recreational facilities and transportation were not available to the Negro players and service was refused.

After Ernie made his statement, the East All-Stars returned to the Fontainebleau Hotel and packed to leave. I made arrangements to catch a flight that afternoon back to Buffalo. All of the East All-Stars congregated in my room while we waited to get out of town. Word of our boycott quickly spread to the white players on both the East and West squads. A practice had been scheduled for that afternoon, and when none of the black athletes reported, the coaches for both teams reached out to find out what was going on.

Coach Lou Saban, who was my coach with the Bills and also the coach of the East All-Stars, called me to find out what was going on. While Lou and I did not always see eye to eye, he understood fully when I told him that the black players had faced discrimination in the city. The game's promoter, Dave Dixon, had heard the black athletes were planning to leave and asked for a chance to speak with our group before we left.

Coach Saban arranged for Billy Shaw and some of the hotel bell hops to drive the Negro East All-Stars over to meet the Negro West All-Stars at the Roosevelt Hotel. The meeting was held in Room 980, Chuck Burr's office. Chuck was the Buffalo Bills publicity director, who was now working in a similar capacity for the promoters of the All-Star event. Ernie Ladd and Earl Faison did not attend because they said, regardless of what Mr. Dixon had to say, they were leaving because they felt staying in the city was a safety issue.

Mr. Dixon brought along Ernest Morial, who was the head of the local NAACP Chapter. Mr. Morial would later become the first black Mayor of New Orleans and his son the first black Senator from Louisiana. I've always felt that Mr. Morial was brought in as the token Negro to support Mr. Dixon's cause. Dixon fought hard for the game to stay in New Orleans, as the loss of the game would damage the city's chance for a professional football team. As last-ditch incentives to stay, we were offered cars, cash, and just about anything else.

Ron Mix, the San Diego Chargers lineman, was the only white player to attend the meeting. He'd thought we could bring more attention to the situation by staying in New Orleans despite the poor treatment. But after hearing our experiences, Ron knew he couldn't sway us and said he would support our decision no matter what we chose to do.

I questioned Mr. Dixon and Mr. Morial's conveniently timed recognition of the problem of ill-treatment toward Negroes. I asked how they could invite us there knowing what we were going to face. We were still in the Deep South and in the heart of Klu Klux Klan country. Did they think the chance at a professional football team would automatically change people's feelings toward race?

Negotiations with Mr. Dixon and Mr. Morial eventually led to a call by some in attendance to hold a re-vote. Our numbers were down to ninteen players now due to Ernie and Earl having already left town. The second vote was 16-3 to boycott the game.

The three dissenting votes came from the three rookies on the roster. My thinking was that they wanted to use the All-Star game platform to cement their status as some of the league's best players. I also figured they didn't have enough caché to avoid the wrath of an unhappy team owner or league office.

Once we settled the matter, everyone quickly made their way out of town. I collected my luggage at the Fontainebleau and headed straight to the airport. Unfortunately, the Eastern Seaboard was snowed in, and I had to wait around the airport lounge for a flight out. At about 10:30 p.m., news of the boycott broke on the local news telecast that spoke of a Negro player revolt. Suddenly I felt like everyone in the airport was looking at me, and for the first time in my life I feared for my safety. All of the stories I had heard of violence towards Negroes in the south came rushing back to me. It wasn't until I was on the plane back to Buffalo that my nerves finally relaxed.

When news of the boycott made its way to the Commissioner and the team owners, a contingency plan was suggested. Houston Oilers owner Bud Adams offered to host the game at Jeppesen Stadium in Houston. While not always great, race relations were considerably more progressive in Houston than in New Orleans.

Commissioner Foss was well aware of the financial loss that the game's relocation would cost both the league and New Orleans. Still, feeling the pressure from the Negro athletes, AFL Commissioner Joe Foss released a statement to the press backing the players and announcing that the game was now being played in Houston. In his statement, Foss explained the situation:

> Dixon assured me that New Orleans was ready in all aspects for a game between racially mixed teams. Evidently, it isn't. They contacted as many businessmen as possible and got them to agree to treat the Negro players well, but they just couldn't get to everyone. Negro players run into problems in nearly every city. But I guess what went on in New Orleans was more than they could be expected to take. I can't say that I blame them.

The contest was held at Houston's Jeppesen Stadium on January 16, 1965. By the time all the players had been re-routed to Houston, there was an overwhelming sense that many of the league's owners were unhappy with the Negro players. They had hoped to eventually add New Orleans as an AFL franchise, and our boycott now put that in jeopardy.

When the game was finally played, the West All-Stars won by a score of 38-14 on a 73-yard touchdown reception by Keith Lincoln, the game's MVP.

At the time the boycott was just a small story in the local newspapers and not considered a big event. But, considering the social climate and the fact that an event of such magnitude had to be suddenly rescheduled due to a boycott by Negro athletes, many thought it should have registered on a greater scale with the public.

Shortly after the game, I became the target of anyone angry over the game having been moved from New Orleans. Even though Ernie Warlick was acting as the public face of the boycott, everyone blamed me. Nick Buoniconti, the linebacker for the Boston Patriots, complained about me and the boycott during a newspaper interview that called the whole incident a "raw deal." Nick's gripe was that the boycott hurt the AFL as a league and subsequently our pension system. He had hoped a new franchise in New Orleans would generate more revenue for the league and add new players to the pension system. As more players joined the pension system, more money would be added to the fund, which would benefit all players in the system. While I understood Nick's thinking, I felt he was clearly being shortsighted. His argument was an easy one to make as a white man.

I responded to Nick's statement by giving a newspaper interview of my own. I said that Nick Buoniconti was not a qualified spokesman, as he was not present at any of the meetings. Even though he was aware of the situation at the time, he did not voice his opinion for or against the walkout. It appeared that he condoned the treatment of his Negro teammates in New Orleans.

In February of 1965, the Buffalo Bills traded me to the Denver Broncos. I'd had my troubles with Bills' management during the prior season, so my trade would not be deemed unusual. But the fact that Abner Haynes and I, while still at the top of our games, were both soon traded following the boycott, seemed more than suspicious. We both ended up with the Denver Broncos, who were hemorrhaging money and on the brink of folding. They needed an infusion of star talent to help ticket sales and were the only team willing to take a chance on the troublemaking Negroes from the All-Star Game. While not popular with most non-Negroes at the time, the boycott brought needed attention to racial discrimination in America and is the event I am most proud of ever being a part of.

Cookie, Abner, and the other Negro athletes who boycotted the game in New Orleans knew they'd put a bull's-eye on themselves. Still, they did what needed to be done for their racial community and not what was good for them in the moment. As usual, Cookie was deemed the rabble-rouser and took the brunt of the criticism. His career would never be the same once he left Buffalo, but he stood by his decision.

History would vindicate Cookie and the other Negro athletes when, in response to their actions, New Orleans was forced to desegregate. The change they brought about eventually led to the NFL awarding the city the New Orleans Saints franchise, and their eventual owner would be the All-Star Game's promoter, Dave Dixon.

Years later, Ron Mix was interviewed about his memory of the boycott and said, "The truth is, New Orleans ought to erect a statute to Cookie. The city wanted an NFL team but wasn't going to get it unless it desegregated. The boycott led to a change in the laws."

When it occurred, the boycott barely registered as a blip on the radar of public perception, but it led to the formation of the Dr. Harry Edwards Olympic Project for Human Rights, held during the 1968 Olympics.

The famous photo of American athletes Tommy Smith and John Carlos standing on the Olympic podium with their fists raised in a black power salute was viewed by many as the next step in the progression of minority athletes taking a stand against discrimination.

Even now, in 2011, when race relations are more progressive, athletes are using their celebrity and commercial power to take stands against discrimination. For instance, many Hispanic baseball players, including Milwaukee Brewers pitcher Yovani Gallardo, have threatened a boycott of the 2011 Baseball All-Star Game in Arizona after Arizona enacted several laws that were discriminatory towards people of Hispanic heritage. While the Negro athletes in New Orleans were the first to take a political stand using the grand stage of sports, history has shown that they would surely not be the last.

An Invitation to History

Immediately following Cookie's return to Buffalo after the re-scheduled All-Star game, he received an invitation to attend another historic event. Pennsylvania Senator Joseph Clark had invited Cookie to attend the Presidential Inauguration of Lyndon B. Johnson. Feeling honored that Senator Clark had extended this invitation, especially following the recent passage of the Civil Rights Act, Cookie readily accepted the offer.

I met Senator Clark on Sunday, November 17, 1963, during a home game against the San Diego Chargers. The Chargers were visiting Buffalo for our second contest that season, and we hoped to avenge the opening day loss we'd suffered in San Diego by a final score of 14-10. It did not work out as planned. I scored the only Bills touchdown with a first-quarter score from the one-yard line. Though I finished the day with 95 yards rushing and 36 yards receiving, that wasn't enough to overcome the three-headed scoring attack the Chargers had with Lance Alworth, Keith Lincoln and Paul Lowe. The final score was Chargers 23-13 over the Bills, but what I remembered most vividly about that day was meeting the Senator.

Senator Clark introduced himself to me on the sideline, and he told me that we both had a connection to my hometown in Pennsylvania. He said that I might not remember, but I'd actually helped his grandmother, who was also a resident of Brackenridge. The Senator's story reminded me of the day I'd walked home from high school and saw a white-haired woman, who appeared to be in her eighties, attempting to mow the lawn. She could barely push the mower, and the area she needed to cover was quite large. After seeing the difficulty she was having, I took over and moved the lawn in addition to performing other chores she needed done around the house. From time to time I would walk by Mrs. Clark's home and offer my assistance for anything she couldn't handle herself.

I had long forgotten my interaction with Mrs. Clark, which seemed like it happened in a different lifetime, but the Senator had clearly been moved by my actions. Following the game, he said that one day he would find a way to repay my kindness to his family. I told him nothing was expected in return, but would find out later that the Senator was a man of his word.

Senator Clark and I remained in contact, and our second conversation was a week later following the assassination of President John F. Kennedy on November 22, 1963. I told the Senator that I felt that President Kennedy had been on the way to improving civil rights. Although President Kennedy had not actually signed or promoted any legislation to further civil rights, he had started to make headway in changing federal hiring practices regarding race, even appointing five federal judges who were black. Senator Clark said that despite Kennedy's assassination, the civil rights movement would continue. He added that Kennedy's death might even spur other politicians to push for civil rights legislation in his memory.

As it turned out, Senator Clark was right. Kennedy's Vice-President and successor Lyndon B. Johnson continued Kennedy's mission with the passage of the Civil Rights Act on July 2, 1964. President Johnson won re-election against Republican candidate Barry Goldwater, still riding on the coattails of Kennedy's popularity, some would say.

Senator Clark had continued to follow my career and was one of the few people to call me and express his support for the stand that I and the other black athletes took in New Orleans. During that call of support, he invited me to attend the Inauguration of President Johnson. I was still feeling a great sense of pride over what we had accomplished in New Orleans and felt there could be no better way to represent the positive changes being made in America than to be a prominent black face at a presidential inauguration. My grandparents, born slaves, never would have been able to fathom that a black man, much less their grandson, would be an invited guest at an inauguration.

I called my friend Samuel Green and invited him to attend as my guest. Sam was a law school student in Buffalo, and I thought this chance to rub elbows with the Washington elite would interest him. I had an ulterior motive for my invitation, too, because in the back of my mind I had concerns about holding my own in extended conversations with such powerful politicians. Though I never had a problem with public speaking, the fact that I never completed high school made me self-conscious about participating in the week's events. There still was that small amount of doubt in the back of my mind that I would be accused of saying or doing something wrong. I did not want to be portrayed as unintelligent or ill-mannered, and felt Sam would be a safety net.

There were several inaugural balls held in the days before Johnson's swearing-in ceremony. Sam and I attended all of the parties. My concerns turned out to be unfounded, as I held my own speaking with the who's who of Washington politics. I held court wherever we went, discussing not just sports, but everything from international politics to current events. I signed numerous autographs that week, including several for members of President Johnson and Vice President Humphrey's families, and at no time did I feel uncomfortable or unwelcome. As a joke, I told President Johnson that he better watch out because in four years he might be facing competition from the unbeatable political ticket of Jack Kemp and Cookie Gilchrist. He paused for a second, as if it actually gave him concern, and then started to laugh.

After several days of pre-inauguration parties, when the actual ceremony rolled around on January 20, I was exhausted. But the adrenaline rush of being in on this historic event kept me going. It was the same feeling I got when I suited up for a game.

Sam and I waited at the hotel for our ride to the ceremony, but it never arrived. We had been promised a car and driver when we first arrived in Washington, but no one ever came for us. Repeated calls to the contact phone numbers I had been given went unanswered. I called Senator Clark's office, but he had already left for the ceremony.

As we sat at the hotel and watched the ceremony on television, I started to suspect that some powerful Southern politicians were still upset about the All-Star Game Boycott of New Orleans. I would later learn that Senator Russell Long of Louisiana had complained to President Johnson about my planned attendance at the ceremony and asked that I be removed from the guest list - all because he felt I had hurt Louisiana's chance at getting a professional football team.

Once Senator Clark found out what had transpired, he apologized profusely. I understood that it wasn't his fault, but I was still upset over what had transpired. What upset me most was how hypocritical I found the whole incident to be. The politicians loved having me at their parties to recall my football stories and sign autographs for their children, but apparently I wasn't good enough to attend the swearing-in ceremony. Was I brought there only for their amusement, or was this simply a last-minute snub orchestrated by Senator Long? The answer eluded me.

I looked at this event as still another learning experience. The Washington powerbrokers who'd kept me from the ceremony had advanced educations and privileged upbringings, but I realized I never should have worried about what they thought of me and my lack of education. Their actions and closed-minded behavior proved it was they who were in fact the unintelligent and ill-mannered members of society.

Cookie's exclusion from the inauguration ceremony was a clear message that many in the South were still upset over the All-Star boycott. The message repeated what he had learned early in life: that there were repercussions for being a black man who stood up for what he thought was right - especially if it were in direct opposition to what "society" considered appropriate or accepted behavior for a black man.

What Cookie took from this experience was that despite not having a high school diploma, his life experiences had given him a degree from the school of hard knocks. Despite being a black man, his star status made him privy to opportunities normally afforded only to whites. Because of his status, he was able to walk between both the black and white worlds during the racially charged time of the civil rights movement. This opportunity to see both sides of the coin was a better education in the ways of the world than he ever could have received from attending Michigan or Notre Dame.

These life experiences would have to serve him well: once football ended, he would find himself looking for a new means of support. Most job applications, after all, don't recognize a master's degree from the school of hard knocks.

Rocky Mountain High

Cookie was just coming off of the high of winning both the rushing title and the league championship with the Bills. In addition to these professional accomplishments, he felt personal pride regarding what he and the other black athletes accomplished by taking a stand against the discrimination they faced in New Orleans. Their resolve to boycott the New Orleans-hosted All-Star event forced the game to be moved to Houston and brought attention to the continued racial discrimination going on in the Deep South despite the passage of the Civil Rights Act. Cookie felt that he had finally made a permanent home for himself in Buffalo and was inspired by the recent strides in the civil rights movement. All of that would soon change.

In February of 1965, I was informed that I had been traded to the Denver Broncos for fellow fullback Billy Joe. Billy Joe was the 1963 AFL Rookie of the Year for the Broncos, but had a lackluster sophomore campaign in 1964 and so had become a trade option for the team. The Broncos were having a hard time drawing fans, and their season ticket sales had dwindled to the point that the team was considering bankruptcy or relocation. The infusion of Abner Haynes, who was acquired through a trade from the Chiefs, and I would hopefully give Denver the drawing power they sought.

During the Bills' 1964 Championship run, I thought that all of the disagreements I'd had with Bills management had been settled with my public apology. We'd mutually agreed to start the 1965 season with a clean slate, but apparently the Bills had already decided to get rid of me. They'd picked a moment when my value was still high due to my league rushing title. If they had released me on waivers, the Bills would have received nothing in return. By keeping me on the team and showcasing my skills throughout the rest of the season, they could now get something of value in return.

I sometimes wondered, if Abner and I had not taken a stand against racial discrimination in New Orleans, would we have finished our careers in Kansas City and Buffalo, respectively. We were the most outspoken players when it came to the New Orleans boycott, and we just so happened to be the only ones traded so soon after the All-Star game. We had placed bull's-eyes on ourselves by being vocal when those in power would have preferred that we just went along. Because we forced their hand, they made the politically correct public decision to move the game to Houston. But behind the scenes, their anger was clear. The boycott destroyed the AFL's chance to add a new franchise in New Orleans and the opportunity to add financing to the league's war chest. The money that a New Orleans franchise would have added to the league's coffers was needed to help fund the ongoing war with the NFL over talent acquisition, and for simple survival within the sport. While not happy with the trade nor with the fact that the Bills had not kept their word, I wore this bull's-eye like a badge of honor.

The fact that we were both traded to the cash-strapped Broncos was telling. Denver jumped at the chance to acquire two marquee players in the hope that we would draw more fans to the stadium. The Broncos did not see the blackness of our skin, nor did they care about our views regarding race. When they looked at Abner and me, they saw the only color that mattered to a franchise in financial trouble, and that was the green color of money.

Out of all of the AFL franchises, the Broncos were in the worst financial shape. They were fighting for survival, so the fact that I came with the tag of being "uppity" or "difficult" mattered little to them. The new Denver backfield of Abner and me immediately drove season ticket sales from 8,000 to just over 22,000. This infusion of All-Star-caliber talent kept the Broncos in business and in the city of Denver.

Once the trade to Denver went through, I signed a two-year contract with a no-cut clause for an annual salary of $37,500 and an additional $5,000 signing bonus. In a show of gamesmanship I asked to wear Denver jersey number two, which was one number better than Billy Joe's old jersey number, three. Billy Joe kept the playful rivalry alive when he arrived in Buffalo and selected number 33, which was one number better than the number 34 I wore while with the Bills.

The Broncos coach was the great former Cleveland Browns receiver, Mac Speedie. At first glance, coach Speedie and I did not seem to have a lot in common, but in truth we were more alike than anyone could imagine. In Cleveland, Speedie had been a star, playing under coach Paul Brown. But he and coach Brown for the most part had not seen eye to eye. Coach Brown didn't care for Speedie's touchdown celebrations on the field and felt that he was sometimes over the top. In 1952, Speedie started his last and most productive season with the Browns by arriving to training camp with a pet skunk he'd named Paul. After leading the team with 62 receptions and receiving the team's MVP award during the 1952 season, Speedie surprised everyone by signing a contract with the

Saskatchewan Roughriders of the CFL. Despite still being productive on the field, Speedie predicted that coach Brown was about to faze him out of the Cleveland lineup due to their disagreements over salary.

Speedie's designation as an All-Star selection in his first two years in the CFL proved that he was still at the top of his game. But a broken leg suffered prior to the 1955 season ended his career on the field and marked the start of his transition into coaching.

You'd think, since we were both driven to play in Canada by the actions of Paul Brown, we would have had a common bond and a mutual respect, at least within the world of football. This was not the case. During my time in Denver, coach Speedie and I never saw eye to eye. As a player, he had been a colorful character, but the stress of being a head coach on a losing team had erased any memory of that carefree time in his career. In order to fight for his coaching life, Speedie had no margin for error and ruled with an iron fist. It was clearly now a case of "Do as I say, not as I do."

My first training camp with Denver did not go smoothly. The Broncos held their pre-season camp in Golden, Colorado, and I reported several days late. This resulted in my first run-in with coach Speedie. I had some personal affairs that I needed to tie up back East before heading to Denver for the upcoming season. When I arrived, coach Speedie said he was going to fine me for my tardiness, and that he would take the money out of my bonus. I tried to explain to the coach that I had legitimate reasons for my lateness, but he refused to listen. Never one to shy away from a situation, I started a war of words with coach Speedie through the press. I read his complaints about me in the morning newspapers and then provide comments to the press for the next edition. This went on for several days.

Finally I'd had enough, and I asked for a trade to the Oakland Raiders. While I waited for the Broncos to respond to my trade request, I stayed away from training camp. I was deemed a hold-out, and the team filed a $400,000 breach of contract suit against me. The basis for their suit was that by withholding my services, I would cripple the team financially. When Abner and I were added to the roster, Denver's ticket sales had soared, and if I didn't play, the fans would feel cheated, creating a public relations nightmare. Following a few days of negotiations, cooler heads prevailed and I reported to camp. The Broncos withdrew the lawsuit and all of the fines. Now the business of playing football was at hand.

That team had some really talented players, including Lionel Taylor, Goose Gonsoulin, and Willie Brown. I had already met many of the team's star players at prior All-Star games or during different league-sponsored events, but when I arrived in camp, I had no established relationships.

I used my time in Denver to start new friendships, and also saw this as an opportunity to mentor the team's younger players. I struck up a friendship with Odell Barry, who was the Broncos' young punt returner. During the season, Odell and I appeared joined at the hip and could usually be seen driving around Denver in my new Cadillac. As part of my contract I'd required the Broncos to supply me with a new Cadillac equipped with a mobile phone. The mobile phone was quite a conversation piece in 1965, but it could also be a curse because I was making it easier for people to contact me. There was one time that Odell answered the car phone just as I was telling him to let it ring. When the person on the other end asked for me, Odell replied, "Let me see if I can find him." But we were being called on a car phone, where could I honestly be other than next to him? Other than that incident, we got along famously and I tried my best to impart my prior experiences, on and off the football field, to the next generation of the AFL.

We opened the season on September 11, 1965, in San Diego against the Chargers. Coach Speedie named Mickey Slaughter the starter at quarterback, and his three-touchdown performance made it seem that Speedie had made the right call. In that game Abner and I each scored a touchdown, but despite our team's offensive output the Broncos lost by a final score of 34-31.

The second game of the season brought the Buffalo Bills to Denver. I wanted to have a standout game against my former team to make them regret their decision to trade me. Unfortunately, the game was one of the most disappointing of my career, as I only rushed for 26 yards on 12 attempts. Mickey Slaughter had an uneven performance at quarterback, throwing two touchdowns and five interceptions. My replacement in Buffalo, Billy Joe, scored a touchdown on a pass thrown by Jack Kemp and drilled home the fact that the Bills had moved on. The Bills won the game by a final score of 30-15 and were on their way to a second straight AFL championship.

In the third week of the season, we secured our first win in an away game against the Patriots. Wendell Hayes and I led the ground attack for the Broncos behind my 142 yards on the ground and his two rushing touchdowns. We were riding high on our 27-10 victory over the Patriots, but this would be only one of four wins during the 1965 season.

I made my eagerly anticipated return to Buffalo on October 24, 1965, and wanted to have a great game in front of the Buffalo fans. The game started off with a Billy Joe 78-yard touchdown reception from Jack Kemp. The Bills' offensive onslaught did not end until they emerged with a 31-13 victory.

Despite the loss, I did all I could to lead the team, rushing for 87 yards and adding an additional 55 yards receiving. The team now had a 3-4 record and was starting to free-fall in the standings.

Our last win of the season came in week ten against the Houston Oilers. The game marked my second 100-yard rushing performance of the season when I added 119 yards on the ground, but the star of the game was Abner Haynes, who rushed for a touchdown and also returned a punt for a score. We left Houston with a 31-21victory, but would finish the season on a four-game losing streak.

Despite the talent on the team, the constant change at the quarterback position made it difficult for the team to succeed. Three different quarterbacks started games for the Broncos in 1965: John McCormack, Jacky Lee, and Mickey Slaughter. Even with the season's quarterback carousel, the Broncos finished third in the league in team passing and second in rushing offense. Still, despite being among the league leaders in two major offensive categories, we managed just four wins and well out of the playoffs.

I finished the season with 954 rushing yards and was the runner-up to the Chargers' Paul Lowe for the league rushing title. I tied Lowe, Wray Carlton, and Curtis McClinton for the league lead in rushing touchdowns with six and secured another All-Star appearance. The one thing I did lead the league in was rushing attempts with 252, which marked thirty more attempts than Paul Lowe, who was second. The sizeable number of rushing attempts, added to the wear and tear I'd suffered in previous seasons, was starting to catch up with me. My knees were starting to swell and ache following each game, and I was finding it more and more difficult for my body to recover from the constant abuse it was facing on the gridiron. The 1965 campaign would be my last full and productive season in professional football.

Though Cookie remained one of the most productive players in the entire AFL, the strain on his body was apparent in his statistics: his yards per rushing attempt dropped to 3.8-yards per carry. Cookie's 928 total rushing attempts over the past four seasons was far and away more than any other player in the league, and it was taking a tremendous toll on his body. Cookie played with a sense of reckless abandonment, giving everything he had to the game, and it was starting to show. He was being run into the ground and towards retirement.

The punishment he so liked to dish out on the field was taking more of a toll than he would want to admit. The tackles that in the past he would regularly break for a few extra yards were becoming fewer and far between. Father time was starting to gain on him and this would be the one opponent Cookie could not outrun.

Cookie as a member of the Har-Brack High School football team.
Photo Courtesy of The Gilchrist Family

Cookie breaking a tackle as a member of the Toronto Argonauts.
Photo courtesy of the Toronto Argonauts.

1962 Bills Press photo depicting Cookie taking a hand off from quarterback Al Dorow (12) and running behind a block set by Wray Carlton (30).
Photo by ©Robert L. Smith Orchard Park N.Y.

December 8, 1963. Cookie conferring on the bench with teammates Daryle Lamonica (12) and Elbert Dubenion (44) during a Bills home game against the New York Jets. Cookie rushed for a then record 243 yards and scored five touchdowns leading the Bills to a convincing 45-14 win.

Photo by ©Robert L. Smith Orchard Park N.Y.

Cookie fighting to break the tackle of the Chargers Bud Whitehead.

Photo by ©Robert L. Smith Orchard Park N.Y.

Cookie running for a touchdown against the Houston Oilers at Jeppesen Stadium.

Photo by ©Robert L. Smith Orchard Park N.Y.

Cookie kicking a field goal at War Memorial Stadium during the 1963 season.
Photo by ©Robert L. Smith Orchard Park N.Y.

October 5, 1963. Billy Shaw blocking for Cookie during a 23-20 win over the Raiders at War Memorial Stadium.
Photo by ©Robert L. Smith Orchard Park N.Y.

December 20, 1964. Another photo from the victory over the Patriots at Fenway Park.
Photo by ©Robert L. Smith Orchard Park N.Y.

Billy Shaw and Cookie relaxing in the locker room prior to a road game.
Photo by ©Robert L. Smith Orchard Park N.Y.

Promotional picture of Cookie taken prior to the start of the 1964 season.
Courtesy of Buffalo State College Archives-E.H. Butler Library

Cookie playing against the Houston Oilers at War Memorial Stadium.
Photo by ©Robert L. Smith Orchard Park N.Y.

December 20, 1964. Cookie celebrates the Bills' 24-14 win over the Patriots with several unidentified members of the Boston Police Department.
Courtesy of Buffalo State College Archives-E.H. Butler Library

October 24, 1965. Cookie returns to War Memorial for the first time as a member of the Broncos. The Bills defeat the Broncos 31-13.
Photo by ©Robert L. Smith Orchard Park N.Y.

Reflecting on a Broncos Loss at home during the 1965 season.
Courtesy of the Denver Broncos

OJ, coach Lou Saban and Cookie following a Buffalo Bills game.
Photo Courtesy of The Gilchrist Family

Heavyweight Showdown

Cookie's time with the Broncos brought him a new friendship with another recent high-profile transplant to the Denver area. Sonny Liston, the former Heavyweight Champion, had also recently moved into the Mile High Region looking for his own fresh start. In his hometown of Philadelphia, Sonny had been branded a troublemaker due to several run-ins with police. He hoped the change of scenery would help him ditch the stigma of always being on the wrong side of the law. Sonny and Cookie quickly connected over their shared desire for a fresh start and the common bond of being branded the "Bad Boys" of their respective sports.

I had met former Heavyweight Champion Sonny Liston several times in the past, but our interactions were limited to brief meetings during award banquets. Sonny had moved to Denver to escape the police harassment he faced living in St. Louis and Philadelphia. He'd been arrested several times during his life, starting with a prison sentence in St. Louis for robbing a gas station. During this incarceration, the prison priest, Father Stevens, introduced Sonny to boxing. Sonny was a natural at the sweet science of boxing, especially with his tremendous reach and punching power. Father Stevens helped Sonny secure early parole from prison and started on the path to boxing success.

Sonny never denied his involvement in that robbery, nor did he make excuses for his actions. He accepted responsibility for the crime he committed and paid his debt to society. Nevertheless, a reputation as a troublemaking convict would follow him throughout his life. Whether deserved or not, the word "troublemaker" always seemed to come up if Sonny or I were mentioned in the media. Regardless of what the point of the story was, there would be a mention of either Sonny or me having done something negative. In my case, I could have saved a kitten from a tree, and still a paragraph would follow reminding everyone that I'd refused to report to training camp due to a contract holdout. Sonny and I shared this common bond of being branded troublemakers by the media.

As Sonny made his way through the boxing ranks toward a heavyweight title fight, he was arrested several more times. Rumors of an organized crime link within his boxing management made him a target for police wherever he resided. I remember his stories of being detained by police and accused of disorderly conduct, just for stopping on the sidewalk to sign autographs. In spite of these outside distractions, Sonny defeated the heavily favored Floyd Patterson for the Heavyweight Title.

Sonny's decision to relocate to Denver came right after his victory over Patterson. He was quoted as saying he'd "rather be a lamp post in Denver than the Mayor of Philadelphia." Though he retained his Heavyweight Title in a re-match with Patterson, he eventually lost to an up-and-coming fighter named Cassius Clay, who would later convert to the Muslim religion and rename himself Muhammad Ali. A year later, Sonny was given a heavyweight re-match with Ali, but lost again. There was a good deal of suspicion in the boxing world speculating that Sonny threw the fight by taking an early dive on a weak Ali blow, allegedly due to fear of the Nation of Islam, who were now in control of Ali's career.

Our friendship was at its height during the period right after his re-match with Ali. Sonny was still deciding whether to hang up his gloves and start his retirement. He was investigating what business options would be open to him, and we even discussed opening a restaurant together. I had an idea for a hamburger joint near the Broncos stadium. When I brought the idea up to Sonny I thought we could market the restaurant with a picture of he and I in black cowboy hats above the name "Cookie and Sonny's Bronco Burgers." I suggested that we embrace our bad-boy image in the marketing campaign, imagining that we would be the Butch and Sundance of the restaurant business.

One night the partnership idea, and very nearly our entire friendship, fell apart. Sonny and I had been out on the town and were chatting with a few young ladies we had just met at a local club. As the night progressed and the drinks flowed, Sonny started to get overly obnoxious toward the ladies. I tried to calm him down, but he continued his rant and an argument between us ensued. In an attempt to sucker punch me, Sonny took a wild swing at me. Fortunately for me, he missed: had he landed that punch, even in his inebriated state, it would have done tremendous damage. Sonny kept coming at me, so I struck him with one punch to the face, knocking him out cold.

The boxing training I'd received during my youth from Dr. Montgomery came in handy that night. Dr. Montgomery always said I had the stuff to become the Heavyweight Champion, but this was the closest I ever got to a title fight, and I wouldn't tempt fate by trying for a re-match any time soon.

The next day, with the effects of the alcohol erased, we moved past the previous night's altercation. We chalked it up to a wild night of women and too much to drink. I decided to stop pursuing the restaurant partnership since I had finally met my match when it came to Sonny's uncontrollable and larger-than-life personality. Looking back, I think we were too much alike in many respects, but it was his love of drinking that was my cue to end our business aspirations.

Sonny decided to get back into the ring and had several more successful fights, running up a streak of 14 consecutive wins before meeting defeat at the hands of a contender named Leotis Martin. That defeat derailed any chance at another title fight for Sonny, but it wasn't his last professional bout. That would be in 1970, against top contender Chuck Wepner. Throughout the bout, Wepner suffered the fury of Sonny's striking ability. The referee had to stop the fight when Sonny broke Wepner's cheekbone and nose, an injury that required seventy-two stitches to repair. The sight of the vicious punishment Wepner suffered made me thank my lucky stars that Sonny never landed the punch that was meant for me.

Sonny and I kept in touch after he relocated to Las Vegas. I was shocked when the news broke that Sonny was found dead at his Las Vegas home on January 5, 1971. The death certificate listed heart failure and lung congestion as the cause of death, but due to the needle marks found on his arms, a heroin overdose was inferred by the local authorities. The hard partying lifestyle appeared to have caught up with the Champ, who had compiled a career record of 50 wins against 4 losses, with 39 of the wins by knockout. His headstone is inscribed with the simple epitaph "A Man," which I find very ironic since he was the most complicated individual I have ever met.

Cookie had finally come face to face with another athletic great whose background and career successes rivaled his own. When Cookie looked at Sonny's life and career, he felt in many respects like he was looking into a mirror. This complicated king of the ring gave Cookie a fresh perspective on his own life and career decisions. The Champ's untimely death was not an image Cookie wanted to see for himself, and it was one of the factors that eventually drove him toward the creation of the United Athletes Coalition.

The Merger and Miami

The war being fought by the upstart American Football League against the established National Football League was coming to an end. The same was also true of Cookie's stint in Denver. He had another year left on the two-year contract he signed with Denver, but, once again, it was acting on his conscious that would be his undoing.

On June 8, 1966, the AFL and the NFL issued a cease-fire when they announced a merger of the two leagues. Though the two leagues would not merge their operations until 1970, for now they would hold a common draft and a championship game between the AFL and NFL winners. Kansas City Chiefs owner Lamar Hunt would eventually name that game the Super Bowl, an idea that came to Hunt after he saw his children playing with a rubber ball called a Super Ball.

There was a plan in place for the placement of expansion franchises in several cities, including Miami, for the start of the 1966 season. The new combined league would be led by NFL Commissioner Pete Rozelle and would retain the NFL name. Eventually divisions called the AFC and NFC would break down the new NFL. The AFC division would be the AFL teams, with the addition of the NFL's Pittsburgh Steelers, Baltimore Colts, and Cleveland Browns, who would transfer in order to even out the number of teams in the new divisions.

Many thought the AFL had gone to the NFL to seek the merger. In fact, the NFL came to the AFL ownership and said the competition between the two leagues was making the business of professional football unprofitable. The two leagues had been trying to outbid each other for the top talent from the college ranks, and the new player salaries were increasing at an alarming rate. Prior to the merger negotiation, the NFL had become aware that the AFL had secured a large television contract with NBC, increasing their war chest. New NY Jets owner Sonny Werblin also fired a shot across the NFL's bow when he signed Joe Namath out of the University of Alabama to an unheard-of $400,000 contract. It was clear to the NFL that the AFL was there to stay, and that it had a take-no-prisoners attitude. While these events were significant in pushing the leagues toward a merger, there was one incident that was seen as the main catalyst.

Even though they were in competition with each other, the two leagues had maintained a gentlemen's agreement to not sign each other's free agents, thereby trying to keep the salaries of established players down. Wellington Mara of the New York Giants broke that agreement when he signed my former Buffalo teammate Pete Gogolak to a free agent contract for the 1966 season. Gogolak was the first of the soccer-style kickers in football, and his accuracy revolutionized the position. Once the Giants broke the unwritten agreement between the two leagues, the AFL decided to go after the NFL's established star players. The AFL signed Roman Gabriel, John Brodie, and Mike Ditka to what they called "future contracts," which meant they were signed in advance of their current NFL contracts expiring. The salaries offered to these players in future contracts far and away exceeded their current NFL salaries and led to an exodus of players from the NFL to the AFL. The NFL owners knew that if the war between the leagues didn't end, they would both risk financial ruin. Football historians consider the Gogolak signing the singular event that brought the NFL to propose a merger of the leagues.

In order for the merger to go into effect, Congress would have to approve the new league by issuing an antitrust exemption. The exemption legislation was pushed through by two Louisiana political heavyweights, Hale Boggs and Russell Long. In appreciation of the politicians' support, the city of New Orleans was awarded an expansion team.
The new franchise was named the Saints, and New Orleans finally had the professional football team they had been yearning for.

The excitement of the merger was sweeping through the world of sports just as I was preparing for my second season with the Denver Broncos. My former Buffalo teammate Willie Ross contacted me, looking for my help. Willie was without a contract and thought I might be able to help him get a tryout with the Broncos. While I made no promises, I told Willie I would recommend him to the team.

I arrived for training camp ten days late and was again in the doghouse with coach Speedie. Willie had also made the trip to Colorado in the hope that the team would allow him to tryout. My first order of business was to talk to coach Speedie about a tryout for Willie. When I entered Speedie's office, the first thing he said to me was that he had already fined me $1,000 for my late arrival to training camp. I told him I was prepared to accept the fine and that I had come to talk to him about a tryout for Willie.

Coach Speedie said that we were loaded at the running back position, and he did not see a need for another player at that position. He even added, "Isn't that the guy that took your place on the field when you quit on your Buffalo teammates?" While he was correct, the personal jab added fuel to the fire of our already heated relationship. He also made a comment related to Willie's Muslim faith: he didn't want that militant Muslim attitude around the team, he said, because he already had enough trouble just dealing with me. The argument escalated when I tried to explain to Speedie that just because someone was Muslim it didn't make them a militant. The two factors of Willie being a black man and a follower of the Muslim religion led Speedie to jump to the incorrect conclusion that Willie must be a follower of the black supremacy movement.

This example of coach Speedie's closed-minded and ill-informed thinking finally pushed me over the edge. While we had never gotten along, Speedie had now made this personal, and I requested a trade before leaving his office. Within a day, the newspapers were all over the incident, and were calling me for a comment, but I refused. The next day when Speedie was being interviewed by the local beat writers, my request for a trade was discussed along with my refusal to report to training camp. Speedie made a comment about my absence saying, "Well, Christmas came early for me this year."

After that I decided that I would never again play for coach Speedie. I would not play for someone who would discriminate against people just because of their race or religion. He had never even met Willie and yet he dismissed his abilities simply based on the color of his skin and the deities he prayed to. When the Broncos insisted they wouldn't trade me, I issued a statement asserting that I would rather retire than play for coach Speedie. On August 2, 1966, I was placed on the reserved/retired list. This gesture was the equivalent of a suspension, as the league did not have a suspended designation.

The Broncos and I were issued a warning by then-acting AFL Commissioner Milt Woodward informing us that if I was not removed from the reserved list by August 16, I would not be eligible to play for the Broncos that season. The Broncos tried to trade me to the Oakland Raiders during this dispute, but found the Raiders' proposal to be less than fair value.

Coach Speedie resigned his head coaching position after losses in the Broncos' first two games of the season. Speedie was given a scouting position within the Broncos organization and never coached again, finishing with a career record of 6-19-1. Once Speedie was no longer in charge, I thought the Broncos would be more open to accepting a trade offer. Several weeks into the season, there was no movement, and I contemplated bringing legal action against the league. I let the Broncos know that if I wasn't traded, I would file a lawsuit against them and the league. The new merger of the two leagues still depended on the Congressional antitrust exemption, and my proposed lawsuit could have put that in jeopardy, and would at least have slowed it down through continued depositions and subpoenas. The Broncos brought their concerns regarding my threat of a lawsuit to the league, and together they determined it was better to avoid any legal challenges prior to the merger's completion.

On October 16, 1966, the Broncos visited the expansion Miami Dolphins for a game at the Orange Bowl. The Broncos lost, but during the visit, they found a willing partner for my contract and negotiated my trade. The Dolphins would give the Broncos a third and fifth-round draft choice in the next year's draft in exchange for my services. On October 18, I was activated by the Dolphins from the Reserved/Retired list. My salary for the year would be the $37,500 salary designated in my Denver contract, prorated over the eight remaining games.

The Dolphins were owned by lawyer Joe Robbie and entertainer Danny Thomas. Having been in the world of entertainment, Thomas knew the importance of marketing. I was brought in to be a fan attraction, much like the Dolphin's mascot, Flipper the Dolphin, who sat in a tank at the end of the Orange Bowl field. Even this late in my career, my name still had drawing power at the gate.

My first game of the 1966 season was on October 23, 1966, in Houston against quarterback George Blanda and the Oilers. Entering the game the Dolphins had a 1-5 record with their only win coming the week before against the Broncos. During the game, I didn't tear it up on the ground, though I accounted for a receiving touchdown on a 13-yard reception from Rick Norton. The Dolphins secured their second win of the season with a final score of 20-13, which was almost not enough against the Oilers' one-man show of George Blanda. George threw one passing touchdown, kicked the extra point and added two more field goals, accounting for all of the Oilers' scoring. If anyone else on the Oilers had scored that day, we would not have been victorious.

During the previous season in Denver, I had begun to have problems with my knees and became accustomed to the constant throbbing and dull ache I felt during the season. After each game I applied ice to my knees to soothe the swelling and pain. I had hoped that the extra rest I got during my prolonged suspension had helped my body heal, but as soon as the game was over, the pain was back. My body was telling me it had taken too much abuse on the football field. Still, despite the continued punishment to my body, I was determined to hold onto football as long as I could.

The touchdown I scored in my first game with the Dolphins was not a sign of good things on the horizon. Following the victory over the Oilers, we lost our next game against Buffalo 29-0. I only accounted for ten rushing yards on six attempts and considered the game a complete embarrassment. The Dolphins continued the losing streak by racking up five more losses against the Chiefs, Jets, Patriots, Broncos, and the Chiefs once again.

Our last game of the season was against the Oilers, and we entered the contest with a record of 2-11. I tried to get the team up for the game by telling them to have personal pride, and that we needed to end the season on a high note. The Oilers started Don Trull at quarterback, and he had a great game, throwing three touchdowns and even rushing for one more. Although I account for no scoring that day, I did contribute with sixty yards receiving and twenty-four yards rushing. We squeezed out a 29-28 win against the Oilers and finished the season with a 3-11 record.

The two things I learned while playing in Miami were that I was unhappy living in South Florida, and that the Dolphins would need time to grow as a team before they could achieve success. At the end of the season I could barely walk without limping, and I was conflicted about whether to return to football the following season. Should I put my body through the punishment of another season in Miami with no real chance of winning?

My personal life was also not faring any better. I was lonely and missed my family and friends, who were back in the Northeast and Canada. I decided that if I did return, it would be my last season and my chance to go out on my own terms.

Cookie saw the writing on the wall. He could no longer ignore the pain he felt with every step he took. The game had always come so easily to Cookie - he'd never thought the accolades and big-money contracts would end. Cookie had seen too many before him forced out, whether due to diminished skills or a career-ending injury. He was determined to walk away under his own power before the game passed him by.

A final season would give him the chance to say farewell to the game he once dominated, while securing one last contract for his retirement. The only question now was whether the farewell would come from South Florida.

Muhammad Ali and Main Bout

Cookie was about to come to the defense of another brash young athlete named Muhammad Ali when Ali became a target of the United States government. Cookie related to Ali's outspoken demeanor, as they were both unafraid to speak their minds and stand up for what they felt was right. Ali had started his boxing career under his birth name, Cassius Clay, but when he became a follower of the Nation of Islam, he changed it to the name he would become known as the world over, Muhammad Ali. Ali's religious beliefs compelled him to declare himself a conscientious objector to the Vietnam War and he thereby became a target of the United States government. Cookie and the other leading athletes of the day would come to his side, not necessarily because they followed the same religious beliefs, but because they felt he was a young black man who had the right to express his opinions and beliefs without fear of persecution.

The young Muhammad Ali started life as Cassius Clay in Louisville, Kentucky. Clay won several local Golden Gloves titles before winning the light heavyweight Gold Medal at the 1960 Summer Olympics in Rome. As his boxing victories began to amass, Clay became more well-known for his constant self-promotion and the fact that he claimed triumph over his opponents even before the matches started. On several occasions, Clay even correctly predicted the round that he would knock out his opponent.

Clay finally got a title shot against Sonny Liston on May 25, 1964. Prior to the fight, the event promoter learned that Clay had become a student of Malcolm X, the Nation of Islam leader. The thought of a fan backlash and the possible cancellation of the fight led Clay to withhold the fact that he had converted to Islam and changed his name to Muhammad Ali. At the pre-event press conference, Clay was asked whether he had switched to Islam, but he sidestepped the reporter's questions with the same elusiveness he used to avoid his opponent's punches. That press conference is where Clay gave his famous quote "I'll float like a butterfly and sting like a bee," in response to a question about his fight strategy.

Clay won the bout when Liston refused to come out of his corner for the seventh round. Clay boasted victoriously, "I shook the world." He was now the Heavyweight Champion, and due to the fact that he was black, outspoken, and a member of a radical religious movement, he had placed himself in the crosshairs of the media.

After the defeat of Liston, the newly christened champion announced his religious affiliation with the Nation of Islam and his name change to Muhammad Ali. In 1965, he held two title defenses, with a re-match against Liston, who was knocked out in the first round, and a 12-round TKO of Floyd Patterson.

In early 1966 Ali was classified draft eligible for the Vietnam War. Upon learning this information he declared himself a conscientious objector. He stated that he had no quarrel with the Viet Kong and that the conflict was in direct violation of the Holy Qur'an.

Once Ali announced his affiliation with the Nation of Islam and his profile grew, every move he and his management made was put under a microscope. Ali had a March 29, 1966, fight scheduled against Ernie Terrell in Canada, which was scheduled to be carried by Main Bout, Inc. Main Bout was a boxing promotion company that was started by lawyer Bob Arum and Cleveland Browns running back Jim Brown. This new business relationship came about when Arum chatted up Brown after a 1965 Ernie Terrell-George Chuvalo boxing match they both attended. Following the Terrell win, Arum commented to Brown that a Terrell vs. Ali match would have huge box-office appeal. This was Arum's way of getting Brown to persuade Ali, who was a close of his, to fight Terrell. For his powers of persuasion, Brown was given a ten percent stake in Main Bout, Inc., which would hold all of the closed-circuit television rights to the match between Terrell and Ali.

Ali's refusal to participate in the war forced him to fight in venues outside the United States, so the fight was scheduled to take place in Toronto, with plans to broadcast the match to the U.S. on closed-circuit television. Brown relied on his prominent contacts through the world of sports to handle the distribution of the closed-circuit rights to the fight within different cities across the United States. He contacted me to handle the distribution rights in the Buffalo area, and I readily agreed.

I had met Ali before he changed his name and religious affiliation and thought he was a great fighter. While I did not always agree with his politics, I believed in his right to freedom of speech and religion.

As the fight date approached, many of the potential outlets for the broadcast, including the two largest theatre chains at the time, B&K and Stanley Warner, began to waver due to Ali's refusal to enter the armed services. These outlets had been receiving pressure from their customers regarding Ali's position on the war in Vietnam and felt that not broadcasting his fight would be a way to boycott his unpopular politics.

Jim Brown had a quite different take on the backlash from the different venues. He felt that the real reason the venues were refusing to handle the broadcast was the fact that primarily black investors owned Main Bout and that Muslims held several key positions in the company.

I had several outlets in the Buffalo area refuse to show the fight. They too justified their refusal by claiming they wanted to avoid offending patrons who'd expressed displeasure with Ali's political views.

I called Jim's Cleveland office to discuss the opposition I was facing in promoting the fight in Buffalo. I was informed that Jim and the four other shareholders of Main Bout were holding a meeting in New York to discuss the boycott of the broadcast venues.

In addition to Jim's ten-percent ownership in Main Bout as the vice-president in charge of public relations, the company also had two other prominent black shareholders. Herbert Muhammad was Main Bout's President and held twenty-five percent of the company's shares. Herbert's father also happened to be Nation of Islam founder Elijah Muhammad. John Ali held the title of treasurer for Main Bout, and also controlled a twenty-five percent stake of the company. John was also a prominent member of the Nation of Islam, acting as their National Secretary.

Bob Arum and Michael Malitz, the sole white members of the company, each held twenty-percent stakes in Main Bout and acted as the company's vice president and secretary, respectively.

I jumped the next flight to New York and became a voice in the discussions. As we sat discussing the problems we were facing in getting the fight televised, the only white faces were those of Bob Arum and Michael Malitz. For once, another race was brought in to be the token face to a corporation or a cause. The strong hold that the Nation of Islam had over Muhammad Ali was seen throughout the discussion. They would dictate when and where he would fight and had now put a stranglehold on the sport of boxing.

As the meeting continued, I spoke up to share Jim's fear that Main Bout was being shut out of the boxing market due to race and the fear of the Nation of Islam. Jim was saying that it was all about keeping a black man down and away from running a successful business. He argued that rejecting Ali's refusal to join the military was the public's way of expressing their underlying anxieties regarding the black owners of the company. Though I did feel that Ali's politics turned off a large segment of Middle America, following the discussion, I also felt that Jim's concerns were founded.

I brought up the idea of asking other prominent black athletes to boycott their respective sports until Muhammad Ali was allowed to fight again within the borders of the United States. This kind of boycott would also bring light to the fact that Main Bout was having difficulty operating due to underlying racism. I outlined what had transpired during the All-Star game boycott in New Orleans and said that if we could get the prominent athletes to stand together, we could be successful in bringing about change.

Regardless of the fact that this situation was related to a business proposition, it was still an issue of racism. The thought occurred to me to bring in a prominent politician, such as President Johnson, to help publicize our situation. During my career I had become acquainted with several powerful politicians, including the current president. The members of Main Bout's board agreed that a politician was the way to go, but they wanted to have a black politician as the spokesman for the group.

The next call I made was to Adam Clayton Powell Jr., the Democratic congressman from New York, and the most powerful black man in politics.

Powell listened to Main Bout's concerns and agreed to support our cause. A press conference was quickly scheduled for the next day, March 10, 1966, in Powell's Washington office. A flurry of phone calls was made by Jim and me to get other athletes to stand with us at the press conference. Jim and me flew to his office in Cleveland to meet up with the athletes who agreed to stand with us. Fellow football players Bobby Mitchell, Lonny Sanders, John Wooten, Walter Beech, and Willie Wood joined us in Cleveland.

During this stopover, I approached Ali and the Main Bout Board about buying into the company. I had a financial interest in the upcoming fight's TV rights, and wanted to become part of Ali's management team. I said to Ali that I could even help him train for his fights by becoming his sparring partner. As a joke, I even added that I would take it easy on him and promised to not knock him out.

Ali told me I needed to take up the matter with Herbert Muhammad and the other board members. Herbert Muhammad flatly refused my offer and said all of the shares were spoken for. I then approached Jim about selling half of his stake in the business, but he refused as well. The more I looked at it, it seemed like the Nation of Islam would only deal with those outside their ranks out of necessity. Jim had already set them up with another major athlete to help promote their cause and act as a mentor to Ali. My services would not be needed on a regular basis, but only to lend a face to this battle. The TV rights I was awarded in Buffalo would be my thank you for lending my name and image to their fight, and that was the best financial agreement I would be offered doing business with Main Bout, Inc.

Once we arrived in Washington, we all met in Congressman Powell's office. I led the discussion by saying that all in attendance were willing to boycott their respective sports in response to Muhammad Ali's treatment and the fact that Main Bout was being shut out of several arenas due to racism. Powell responded by saying that while an athlete's boycott may be an option in the future, the point of the press conference was to let the general public know that Ali and Main Bout were facing harassment and racism. Powell asked me to lead the procession of athletes into the press conference room. Powell and Jim entered last and sat before a microphone while I stood behind them with Bobby Mitchell and the other athletes.

Jim and Congressman Powell were the only ones who spoke at the news conference. Jim talked about how behind-the-scenes groups had tried to discredit Main Bout by alleging illegal activities and organized-crime ties. "Main Bout is a perfectly legal operation," he declared. "The only difference is that this is the first time that Negroes are getting in on the big-money end of a fight."

Congressman Powell then vowed to use the full resources of his office to investigate the claims of racism and determine whether federal law could be invoked to remedy the situation.

We were less than three weeks from the fight and hoped that this public stand would bring attention to the situation. Ali's opponent Ernie Terrell had withdrawn from the fight during all of the controversy and been quickly replaced by George Chuvalo.

The fight went off in front of 12,000 fans at Maple Leaf Gardens, and Ali emerged victorious after a 15 round decision. The fight was profitable, but nowhere near what it would have been if the two largest theatre chains hadn't walked away. Our press conference and public outcry did not bring any of the venues back to the table, but we showed that we were ready to fight for equal rights and freedom of speech.

Muhammad Ali fought and won three more times in 1966, all outside US borders. Ali returned to fight in the US when he faced Cleveland Williams on November 14, 1966, at the Houston Astrodome. Ali won this fight, but his fight with the US government and the public's opinion was just beginning.

I continued to follow Ali's career. We spoke from time to time, and I always told him to stay the course with his beliefs and never to bow to public pressure. I respected Ali's frank and outspoken nature and saw a lot of myself in him. Though Ali was already strong in his convictions,

I thought my positive reinforcement would help to strengthen those beliefs. At different times in my career, I had made several controversial decisions and had always wished that someone had been there to lend similar words of encouragement. I made it a point to provide him with the support I would have wanted for myself.

On April 28, 1967, Ali was arrested after three times refusing to respond to his name during a military induction ceremony. At the trial, he was found guilty in less than a half hour. Ali remained free on bail while he appealed the conviction, but for a three-and-a-half-year period was unable to fight because his boxing license had been revoked. In addition to the support Ali received from Jim and me during this difficult time, he also received the support of the biggest names in sports, including Bill Russell and Kareem Abdul Jabbar. We all spoke out in support of Ali's right to freedom of speech and religion.

Ali eventually resumed his boxing career in 1970 and continued his winning ways with a third round TKO of Jerry Quarry. His winning was not exclusive to the boxing ring, as The United States Supreme Court eventually overturned his conviction.

Ali continued to fight until his retirement in 1981 and won the Heavyweight title on three separate occasions. In 1984, he announced that he was suffering from Parkinson's disease and as time passed his condition would deteriorate. I wondered if the repeated head trauma he suffered in the boxing ring had brought on this condition. Would he become punch drunk like so many of the boxers who had entered the ring before him? As I progressed towards retirement, I had started suffering from repeated headaches and periods of forgetfulness. Was I, like Ali, feeling the effects of participating in a violent sport? I guess only time will tell for both of us.

Cookie found a kindred spirit in the outspoken Muhammad Ali. While they didn't share the same politics, they had a common bond in being outspoken black athletes who each had reached the top of their respective sports. Cookie was disappointed when he was refused a chance to become part of Ali's management group, but continued to support Ali in his pursuit of his legal rights.

Cookie's relationship with Ali also prompted him to question the role that violent sports like boxing and football might have on an athlete's mental and physical well-being later in life. The experience of seeing numerous former friends and teammates suffer from diminished health and, sometimes, dementia much earlier than the general public, led Cookie to question the safety of these sports and consider more seriously what his own future might bring.

The Last Hurrah

Cookie had decided the upcoming 1967 season would be his last on the gridiron. While training for his farewell, he also began to ponder what he might do once he retired from football. Cookie had left school after the eleventh grade, and, other than playing football, he had no other formal training. When he came to realize that he was only prepared to be Cookie Gilchrist the football player, the thought scared him more than anything that he had faced on or off the field. Cookie's athletic skills had always made him a sought-after talent, even though he had been branded as a difficult troublemaker. Cookie had always thought that football needed him to survive, and as the end of his career approached, he realized it was actually the other way around. He would be replaced as soon as he walked off the field, and he might not be able to fill the void that the loss of the game would leave in his life.

The end of the 1966 season brought the first Championship game between the AFL and NFL Champions. On January 15, 1967, the NFL powerhouse Green Bay Packers, led by coach Vince Lombardi, defeated the Kansas City Chiefs by a final score of 35-10. The game was held in Los Angeles and was not even a sellout. Any fan could have walked up to the ticket window and purchased a seat for twelve dollars - a far cry from future Super Bowl game tickets, which are the most expensive and sought-after tickets in the world.

Prior to the game, the Packers were told by the NFL owners that a loss to Kansas City was unacceptable. Even though the two leagues had negotiated a merger, there was still bad blood between them, making this game personal. The NFL wanted to prove to the world that they were indeed the superior league by beating the "Mickey Mouse League," which was what they called the AFL behind closed doors.

Following the game, Coach Lombardi was bombarded with questions from reporters looking for a quote asserting the NFL's superiority. He was quoted as saying, "I don't think Kansas City compares with the best teams in the NFL." He added that he felt that Dallas, the NFL runner-up that year, was a much better team than any within the AFL. Lombardi's post-game comments gave me and everyone else that played in the so called "Mickey

Mouse League" the bulletin board material we needed for the next time the two leagues played, which would come during the 1967 preseason.

As the 1967 season was rolling around, I was informed that I had been traded from Miami back to the Denver Broncos along with George Wilson, Ernie Park, and Earl Faison, in exchange for Abner Haynes, Jerry Hopkins, Danny La Rose, and a sixth-round draft pick. The trade wasn't that surprising since I hadn't had a great season in Miami, but the fact that my former coach Lou Saban pulled the trigger on it was. Lou had left the Bills following the 1965 season when they won the second of back-to-back championships. A week after winning his second title with the Bills, he walked away from Buffalo to coach Maryland in the college ranks. While coaching at Maryland, Lou decided he preferred coaching in the professional ranks and jumped at the Broncos head-coaching offer. I took it as a great compliment that, despite our past differences, he thought enough of my ability to bring me back to Denver.

In the off-season the two leagues held their first common-player draft. The Broncos selected with the sixth overall pick a young tailback from Syracuse named Floyd Little. I had clearly been brought in to be a mentor to this new superstar-in-training as well as a bridge for the team until he was ready to take over the bulk of the workload.

When I first met Floyd, I could see that he had the physical ability to become one of the great running backs, but more importantly, he also had the ability to be a leader on the field. Syracuse had a history of producing high-caliber running backs including Jim Brown, Ernie Davis, Jim Nance, and Larry Csonka. Floyd would eventually set the league on fire, earning himself a place in Canton with the greats of the Pro Football Hall of Fame.

The 1967 preseason schedule pitted us in a home game against the NFL's Detroit Lions. Floyd didn't play in this game, as he was leading the previous college All-Stars in an exhibition game against the Champion Green Bay Packers. Prior to our game, coach Saban read us the riot act and said that we could take this opportunity to let the NFL know that the AFL was the superior league. The preseason and the end-of-year championship game, later called the Super Bowl, would be the only time the two leagues played each other until the final merger of the two league's schedules in 1970. This was our chance to make a statement for the AFL.

When we rushed onto the field, I can say without a doubt that the entire Bronco team wanted to punch the Lions and the rest of the NFL in the mouth. The great Lions' defensive tackle Alex Karras had been extremely condescending during the coin toss, telling my Denver teammate Dave Costa that if the Lions lost, he would walk back to Detroit.

The first quarter was scoreless for both teams, but we drew first blood in the second quarter with a 35-yard field goal by kicker Errol Mann. I followed that by finding the end zone with a one-yard touchdown run. At halftime, we were shutting out the Lions by a score of 10-0, and the looks of shock were visible along the Lions' sideline. In the third quarter, both teams traded punts with no scoring from either team. Early in the fourth quarter, the Lions did get on the scoreboard with a touchdown pass from quarterback Milt Plum to receiver Bill Malinchack. The score was now 10-7 in our favor, but the Lions were now within a field goal of tying the game. Our defense settled down and kept the Lions from scoring any additional points. We scored one more field goal on another Errol Mann kick within the last two minutes of the game, leaving us with a final score of 13-7 in favor of the Broncos.

The Broncos had secured the first win for the upstart AFL over the established NFL. Even with the constant pain in my knees, I had managed 89 yards rushing on 13 carries with a touchdown. My hard training and focus during the off-season was paying off on the field. Though only a preseason game, both teams had played as if it was for the Super Bowl. The victory was a wake-up call to the NFL that the so-called "Mickey Mouse League" meant business.

The preseason schedule continued the next week with another home contest against the NFL's Minnesota Vikings. Floyd started at tailback, and I was the starting fullback. We won the game by a score of 14-3, with Floyd and me both scoring touchdowns. I was determined to go out on top and would punish whoever got in my way, and that day I took out my aggression on Jim Marshall and Alan Page, the defensive ends of the Vikings. Page would later be named to the Pro Football Hall of Fame, but as a defensive tackle. During that game I exploited him at the defensive end position while running continued sweeps, forcing the Vikings to move him at halftime to defensive tackle, where he remained for the rest of his Hall of Fame career. Following our second win against an NFL team, I was sure they were feeling the backlash of Coach Lombardi's condescending comments following the first Super Bowl.

The following week brought our last preseason game against the hated Oakland Raiders. The game was being held in Nebraska in honor of their centennial celebration. The League picked a rivalry game to give the local crowd a great show. We won for the third week in a row with a final score of 21-17 over the Raiders. Throughout the game I brought the pain to Raiders' defensive end "Big Ben" Davidson. As we continued to run the sweep play, I would come around and try to bury Big Ben. This was not an easy task as he stood a ferocious six feet eight inches tall. Floyd later said Big Ben took so many of my hits, he eventually just moved out of my way. Following the game, my knees were again swollen and painful, but I was feeling good about my decision to return. I was having fun playing the game again and relished the opportunity to suit up for this one last season.

Our first regular season game was scheduled for September 3, 1967, in Denver. We were playing the Boston Patriots and their stars: Babe Parilli, Gino Cappelletti, and Jim Nance. Floyd was clearly the new star of the Broncos, playing tailback and also returning kicks. I only made 10 rushing attempts in the game for 21 total yards. Then my body finally gave out. My left knee made a horrible popping sound, and the pain that ensued was excruciating. We won the game 26-21 on Goldie Seller's 29-yard interception return for a touchdown late in the fourth quarter, but my season was over.

The week following the game, the team's doctors performed exploratory surgery and said I had almost no cartilage left in the knee, and that I'd partially torn my ACL. Following the surgery to repair the damage, I was put in a full-leg cast and told my season and possibly my career were over. Whether or not my career was over was going to be a wait-and-see proposition. Sports medicine was not as advanced as it is today - I think if we had had today's technology my career might have continued.

Due to my inability to finish the rest of the 1967 season, the Broncos placed me on waivers. Knowing that I was damaged property, no other team made a claim for my contract.

I had already decided to call an end to my career after that season, but events did not play out as I envisioned. Now I was conflicted over whether to come back and make 1968 my final season, but my injury would dictate that decision. I continued my rehabilitation in Denver, while still doing my best to give guidance to the younger members of the Broncos. The team did not fare well, and lost the nine games following my injury to end the 1967 campaign with a final record of 3-11.

The 1968 season would bring the addition of the Cincinnati Bengals to the American Football League. The Bengals were going to be owned and coached by former Cleveland Browns coach Paul Brown. My dealings with coach Brown out of high school had left a bad taste in my mouth, and I'd vowed to never play for him. Each team in the AFL was required to leave several of their players open and available for the Bengals to choose from in the upcoming expansion draft. In effect, each team would leave five players unprotected, and the Bengals would have their pick of the litter. The Broncos left me unprotected and available due to the uncertainty regarding my knee injury. I understood their point: why protect a player coming off an injury when you don't know if he'll ever play again?

As was my luck, on January 16, 1968, the Cincinnati Bengals picked me in the expansion draft as one of the original Cincinnati Bengals. But I never suited up for them. The combination of my disdain for coach Brown and my knee injury, which never fully recovered, forced me to hang up my jersey and walk away from the game. It wasn't the storybook ending I had hoped for, but I guess you don't see too many "Happily Ever After" endings in football.

Cookie's path had now been decided for him. The thought of a long rehabilitation was difficult enough, but the idea of being forced to play for coach Paul Brown made the thought of continuing unbearable. Cookie knew that, due to his age and the fact that he was, coming off of a serious injury, few if any other teams would be interested in his services. If he wanted to continue playing, it would only be for the Bengals under the direction of coach Brown. Cookie had never forgiven the coach for taking advantage of his youth and inexperience by signing him to a contract out of the eleventh grade in clear violation of NFL rules. The loss of the promised contract and, more importantly, the loss of educational opportunities due to Brown's actions, was something that Cookie had never gotten over.

And now that his football career had come to an end, Cookie was feeling the loss of his education more than ever before. The imposing figure of Cookie Gilchrist, who'd struck fear into countless opponents on the football field, now faced an opponent that filled him with more fear than he'd known. That fear was generated not by a man, but rather by what the future held for him as an uneducated football hero.

A Man of "ACTION"

"ACTION" was the umbrella name for the United States Government program that included the Peace Corps. Years ago, Cookie had become involved in the world of politics through his relationship with former teammate Jack Kemp and his support of Richard Nixon's Presidential campaign. As a result of his support, Cookie found himself presented with a Presidential appointment as an ambassador for the ACTION program. He would soon find that navigating the world of politics was much harder than breaking tackles on the football field.

I became involved in the world of politics when my former teammate with the Buffalo Bills, Jack Kemp, asked me to help him with Richard Nixon's Presidential campaign. My initial foray into the world of the Washington elite hooked me on the excitement and rush of politics. I thought the world of professional athletics was exciting, but the power wielded by the power brokers of Washington was the real rush. In addition to gaining a newfound interest in politics, my support of Nixon's Campaign also gained me favor within the Republican ranks.

This was not Jack's first endeavor within the world of politics. He'd actually begun working on his political future while he was still playing quarterback in the AFL. In addition to studying the team's playbook, Jack studied the New York Times to prepare for his life after football. Jack's voracious appetite for knowledge and his desire to discuss politics when anyone lent an ear had earned him the nickname "the Senator."

Jack and Tom Addison of the Boston Patriots helped found the AFL Player's Association. After Addison's term as the first President of the Player's Association, Jack was named his successor and remained in that position until he retired from football. I always believed his position with the Player's Association is was what gave him the itch to pursue politics.

Jack spent his football off-seasons working on several Republican campaigns, including Ronald Reagan's 1966 California gubernatorial campaign. Once Reagan was elected, Jack spent his down time in Sacramento, working as a Reagan staff member. In 1969, he took a position working for the Republican National Committee, creating the political inroads he would need to support his own eventual campaign for Congress.

Jack decided to start his political career in Buffalo, where he'd had his greatest success on the football field. His road to political office was difficult, considering he was a Republican vying for a political seat in a suburban Buffalo district that traditionally voted Democrat. The fact that Jack had been a sports hero in Buffalo and now called himself a bleeding-heart conservative helped his cause, but he needed more.

Jack asked me to join his campaign, believing that I would help him draw the Negro vote, which traditionally voted Democrat, on Election Day. The color of my skin coupled with the fact that we now had two of the most high-profile players in Bills' history working together again, would help to promote Jack's campaign.

I made public appearances for Jack's campaign in and around Buffalo. Jack did have this natural strength about him that made voters stand up and listen, but for this first campaign, he needed an extra push with the voters. During the final days of the campaign, Jack took notice of how hard I was working and promised to repay the favor. His charisma and political knowledge, coupled with my support, won him his first term in Congress.

As we celebrated Jack's election, I told a newspaper reporter in attendance that this was only the first step for Jack, and that someday he would be leading the country from the White House. I even added that Jack would have two phones in the Oval Office, a red phone with a direct line to the Kremlin and a black phone that went right to my house. Now that Jack was the new boy on the block within the who's who of Washington, I looked forward to calling in the favor he'd promised.

Once Jack was secure in his new Congressional office, he approached President Nixon looking for a position for me within the administration. I was soon given a position under the government agency called ACTION, which was the parent organization of the Peace Corps. The Peace Corps was created as a volunteer agency through which volunteers would live and work within developing countries. This interaction would provide the volunteers with a better understanding of these other countries, while promoting a positive American presence within these countries. The majority of the volunteers who signed up for the program were white, and I was brought on to help with the recruitment of people of color. The thought was that my outspoken nature and marketability would help draw more volunteers from the inner cities.

The position had an office in Washington, but my major role was to make public appearances on the road. I don't think I was inside my office more than twice. Due to my frequent travel, I was provided with vouchers for the airlines. My love of travel may have gotten the better of me, because after less than a year in office I received a call from Jack questioning my travel records. He asked, *"Cookie, you are keeping track of all of your business trip expenses, aren't you?"*

I replied, *"Jack, I am a man of the people. That's why they hired me - not to be a paper pusher."* But I agreed that better record keeping was needed, so I suggested that the program hire me a personal assistant. The truth was, this was Jack's way of warning me that the program suspected I was using the vouchers for personal travel as well.

During my tenure, I voiced my opinion that not enough was being done to get more minorities involved in the program. I was starting to feel that I had been brought in as the token black face for the program, and that all of my suggestions to further the program were falling on deaf ears. Due to my excessive travel expenditures and my vocal opposition to the program's ineffective recruitment practices, the agency eliminated my position. They determined it was costing too much money to keep me on the government payroll. That seemed to be the same line the team owners told me while I was playing football.

I still think I was one of the first black Republicans with a Washington appointment, and I was certainly the shortest tenured - my term was just under one year. This marked the end of my political career and my Republican Party designation. From that point on, I declared myself a Democrat and only crossed party lines to support Jack, who was just getting warmed up in the political arena.

Jack continued in Congress, and for a time, many viewed him as the heir apparent to Ronald Reagan in the White House. However, following Reagan's presidency, his Vice President, George H. Bush, became the favorite of the Republican Party. Jack withdrew from the race and, for putting the party first, was appointed the Secretary of Housing and Urban Development within the Bush administration.

Following the end of his appointment to the Bush Cabinet, Jack maintained a presence in Washington by making public speaking engagements and continuing to work for the Republican Party. He made one more attempt at the White House, now as a Vice-Presidential candidate on the Bob Dole ticket. The Democratic ticket of Bill Clinton and Al Gore defeated the Republican power duo of Bob Dole and Jack Kemp. Following the election, Jack continued to speak on behalf of the Republican Party and worked on the boards of numerous corporations and charitable organizations. Whenever called upon to support Jack's career and charitable endeavors, I happily complied.

Jack was always a sounding board for my future business ventures. The bond we had forged during our time on the football field lasted the rest of our lives. While I did not always like what Jack had to say - which was whenever he disagreed with me - I always respected his opinion. When he passed away in 2009, I felt like I had lost a brother. No matter what had come between us over the years, I always knew he would be there when I called. After his death, I felt alone.

Cookie's attempt at being a player in the world of politics was short-lived. However, though his position at ACTION was eliminated, he kept the excitement of politics alive through his relationship with Jack Kemp. Football had brought together two individuals from extremely different backgrounds and forged an unlikely friendship that they called upon throughout their lives. While this was one of the strongest relationships Cookie had ever had, it was not the last one that the game of football would forge.

The United Athletes Coalition

Soon after retiring, Cookie realized that life after football is not always kind to the retired player. For many who had come before him, life after football included pitfalls including divorce, poor health, and financial ruin. Cookie had the foresight to see the need for a service to help assimilate retirees -- of all sports -- back into the world of everyday life.

My retirement from football brought with it the removal of order and rules in my life. While playing football, my weekly schedule was prepared for me, leading to a regimented lifestyle. Although I had a history of breaking team curfew or other infractions, the order of it all had always been somehow comforting.

My attempts at becoming an actor in Hollywood had failed and my marriage to Gwen had fared no better. Even though I was not a working actor, I had started to partake in the "Hollywood Lifestyle" of cocaine, liquor, and women.

These new vices were my way of dulling the sharp pain of becoming an afterthought in the public eye. I'd come to realize that once my athletic gifts were diminished, I was just another player for the owners to throw on the trash heap. Many people do not understand that once an athlete shows promise, he or she is groomed for greatness. While there should not be a separate set of rules for anyone, there's no mistaking that we were treated differently. Minor infractions or eccentricities are just ignored when elite athletes are involved. Everyone looks the other way because athletes are judged by a different set of rules.

I am in no way condoning this practice, but this was the way I was treated from the age of eight until I retired. What I experienced during my athletic life was in no way an isolated incident, and this preferential treatment was the main reason for the difficulty I had transitioning into post-career life. People fawned over you and put you on a pedestal because of your abilities, and I found I wasn't ready for the pedestal to get pulled out from under me. Later discussions with other elite athletes like Eddie Matthews in baseball and Sonny Liston in boxing made me realize that this was not just a problem for football players, but for athletes in general.

As I sorted through becoming an everyday person, I started to experiment with narcotics, and my drug of choice was cocaine. The high of the drug would make me temporarily forget about the problem of what I should do next with my life. I never attended college or even graduated high school, which automatically precluded me from job opportunities. There was even a time when I wanted to counsel young athletes, but one of the requirements of the position was that I needed a high school diploma. I was confounded by this requirement, feeling that I would be a great counselor based on my history in professional sports, but the agency in question would not allow it. My lack of education has always been my greatest regret. I saw now that I was ill prepared for life off the field.

My relationships during this transition period were also unsuccessful. I had a tumultuous on-again, off-again relationship with Playboy playmate Jean Bell. Jean was the first African-American woman to grace the cover of Playboy magazine. This was my first serious relationship with a woman of color. I was taken in by her natural beauty, as well as by the excitement of her celebrity status. Our relationship was a difficult one due to our public personas, which were a matter of tabloid fodder. Once it was clear that my star had faded while hers was still on the rise, Jean decided to move on. She had secured some movie roles and was making the rounds at the Hollywood hot spots, while my football prominence and income were on life support. She let me know that she had become accustomed to living in a certain lifestyle, which I would not be able to give her.

While I knew Jean was not the great love of my life, the cutting words that ended our relationship hurt more than any hit I'd taken on the football field. I sank into a deeper depression and found escape within a bottle of whiskey.

Jean moved on to enter a relationship with actor Richard Burton. She is even credited with helping him quit drinking. After their relationship ran its course, they remained friends and she pushed him to pursue the great love of his life, Elizabeth Taylor.

The wake-up call that led me to change my ways came when I learned of the death of a football legend. Len Ford the All-Pro defensive end for the Cleveland Browns had been found in a rundown motel, dead of an apparent heart attack. There were rumors that he had been abusing alcohol, but all I knew was that he died at the age of forty-six, alone and with his life in ruins. A few years after his death, Ford was enshrined into the Pro Football Hall of Fame in Canton.

If this could happen to someone of his magnitude, I realized, I wouldn't be far behind if I kept up my behavior. I became determined to do my best to keep this kind of tragedy from happening to other athletes, especially myself.

I sat down and tried to figure out what was needed to help athletes make the transition into retirement. The first thing that came to mind was marriage counseling. While playing football, I was away from my family for large periods of time. During the periods when we were living under one roof as a traditional nuclear family, the transition was always difficult and I thought, in retrospect, that marriage counseling might have helped smooth that transition.

Marriage counseling was only one step in the mental health process that I thought would be beneficial to athletes. Private therapy sessions to work on feelings of depression due to the loss of the game and the adulation associated with it would be a large part of the mental health plan. The last component in the mental health services would be a substance abuse program designed to help athletes who were addicted to drugs or alcohol, whether due to depression or due to the chronic pain they experienced from the injuries they had suffered on the field. This mental health plan would need to be the cornerstone of any endeavor to help athletes make the jump into civilian life.

The next component of the program, I thought, would be a division to help players find job opportunities and develop new marketable skills. If an athlete had an idea for a new business, we would have an investment advisor on staff that could help them develop a business plan. I saw the need for this service based on the failure of my own entrepreneurial ventures, due to my lack of business experience and knowledge of financial management.

Stories of former players becoming destitute and sleeping on park benches had to become a thing of the past. The program would provide financial support and housing for those in need. At the time, no league offered anything like the services I proposed. If ex-athletes fell on hard times, their only option was to apply for state welfare assistance. Now they would have another option, where they could get help from their peers while maintaining their dignity.

This program, if managed properly, would revolutionize professional athletics. The services for those in need of financial assistance or job training would be revolutionary. The best way to change the course of an athlete's future was through a proactive approach to the problem. Starting the counseling process in high school or college by advising young athletes as to what was in store for them, would give them a better chance at a productive post-career life. This additional insight would give them the time and information needed to obtain the proper skills and financial management for everyday life.

I sought counsel from my friends in football. One of the people I spoke with about the program was Richard "Dick" Bass. Dick had been a pro bowl running back for the Los Angeles Rams. He thought the plan I had come up with was sound, but suggested an additional dimension to the program. He suggested a summer camp for youths where we could promote the power of athletics with current and former athletes. This would help keep kids focused and promote the coalition's message, thereby preparing young athletes for the future. It would also be a positive experience for all who attended, whether or not they became a future All-Star, because they would have the opportunity to meet and interact with their sports heroes. The biggest benefit was that we would be creating a safe haven to keep young people, especially in the inner cities, off the streets and out of trouble through athletics.

Later, Dick's idea to start the youth camp within the program seemed ironic. It came out that he'd allegedly fathered a child named Kody Scott, who was born of a brief romantic liaison. Dick did not know of Kody's existence, and his mother raised him along with his siblings from another relationship. Kody became wrapped up in the Los Angeles gang culture when he became a disciple of Stanley Tookie Williams, the founder of the Crips street gang. Kody became known as "Monster" for his violent persona, and rose to the head of his own crew, the Eight Trey Gangster Crips. He spent large parts of his adult life in prison and changed his name to Sanyike Shakur when he joined the Republic of New Afrika. Following his association with the Republic, he started to change his views on what his role and that of other African-American people should be. He started to preach the Republic's message of a call for the United States government to provide reparations for the slavery of their African-American ancestors.

Despite this newfound path, Kody had more run-ins with the penal system following the Los Angeles "Rodney King Riots" and still remains incarcerated. It makes me wonder whether, if Kody had been exposed early on to a positive influence and not left to fend for himself in the underworld of Los Angeles gang culture, his life might have turned out differently. We will never know the answer to that, but I did know that Dick's idea for a youth camp was a good one, and that I needed to incorporate it into the program.

Armed with the main components for the program, I decided to put my plan into action. The name I chose for this endeavor was The United Athletes Coalition of America and Canada. The Coalition was created as a non-profit organization, and I asked for the full support of my friends in the fields of both sports and entertainment.

I knew it would be an uphill battle to change the public's perception that former athletes were set for life and that they didn't require financial assistance. Fans could only recall hearing the newspaper stories of the large contracts that the top athletes signed. They would say to themselves, *"Why should I look to help someone who made more money in one year than I might make in my entire life?"* I had to publicize the fact that most athletes make much less than the top players and might not even qualify for health or pension benefits. In fact, the creation of organized player unions was something that was fairly new to the major sports. The baseball and football players associations only came into real power in the 1960s, and the players who pre-dated these organizations had been left to fend for themselves.

I now set out to use everything at my disposal to pull back the proverbial curtain in order to show everyone what really happened once the cheering stopped.

Cookie realized from his own experience that young athletes would never foresee the mortality of their careers; they'd always assume that one more contract would be coming to keep them afloat. He knew this better than most: early in his career, if he had a hundred dollars, he would spend two hundred, always thinking he could play forever. Now, having seen the cautionary tale of Len Ford, Cookie was determined not to become another victim of the celebrity lifestyle. Armed with that fear and determination, he put his plan into action. Unfortunately, he would soon find that the stigma of being "uppity," "difficult" Cookie Gilchrist would overshadow the merits of the project.

Funding and Futility

Cookie was on a mission to bring his dream of making the United Athletes Coalition into a reality. To change the culture of professional sports would not be an easy task, and Cookie had no illusions to the contrary. The ideas and services Cookie proposed would be revolutionary, yet the only thing that the ownership in the different sports involved could see was the large expenses it would create. Cookie knew that, in order for the Coalition to survive, athletes would have to stand united and push to make the services the Coalition offered the accepted standard in the world of sports.

As I set out to put my plan for the United Athletes Coalition into action, the first person I contacted was John Agro, the attorney for the CFL Players' Association. After I described the program to John, he said the ideas were sound and agreed to help me get the program on track.
Now that John was on board, I hoped that his backing and his well-earned reputation would get people to look past my involvement with the project. The shadow of being branded a troublemaker had followed me throughout my career, and I did not want this program to fail just because my name was attached to it.

John started to lay out what the corporate structure of the Coalition would be, and he set up a flow chart for the responsibilities of the employees and volunteers. I started making calls looking for support for the coalition. One of the first responses I received was from Pete Rozelle, the Commissioner of the NFL. Rozelle's response was as follows: *"Your plan for player counseling is a most constructive one, but not feasible for financial participation by this office now. Should this situation change in the future, I feel the type of program you suggest would be extremely worthwhile."*

I felt the NFL's response was basically saying, *"Your program is appropriate and needed, but since it cuts into our profits, we have to pass."*

This letter was dated in September of 1973, well before the NFL surpassed Major League Baseball as America's favorite sport and cemented themselves as one of the most profitable sports leagues. As the NFL's fortunes rose, they never chose to enact or support any program that might possibly affect their finances negatively. They were never proactive and chose to always be reactive to situations, most notably when the issue of concussions and their future impact on a player's health came to public attention. The NFL stuck their head in the sand and did nothing until Congress investigated the issue.

THE NATIONAL FOOTBALL LEAGUE

410 PARK AVENUE, NEW YORK, N.Y. 10022 • PLaza 8-1500

25 September 1973

Mr. "Cookie" Gilchrist
400 South Beverly Drive
Suite 215
Beverly Hills, California 90212

Dear "Cookie":

As I told you on the telephone, your plan for player counseling is a most constructive one, but not feasible for financial participation by this office now.

It would not be possible for me to secure budget approval for an expenditure of this size so far into the year. The reasons for this are the fact that we now have Buddy Young and Bill Granholm aiding players on a full time basis from this office, a Security Department that serves as a business and investment checking service for the players and because relations between the club presidents and the people operating the Players Association are strained.

Should this situation change in the future, I feel the type of program you suggest would be extremely worthwhile.

Regards,

PR:te

PETE ROZELLE
Commissioner

Before those hearings, if a player suffered a head injury but could still walk, they were sent back into a game and told to suck it up or shake it off. After the Congressional Hearings, and with the threats of lawsuits, the NFL was finally forced to recognize that after a player suffered a concussion, they needed to provide extensive medical supervision and baseline testing before the player could safely return to the football field.

Commissioner Rozelle's refusal to help support the Coalition financially was not unexpected based on the NFL's prior track record, but I had held out hope that the merits of the program might have swayed them. I decided to run a sweep around the major sports leagues to get the support of their star athletes, then ask them to apply pressure to their respective leagues.

I started doing interviews in the media in order to draw support for the program and told those athletes who needed help or those who knew of other athletes who needed help to contact me in Denver. One of the first interviews I did was with the Denver Post, and I put a true face on the problem when I told the reporter, *"From what I have witnessed and from what I have felt myself, I would imagine an athlete goes through the same withdrawal symptoms a heroin addict does. All of a sudden, you're walking down the street and no one recognizes you, when not too long ago that same public would have been cheering for you or asking for an autograph. You go into a bank to borrow money for a business venture, and you are turned away. You discover that your lack of education is a very monumental fact."*

All of these quotes were feelings and situations that I had experienced, but other players before and after me had similar stories. Several more interviews in the newspapers and on television followed, but the message seemed to be falling on deaf ears. In every instance, regardless of the fact that each writer found merits in the program, their coloring me as a troublemaking malcontent obscured the overall message.

At that point, I also met with resistance from the NFL Players' Association regarding financial support, though they agreed with the merits of the program. When I petitioned the NFLPA for their support, they were in the middle of transitioning from the leadership of former Baltimore Colts tight end John Mackey to former Colts and Green Bay center Bill Curry. Mackey gave me a statement of support that stated, *"Cookie, your idea to help activate and help former athletes is an excellent one. I wholeheartedly endorse your program and will be available to help in any way I can."* Mackey told me that although the NFLPA could not financially support the program, he would help promote the program whenever he could, and would ask the Curry administration of the NFLPA to do the same.

So far, I had not received any financial commitments to the program and was funding the marketing campaign and the day-to-day operations on my own. As my bank account was almost drained and I was looking for a lifeline of funding, I called my old friend, Congressman Jack Kemp, and we discussed the program's benefits. I asked Jack if there was any way to federally fund the project, but he said no, there was no way to get federal money to fund benefits for former athletes. He did offer to help promote the program and bring it up during a meeting in the House of Representatives.

On February 14, 1974, Jack brought up the Coalition in a formal meeting and made the following statement on the congressional record:

> Mr. Speaker, Cookie Gilchrist and I were teammates with the Buffalo Bills and I admired him as a teammate and as a great fullback, but even more as a man who wants to help other people.
>
> Today he is actively nurturing a vision he has long held to help ease the difficult transition of athletes from the playing field to the business world of American life, which many times is difficult indeed and leads to some real life tragedies.
>
> The Colorado nonprofit corporation he has helped establish, United Athletes Coalition of America, Inc., will attack the problems created by the tremendous popularity of athletics in the United States: first, problems of their overemphasis and consequent distortion of values by young people: second, problems in the maintenance of personal and financial perspective by active professional athletes; and third, problems in the transition by athletes from participation in professional sports to the mainstream of American life at the conclusion of their athletic careers.
>
> UACA will direct its efforts toward:
>
> First. Education and guidance of athletes at the pre-professional levels by using individual present and retired athletes to express their experiences through visitations to colleges, high schools, and elementary educational institutions: through financial assistance to worthy and needy athletes pursuing educational goals in non-athletic areas.
>
> Second. Education and rehabilitation of ex-athletes by establishing information and counseling centers in key cities in order to direct ex-athletes in financial, legal, medical, psychological, and career counseling: make available direct financial assistance to appropriate ex-athletes and their families in the form of controlled grants for alleviating severe personal problems.
>
> Third. Education and guidance of current professional athletes by (A) disseminating information regarding educational and vocational training: (B) disseminating information concerning legal, financial, social problems

common to professional athletes: (C) establish in key cities local offices manned by qualified ex-athletes to give one-on-one counseling and advice regarding problems affecting all areas of life which may be particular to athletes: (D) make available professional expertise concerning personal and financial management for athletes through educational group seminars.

The objectives toward which Cookie Gilchrist and the UACA are working make it important that my colleagues become aware of his efforts.

Jack then entered into the record an article from the Buffalo Courier-Express where I was interviewed and gave my reasons for creating the UACA, before closing his remarks.

When he put the benefits of the program on the Congressional record, Jack came through for the UACA. The program had gone from merely being Cookie's crazy idea to one that was respected enough to be mentioned on the record during a session of Congress. Since the matter was entered into the Congressional record on February 14, I told Jack that it was the only Valentine's Day where he'd remembered to give me a gift.

Following the Congressional endorsement, I received several letters of support from high-profile athletes in the different major sports, but few donations or promises of funding.

The following athletes supported the mission of the United Athletes Coalition of America:

Football:

John Agro- Attorney, CFL Players' Association; Ernie Barnes-Denver Broncos; Odell Barry- Denver Broncos; Dick Bass- Los Angeles Rams; Buck Buchanan- Kansas City Chiefs; Jim Brown- Cleveland Browns; Peter Bennet-Toronto Argonauts; Uly Curtise-Toronto Argonauts; Clem Daniels- Oakland Raiders; Willie Davis- Green Bay Packers; Booker Edgerson- Buffalo Bills; Henry Dyer- Los Angeles Rams; George Dixon- Coach, San Diego Chargers; Marv Fleming- Green Bay Packers; Tom Flores- Oakland Raiders; Jake Guadaur- Commissioner, CFL; Rosey Grier- Los Angeles Rams; Tom Jones-Ottawa Roughriders; Charlie Greer- Denver Broncos; Frank E. Hawkins- San Francisco 49ers; Ralph Goldston- Hamilton Tiger-Cats; Mike Henry- Los Angeles Rams; Alvin Hall- Los Angeles Rams; John Henry Jackson-Toronto Argonauts; Winston Hill- New York Jets; George Hughley-Toronto Argonauts; Sam Huff- Washington Redskins; Jack Kemp- former Buffalo Bill and current politician; Dr Bob Kerlin - team physician, Los Angeles Rams; Dan Klosterman- Calgary Stampeders; Ernie Ladd- San Diego Chargers;

Izzy Lang- Los Angeles Rams; Floyd Little- Denver Broncos; John Mackey- Baltimore Colts; John Madden- Coach, Oakland Raiders; Marvin Major- New England Patriots; Ollie Matson- Los Angeles Rams; Ray May- Denver Broncos; Jerry Mays- Kansas City Chiefs; John McCormick- Denver Broncos; Curtis McClinton- Kansas City Chiefs; Bob McCullough- Denver Broncos; Gene Mingo- Denver Broncos; Bobby Mitchell- Washington Redskins; Haven Moses- Buffalo Bills; Joe Namath- New York Jets; Jim Pace- Hamilton Tiger-Cats; Jim Nettles- Los Angeles Rams; Bernie Parrish- Cleveland Browns; John Pitts- Buffalo Bills; Alex Ponton- Toronto Argonauts; Art Powell- Oakland Raiders; George Ratterman- Cleveland Browns; Joe Robbie- Owner, Miami Dolphins; Walt Roberts- Cleveland Browns; Fred Robinson- Ottawa Roughriders; George Saimes- Buffalo Bills; James Shorter- Cleveland Browns; O.J. Simpson- Buffalo Bills; Bubba Smith- Baltimore Colts; Tody Smith- Houston Oilers; Jerry Sturm- Denver Broncos; Bill Thompson- Denver Broncos; Andre White- Cincinnati Bengals; Fred Williamson- Kansas City Chiefs/Actor; Sidney Williams- Cleveland Browns; Ted Woods- Calgary Stampeders; Mike Balou- New England Patriots; Charlie Janerette- Denver Broncos; Johnny Sample- Baltimore Colts; Herb Adderly- Green Bay Packers; Leroy Kelly- Cleveland Browns; William Sullivan- Owner, New England Patriots; Weeb Ewbank- Coach, New York Jets

Baseball:
Leon Wagner- California Angels; Chuck Mann- California Angels; Dick Baldwin- Washington Senators; Tony Mazziotti- New York Yankees; Richie Allen- Chicago White Socks

Boxing:
Muhammad Ali- Heavyweight Champion; Kid Gavalin- Former Welterweight Champion; Joe Louis- Former Heavyweight Champion; Sugar Ray Robinson- Former Middleweight Champion; Joe Frazier- Heavyweight Boxer

Hockey:
Ken Dryden- Montreal Canadians

Basketball:
Wilt Chamberlain- Los Angeles Lakers; Hal Greer- Philadelphia 76ers; Tom Hawkins- Los Angeles Lakers; Wayne Hightower- Denver Rockets; Ralph Simpson- Denver Rockets

Entertainment and Politics:
Howard Cosell- Sports Announcer; Marvin Gaye- Singer; Ed Gillinwaters- Director, National Athletes Health Institute; Scoey Mitchell- Comedian; Charlie Patterson- Inventor of hockey helmet and head injury prevention activist; Jim Proudfoot- Sports Editor, Toronto Sun; Butch Tavares-Singer; Robert Yegge- Dean, Denver School of Law; Tom Bradley- Mayor of Los Angeles; Harold Ballard- President, Maple Leaf Gardens; Bob Johnson- Editor, Jet Magazine; John Johnson- Publisher, Ebony Magazine; Dick Ebersol- ABC Sports; Murray Olderman- National newspaper columnist; Sammy Davis Jr.- Entertainer

Joe Namath agreeing to support the United Athletes Coalition.
Photo Courtesy of The Gilchrist Family

Out of all of the people to endorse the program I only received one financial pledge. I received a Western Union message from Marvin Gaye with a check for $5,000. The message read as follows: "You'll have to trust somebody, so you may as well trust Cookie. I do. There is strength in unity- check it out. Peace, Marvin Gaye Jr." This was the first person besides me to make a financial contribution to the program, and it came at the perfect time. I had emptied out my own bank account fighting for the survival of the UACA and this infusion of cash would keep the program afloat a little longer while we looked for volunteers and funding. For the most part, the athletes and others who'd endorsed the program just lent their names and words of support. In order for the program to work, people would have to volunteer their time and make a real financial commitment.

MGMDVRT HSB
2-234061E021 01/21/74
ICS IPMRNCZ CSP
2135562100 MGM TDRN LOS ANGELES CA 100 01-21 0358P EDT
ZIP 80202

western union Mailgram

UNITED STATES POSTAL SERVICE U.S. MAIL

COOKIE GILCHRIST
8000 GIARD ST
DENVER CO 80202

YOU'LL HAVE TO TRUST SOMEBODY FOLLOWS SO YOU MAY AS WELL TRUST COOKIE. I DO. THERE IS STRENGTH IN UNITY - CHECK IT OUT. PEACE

MARVIN GAY JR

15:58 EST

MGMDVRT HSB

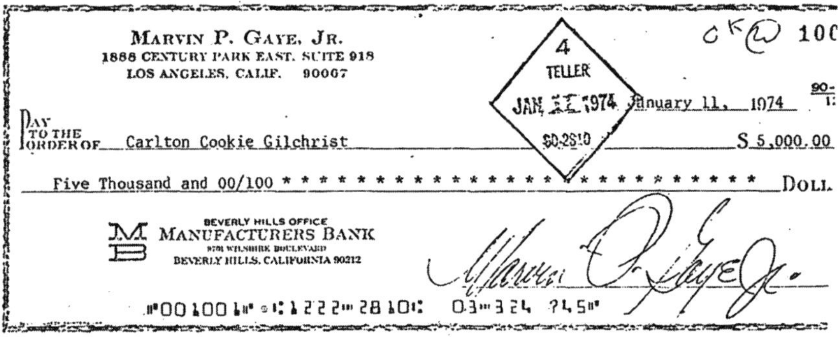

MARVIN P. GAYE, JR.
1888 CENTURY PARK EAST, SUITE 918
LOS ANGELES, CALIF. 90067

4 TELLER JAN 1974 $0.2810

January 11, 1974

PAY TO THE ORDER OF Carlton Cookie Gilchrist $ 5,000.00

Five Thousand and 00/100 DOLL.

BEVERLY HILLS OFFICE
MANUFACTURERS BANK
BEVERLY HILLS, CALIFORNIA 90212

Marvin P. Gaye Jr.

When I explained the program to other athletes, they all said the program sounded great and that they would want to take advantage of the different programs as they transitioned into retirement. I explained to the athletes that without their funding and support, the program would not get off the ground. I said that by making a financial donation now, while they were still making money in their respective sports, they were ensuring services for their retirement and for the others that came before them. To a certain degree, it was like saving for a rainy day. Unfortunately, athletes who are still playing always think they will play forever and that the money train would never end.

One of the few athletes who volunteered his time was Charlie Janerette, a former defensive end for the Denver Broncos. Charlie and I had become friendly when we both played for the Broncos. I approached Charlie about getting involved in the day-to-day operations of the UACA because I felt his educational background, which included a Master's degree from Penn State, would be a benefit to the organization. He happily agreed.

I later found it ironic that Charlie had been one of the biggest supporters of the UACA, because he could have benefited greatly from the program's counseling services.

Years after his involvement with the UACA, Charlie was living with manic depression which he could keep under control with medication. Charlie was an imposing figure at six-foot four and 270 pounds, but those who knew him would tell you he was just a big teddy bear. In fact, Bill Cosby was a high school football teammate of Charlie's, and he patterned the children's cartoon character Fat Albert on Charlie's teddy-bear-like personality. Unfortunately, if Charlie did not take his medication, he would become unruly and his actions would become unpredictable.

On October 26, 1984, two days after walking out of a psychiatric facility, Charlie was shot and killed by a Philadelphia police officer after an altercation. Charlie had actually been stopped by police twice before the shooting for being drunk and disorderly, but was released both times.

The fatal incident started when Charlie allegedly attempted to drive away in the police officer's patrol car, which the officer had left running as he investigated another incident. The officer's account of the incident alleged that when he tried to remove Charlie from the patrol car, Charlie went for the officer's gun. Charlie was shot point-blank in the back of the head in what appeared to be an unjustified shooting. The officer was never charged criminally for Charlie's death, but a civil trial found the officer negligent, and a civil judgment was awarded to Charlie's family. I've always felt that, if Charlie had had the psychological services of the UACA, or any other program through the NFL or NFLPA, available to him, his death could have been avoided.

Sadly, even with a volunteer staff and an infusion of cash from Marvin Gaye's donation, the UACA was on its last legs. The UACA had become an obsession and while I fought to keep it alive, the other aspects of my life were falling apart. I spent all of my money and time on the UACA and let it occupy my every waking moment. Looking back I realize that I was really fighting for my own future, as well as for the fallen athletes who had come before me. I had put all of my effort and finances into this project; if it failed, I too might find myself on the street without any appreciable skills or means of support. As I fought for benefits for other athletes, who were in essence strangers, my family became an afterthought.

I sat down with John Agro in the UACA's Denver office, and we tried to figure out what our next step would be. John suggested that we campaign for financing in Canada due to his connections with the CFL Players' Association and the Canadian government. John made a few phone calls and was able to schedule meetings with members of the Canadian government who were influential in the world of Canadian sports. The next day John and I were on a plane to Ottawa with a proposal we hoped the Canadian government couldn't refuse.

The first meeting we had scheduled was with John Munroe, the Minister of Health and Welfare for the Canadian government. Minister Munroe's office oversaw the regulation of fitness and amateur sports for the Canadian government. When we arrived at the Minister's office, we were informed that he had been delayed and wouldn't be in until later in the day. The Minister's office suggested we discuss our proposal with Lou Le Faive, the President of the National Sports and Recreation Centre of Canada. Le Faive was a very powerful cog in the Canadian sports machine, and I knew that if we could sway him to support the program, we would gain a foothold in Canada.

John and I made our way over to the National Sports Recreation Centre and waited for Le Faive to arrive for our meeting. At that time, Le Faive's claim to fame was that he was instrumental in organizing the1972 hockey summit between Canada and the Soviet Union. John and I were brought into a conference room, where, seated at the table, were Le Faive and Ron Stewart. Stewart was a former CFL running back for the Ottawa Roughriders and would later become a member of the CFL Hall of Fame. He was one of the shortest players I could recall at only five foot seven, but he was also one of the toughest players to tackle. Following his football career, Stewart had completed his law degree and was now becoming involved in the world of Canadian politics.

John began our presentation and discussed the benefits provided by the UACA program. John stated that the UACA was not limited to the United States and that if the Canadian government pledged any money that it would be used to only fund services for Canadian athletes. John ended his part on the business side of the UACA, and I was now to begin talking about what I knew best, and that was what happened to athletes once they finished playing.

I read aloud a list of athletes, and the different problems they suffered in retirement. At first, Le Faive and Stewart seemed drawn in by the hardships of the athletes, and I thought our presentation had gained their support. But as soon as I finished speaking, Le Faive said that while the program had merits, who would want to help an athlete who makes $100,000 a year? He went on to say that that's more than most people make in their lifetime.

I countered his statement by saying that only the top athletes made that type of money, and that most athletes made much less. After arguing back and forth regarding what the public's perception of the program would be, I asked Le Faive if he would provide support for the program. Le Faive said that without a doubt, the program had merits and that they could assist in finding qualified professionals for the UACA to use in Canada, but they would provide no funding.

Their offer was more than any other organization had offered, so, while not thrilled, I considered it a partial victory. I found it odd that during my entire presentation, even when I talked about former CFL teammates suffering in retirement, Stewart never said a word. He was a former player, and I was sure he had seen or heard of former players in trouble. It seemed to me that he was new to the world of politics and did not want to rock the boat. He let the elder statesman, Le Faive, take the lead and he just followed. Stewart did open up a bit when the meeting concluded, and we spoke of our days on the gridiron.

John had set up another meeting for later that afternoon with Tom Bedecki, President of Sports Canada. Sports Canada was another government organization that developed sports policies in Canada. We thought if we could get Sports Canada to accept the UACA program, we could get it adopted as the accepted policy within Canadian sports. Before our meeting with Bedeki, John called the office of Minister Munroe and was told that he was now in, but was too busy to see us during this visit. We were asked to reschedule, but it felt much more like a nice way of saying, "just go away!" I'd had enough doors slammed in my face during my life to know what the Minister's office meant. Canadians were always much less confrontational than Americans, and this was the Canadian equivalent of a door being slammed in our face. It appeared that appealing to Tom Bedecki and the office of Sports Canada would be our last chance to sway the Canadian government.

When we arrived at the offices of Sports Canada, we got right down to business. Bedecki had invited several other members of the Sports Canada offices to join the presentation, but didn't introduce any of them to John or me. John again started the presentation, and this time around stressed the youth aspect of the program, which involved established athletes mentoring the up-and-coming generation of high school and college athletes. When John finished his end of the presentation he also stressed that as the program chairman, he would not put his name and reputation behind a program that was not on the up-and-up. At the time, I did not think much of the comment, but after reflecting on it, I wondered if he was trying to mitigate my involvement with the program. Was he saying, *"Don't be scared off by this being a Cookie Gilchrist project, because real businessmen are involved as well?"*

I then began my end of the presentation for Bedecki and again spoke of the fallen athletes that could have been helped by a program like the UACA. During my presentation, Bedecki and the other members of Sports Canada seemed disinterested, as if they were only listening because they were being forced to out of some sense of obligation. As I discussed the merits of the program, I watched my pleas for the program fall on deaf ears as the clock-watching and looks of boredom continued. After I finished my impassioned speech for the UACA, I was left exhausted and upset that my horror stories of the lives of many former athletes were just words rolling off the backs of Bedecki and his staff.

Everyone sat silent in the room until Bedecki opened up and said; *"So what's the point, Cookie? To help over-the-hill football players? People aren't concerned with them; they're looking ahead and involving themselves with the youth. Anyway, don't you feel it's too late to teach these guys anything? It's like teaching an old dog new tricks."*

I was horrified with his response. He was equating a former athlete with an old dog. I did everything within my power to control my temper and not explode at every person in the room. I held my tongue, because I knew that was what they expected. If I exploded, they could just say difficult Cookie Gilchrist came in and started trouble, and that's why we turned his program away. I would not make it so easy for them to turn me away.

I countered Bedecki's argument and said that teaching these "athletes" new tricks was not going to be as difficult as he made it out to be. The key was to get the athletes to admit that they had problems in the first place. Most of them were too proud, still living on yesterday's achievements and unable to face up to reality. That is, until reality smacked them in the face and the results could be disastrous. I again spoke of how counseling services could help them. If worked correctly, the athletes who were helped by the program would return and counsel others going through the same problems they had conquered.

Bedecki in a condescending tone then said, *"How do you plan to put such a large-scale program into place? It sounds good in theory, but you will never be able to gain the amount of athlete support that the program would require."*

I replied that it wasn't impossible, but that we needed the funding to market and implement the program. The next thing I pointed out was that I had come this far by funding the program out of my own pocket, and that if we had the support of Sports Canada, we could be successful.

Bedecki was unmoved. He said the program was unfeasible, and his office would not provide any type of support.

As Bedecki was trying to end the meeting, I said that all I wanted to do was to help people. The state that sports were in was tragic, I said. They were wasting young people's lives. I mentioned that my youngest son Scott played on a youth football team and that when I attended a game I noticed they had no ambulance or qualified medical professional present in case of an injury. There are noted cases of kids' lives being ruined because of a lack of qualified staffing at sporting events or any event where an injury could be foreseen.

Bedecki's response was that I was exaggerating and that he'd never heard of a serious injury at a youth sports event. We then went back and forth on the issue, and when I brought up specific cases of youths being injured, he would say he was unfamiliar with those stories.

In an attempt to change the momentum, Bedecki remarked, *"Well, Cookie, nobody told these guys to go out and play sports. I mean, no one held a gun to their head and demanded that they play."*

I agreed that no one had forced these guys to do anything, but then, no one warned them of the consequences of what could happen if they did play, either. Sports are glamorized through the media, especially TV. I was asking that the same people who lined the trap with gold be held responsible for those who were caught in its grasp.

Bedecki didn't grasp the arguments regarding the need for the program and turned the conversation back to strictly matters of business. John jumped in then to explain the corporate structure of the UACA and listed the different medical facilities we were affiliated with in the United States. Bedecki said he was looking to see if we had done a recent business proposal with current financial figures. I presented him with the business plan that had been completed just over a year earlier, and he claimed the figures were too outdated. I knew he had been backed into a corner and was just looking for a way out.

We argued some more about whether the business proposal was actually outdated, and I suggested that if they believed in the overall merits of the program, they should at least make a donation to cover the cost of redrafting new business projections. Bedecki smirked and said that I should come back to see him when I had my affairs in order.

As I rose to leave, I pushed the conference table away from me and into Bedecki's chest. As I turned to walk out of the office, Bedecki and his associates started snickering, and I finally let them have it, unleashing a verbal tirade of every curse word I knew. I said, "Once I get this thing going, I will expose all of you motherfuckers who sat on their hands and did nothing to help."

John gathered his papers and did his best to apologize to Bedecki. John's work with the CFL Players' Association required that he stay in Bedecki's good graces. Following my verbal outburst, he would need to do his best to distance himself from me.

On the trip home, John told me we could have gotten more from them if I had not acted out. I replied that they were going to do what everyone in the world of politics and sports did, and that was what was in the best interests of their careers and bank accounts - that is, until someone shames them into doing what is morally correct.

Now that I had lost John due to the conflict I had created in Canada, I sought out the counsel of the one person I felt believed in the program, Marvin Gaye.

Cookie was discouraged by the fact that the UACA was about to fold due to a lack of financing. He was sick and tired of hearing how good the program's ideas were, but that, despite the praise, there were few who were putting their money where their mouth was. Cookie would now have to change his strategy and think outside the box when it came to finding funding for the program. He needed a "Hail Mary" to save the UACA, and he would turn to Marvin Gaye to be his quarterback on this last play.

Marvin and Maple Leaf Gardens

Cookie was searching for alternative means to fund the UACA now that the major sports leagues had passed on the program. The thought of asking athletes to join the organization and pay yearly dues was a consideration, but this didn't seem realistic. He realized that those athletes who could afford the yearly payment didn't need the UACA's services, and those who actually needed the program couldn't afford dues. Cookie wanted to continue to make the UACA a donation- and volunteer-based program, so he asked his friend Marvin Gaye to headline a concert, the proceeds of which would be used to support the development of the UACA.

Marvin Gaye had been an unbelievably generous friend to the United Athletes Coalition and the only person to make a financial donation to the program. Marvin loved the game of football -- he'd even tried to get the Detroit Lions to give him a tryout as a wide receiver at one point. Marvin had become friendly with Detroit Lions cornerback and future Pro Football Hall of Fame inductee Lem Barney and asked Barney to get him a tryout.

Marvin's sudden desire to change his career came when he reached a crossroad. His former duet partner Tammi Terrell had recently passed away from cancer, and he'd just recorded "What's Going On," which Motown Chief Berry Gordy said was unmarketable due to its political message. Many people are unaware that Barney and fellow Lion Mel Farr sang backup on "What's Going On," and eventually received gold records for their work on the recording. Marvin held his ground with Berry Gordy and refused to record any other material until "What's Going On" was released.

It was during the six-month period when Berry and Marvin were fighting over the record's release that Marvin began training for his chance to play professional football. He started weightlifting and added thirty pounds of muscle to his six-foot-four frame. Barney and Farr arranged for a meeting between Marvin and Lions head coach Joe Schmidt. Schmidt was a former star of the Lions defense and also a future member of the Pro Football Hall of Fame. Schmidt didn't know what to make of Marvin, but asked him for film from his high school and college games. Marvin explained to Schmidt that he'd never played any football on any level, but assured him he was very dedicated. Schmidt ultimately refused to grant Marvin the tryout over fear he might suffer a severe injury, remarking,
"If I could sing like you, I certainly wouldn't want to play football."

Meanwhile, Motown relented and released "What's Going On," which rose quickly on the Billboard charts and was hailed by critics as a masterpiece. Once Marvin's musical career bounced back, his desire to play football professionally waned -- but his love of the game and the athletes who played it remained a passion.

I called Marvin in Detroit and explained that I had been unable to secure any additional funding for the program. He offered additional funding out of his own pocket, but I suggested a benefit concert in Canada. Marvin had never performed in Canada, and I thought the demand for tickets to his first performance there would make the show a sellout. Marvin explained he had never played a concert in Canada due to management difficulties with Canadian venues, but I thought that with my connections in Canada we would be able to pull it off. I asked him if he thought he could get any other performers for the benefit, and he threw out a few names, including the Tavares Brothers and Ike and Tina Turner. Marvin said he would make a few inquiries to see which of his friends would be interested in playing the benefit, and I took on the task of finding a venue to hold the event.

As I thought about prospective venues for the concert, the same location came back to me over and over: Maple Leaf Gardens in Toronto. That venue held about 18,000 fans for concerts, was in a major city, and had held several major concerts in the past, including the Beatles. The owner of the Maple Leaf Gardens was Harold Ballard, whom I'd crossed paths with during my time playing football in Canada. Ballard owned the Toronto Maple Leafs and the arena, and had a reputation of being a shrewd businessman, but at time over the top. It was rumored that during one of the Beatles' concerts, held at the Garden during a hot summer day, Ballard had ordered the heat turned up and all of the drinking fountains disabled. According to rumor, he'd held back the start of the concert more than an hour, with the only refreshments available at the Garden's food services, and at three times the standard price.

At the time I was searching for a concert venue, Ballard had just finished serving a federal sentence for tax evasion due to writing off personal expenses as business expenses, such as limousines for his daughter's wedding. He was originally sentenced to nine years in prison, but served only about one-third of the sentence before he was paroled. While Ballard was on trial, he'd made what appeared to be public overtures of goodwill to portray himself in a better light to a potential jury pool. He'd offered Hockey Canada the use of Maple Leaf Gardens for training and games during the Hockey Summit between Canada and the

Soviet Union. He'd even offered to donate the Maple Leafs' share of the gate to the NHL players' pension fund. Ballard's conviction came down right before the games between Canada and the Soviets began, and at the series' completion he sent a full bill for the use of Maple Leaf Gardens to Hockey Canada. These incidents should have been a warning sign not to go into a business relationship with Harold Ballard, but I foolishly thought I could hold my own. That was my first mistake.

I called Ballard's office and explained that I was looking for a venue for a benefit concert for the UACA. Ballard asked me a little about the program and I talked up the counseling services that the program would provide. I explained that a lot of football players are loaded up with painkillers so they can perform on the field despite serious injuries, and that once they retire the team doctors are no longer there to feed the addiction they created. These warriors of the gridiron experience their lives falling apart while they look for that next high. Their finances get wiped out, and some even turn to a life of crime to feed the addiction. I explained to Ballard that the UACA's counseling services would get them into a rehabilitation program and then help them adjust to life after the game. Ballard asked me more about the financing of the program and I explained that the UACA was a nonprofit organization and that all of the proceeds from the concert would be used for the organization. Ballard was also advised that the only monies deducted would be for the expenses of the concert's performers.

Ballard stated that he would allow the UACA to use the Gardens for the sum of $8,500 because of our nonprofit status. The one thing he added was that he had an exclusive agreement with Concert Promotions International to promote any concerts at the Maple Leaf Gardens, and therefore we needed to use CPI to promote our event. I was told that because the concert was a nonprofit event, CPI would only charge for their expenses and it would be a nominal fee.

I later found out that CPI was a company spearheaded by Ballard's son, Bill Ballard, and was a way for Maple Leaf Gardens to double dip by charging performing acts twice for use of the Maple Leaf Gardens.

The Maple Leaf Gardens had an open date on February 6, 1975, and I jumped on it since I felt the $8,500 rental cost was a fair price. If we could sell out the building, the take would be well over $150,000 and would justify the $8,500 rental fee. The contract I signed stated that whether the concert happened or not, Ballard's company would be guaranteed the fee. I think this provision was added because Ballard was anticipating that I would fail to get Marvin to perform and he would in essence clear a profit for doing absolutely nothing.

I called Marvin to tell him that I'd secured a date and venue for the concert. Marvin said that the Tavares Brothers and Ike and Tina Turner had agreed to perform for the UACA. I explained the terms of Ballard's agreement to Marvin, and he too thought it was a fair deal.

The next step would be to promote the event through my connections in the media. The first person I called was Bob Johnson, the head of Jet Magazine. Marvin and I held a conference call with Bob to promote the concert, and he was kind enough to promote our efforts prominently in the magazine.

I knew this would not be enough to market the concert and the UACA, and asked Marvin to be the face of a Canadian Television commercial promoting the concert. The sixty-second commercial opened with Marvin sitting at a desk, and the dialogue was as follows:

Hello, I'm Marvin Gaye, and I'd like to tell you about a fantastic evening of unusual entertainment, February the 6th at the Toronto Maple Leaf Gardens. This will be my first appearance in Toronto and I'll have Ike and Tina Turner and the Tavares Brothers with me. This one-night-only appearance will be on behalf of the United Athletes Coalition of America and Canada, a non-profit organization headed by Cookie Gilchrist. You may remember Cookie from when he was scoring touchdowns with the Argonauts and the Buffalo Bills. Well, he's still scoring, but this time it's for athletes -- athletes at all levels, and especially those who have had a difficult time making the transition from active sports participation to non-participation. Please join Ike and Tina Turner, the Tavares Brothers, and myself February 6th at Maple Leaf Gardens. For ticket information, please contact the Gardens ticket office. See you there February 6th.

Marvin thought the television spot went over well, but wanted to do more. He drafted his own statement about the UACA and released it to the press, hoping that this public proclamation supporting the program would get others interested in providing their support. The press release statement was as follows:

Marvin Gaye says "U.A.C.A.C. IS THE WAY"

All of us, at one time or another, have dreamed of being a sports superstar. After you've shared one of those super thrilling moments from the grandstand as the winning touchdown is scored, or a pitcher gets the last out of a game, or a great player skates the entire length of the ice to score the winning goal...I'm sure you've shared in those moments and memories, just as I have.

But you know, not all of the athletes you watch perform as superstars. Some of them get badly hurt awfully early in their careers. Some of them never do learn how to handle their lives outside of sports. Nearly all of them have dedicated their lives to organized sports right from when they were just little kids. As a result, most of them don't know how to handle the transition from active participant to a place on the sidelines. We cheer for them when they are great. We expect them to come up with super performances week after week despite grueling games and the risk of serious injury. We live some of our most thrilling moments through their performances...and yet once they're hurt or old or just simply worn out, we usually forget them. And it's so sad to see the names of once great athletes in the paper reporting on how they're involved with alcohol, drugs and crime. All because nobody took the time or the trouble to prepare them for the real world outside sports.

Well, I figure that's all wrong. You can't turn your back on a fellow man that society has made into a professional gladiator just because he can't perform anymore. You can't take a life and just throw it on the garbage heap. My good friend, Cookie Gilchrist, is trying to do something for the athletes. He's been there. He knows. He's formed the United Athletes Coalition of America and Canada. Already men like Muhammad Ali, Jim Brown, Howard Cosell, Joe Namath, Sugar Ray Robinson, and O.J. Simpson have pledged their support along with hundreds of other famous athletes. As a coalition of athletes and interested parties, their aim is to help, guide, and advise both professional and amateur athletes right from the very first moment they show promise of becoming a talented athlete, through to their retirement. The coalition wants to get schools, clubs, church groups, little leagues, wherever they can show the children the reality of organized sports and help prepare them for the time when they can no longer be an athlete. In my song, "Save the Children," I said it my way. This is Cookie's way of saying the same thing.

He wants to reach the kids and give them a fair chance of making it after they've played their last game or run their last race. And he needs your help. It takes money to send out all the professional counselors and ex-athletes who have volunteered to help Cookie. It takes money to reach all the children, all the superstars, all the minor leagues, all the broken down ex-athletes.

I'm just one guy that has volunteered to help Cookie. I believe in what he's trying to do. Organized sports has entertained and thrilled me. This is my chance, and your chance, to do something for the men who made these magic moments happen, and for the children who will make them happen tomorrow. Help us, won't you? Even with God as his quarterback, Cookie can't do it alone. Send your contributions, no matter how small, to the UACAC.

God bless you all, Marvin Gaye

Now with the positive press for the UACA and the Toronto concert on the horizon, I felt that the program's fortunes had changed. The initial box office response was overwhelming and it looked like we would sell out the Garden. With the infusion of the funds from the concert, I could actually get down to helping athletes instead of fighting the system that refused to see the problem that organized sports had created.

The concert date came around quickly, and Maple Leaf Gardens appeared to be standing room only. Marvin and the Tavares Brothers showed up to perform, but Ike and Tina were nowhere to be found. I later received word that they were unable to attend due to unforeseen personal issues. While I was never given specifics, they split up about a year later and rumors of the relationship being abusive were rampant.

Following the concert, I went to see Harold Ballard to discuss the final breakdown of the event's costs and to collect the proceeds for the UACA. I mentioned that it was a standing-room-only crowd and that it was great that the event sold out. Ballard claimed that the attendance was only around 11,000, and nowhere near the Gardens' capacity of 18,000. In the contract that I signed with Ballard, I had allowed for the Gardens to handle all ticket sales and in effect had given them control over the final ticket sale figures.

The conflict over the attendance was just the first problem because Ballard then hit me with a bill for $30,032.34 for the rental of Maple Leaf Gardens and another bill for $26,727.65 for CPI's services. I said to Ballard that I had a signed contract for $8,500 for the rental and that CPI was working only for expenses, due to the fact that the event was for a nonprofit organization. Ballard countered that he felt that the UACA was a for-profit organization because he heard that Marvin had collected $25,000 for his performance at the event and he felt this was a straight appearance fee due to the amount. I explained that the reimbursement fee also included the money Marvin had paid for the television advertising and other marketing costs. At the time Marvin was making $75,000 to $100,000 per concert and was willing to provide documentation to Ballard to clear up the matter, but he refused to entertain the discussion any further.

Based on Ballard's ticket sale numbers and the inflated rental costs the coalition would only clear $7,369 instead of the $100,000 Marvin and I had calculated based on our attendance estimates and the original rental pricing. That night I left Maple Leaf Gardens without one dollar from the night's proceeds and with the threat from Ballard that he would tie up the matter in court unless I agreed to his financial terms.

Ballard was a powerful man in Canada and had a firm grip on the media. The next morning I expected to see a headline that read how successful the concert was but instead read the Toronto Sun's bold headline, "Tina didn't show, angry rock fans demand refund!"
The other local paper, the Global Mail, was slightly kinder in printing in

small letters, *"Marvin Gaye lush and lavish, beats disaster."* I took this as Ballard putting his spin on the event in preparation for a fight over the proceeds. This was also to protect his son's company, CPI, which promoted all of the non-sports events at Maple Leaf Gardens and other arenas around Canada. If people realized that I had been able to put on a successful concert without any significant help from CPI, then it could bring on a challenge to CPI's apparent monopoly in the concert business.

About a week later, Marvin and I held a conference call with Bob Johnson to explain our situation with Ballard and CPI. Marvin started off by telling Bob that he totally supported me and that Ballard and CPI were trying to assassinate my character through carefully placed articles in the Canadian press. Marvin told Bob that he was shocked at the treatment I'd received, especially given the fact that I had the original documents stating what the terms of the venue rental would entail. Marvin thought that Ballard and CPI would want to get off on the right foot, thinking that he could be the first of many black acts to come and play in Canada. He then said to Bob it was evident that this was not the case, as he'd seen me taking flack from Ballard and his people all night. He said, *"It's pretty evident that they don't want that to go down, and not only do they not want that to go down, but they are trying to put, as it's been said, 'a nigger in his place.'"*

He further added that he felt CPI was trying to throw a monkey wrench into the incident because they saw that the UACA had the ability to successfully bring black acts into Canada, and that it could therefore be a threat to their existence. He said that I'd done a fine job with the event, which was done as a benefit for expenses only, which we can document. The entire smear campaign against me, he explained, was because CPI wanted to control and exploit the acts, especially the black acts.

Bob then said to Marvin that if he went on the record with this, he could be doing damage to his ability to tour, especially within Canada. Marvin said he had numerous offers for big money dates in Montréal and Winnipeg, but that his allegiances were with the UACA. He said he'd performed for the UACA benefit because he felt the organization's mission was honorable, and he was now speaking up because he saw me being attacked in the press for wanting to help people.

I told Bob the original terms of agreement and the fact that I felt that Ballard and CPI probably never thought the event would take place and assumed they'd collect a rental fee regardless. Marvin jumped back into the conversation and said, *"I imagine them saying, 'Oh, well, here is a nigger trying to do something, and he is not going to get anywhere,' but when it started to look like it would be successful it was a different ballgame."*

Marvin added that with the success that our concert had, the venue would want to bring more black acts into the area. Stevie Wonder had been approached and offered big money to play dates in Toronto, but CPI wanted to make sure they had Cookie out of the way. He is a real threat to their business. If he decides to take them on as a rival promoter and has the only access to the major black acts, it could put them out of business.

I then told Bob that I'd spoken with Bill Ballard at CPI the day before in an effort to settle the matter and get the funds that had been set aside for the UACA. I had only gone the route of promoting a concert because all of my other efforts to finance the UACA had failed, and I felt that CPI felt I was looking to make this my new career, which would make me a rival to their business.

Ballard was combative during our conversation and said, "If you think you can book another arena in North America, you can forget it, because you won't be able to do anything." I tried to explain to Ballard that I just wanted the money for the charity and that would be the end of my career as a concert promoter, but he hung up the phone as I was mid-sentence. Bob Johnson ran our version of events in a March issue of Jet Magazine. Bob called Maple Leaf Gardens for their response to our version of events and their spokesman Peter Larson said that all of the receipts were in a trust account until a settlement could be reached. The article even mentioned that Larsen scowled while stating, "We can sit on the money for a long time, until doomsday if necessary."

Unfortunately, Larsen wasn't bluffing with his statement. My financing had run out and a lengthy legal fight would just make the situation worse. The Ballard family had put the final nail in the coffin of the UACA. I never saw one cent for the UACA benefit show and don't know what happened to the money collected that night. The UACA folded due to lack of financial support.

For many years, I had spoken my mind and I was always called out by someone for it. At first it was players, coaches, and owners; later, it was members of the media. When I started out in football, there was no such thing as an agent. Every year you negotiated the terms of your own contract. If you were unhappy with the terms, there was not much recourse. I knew my value as a football player and pushed the envelope as far as I could during negotiations. Now I wonder, if I were white, would I have just been considered a savvy businessman? Any time I didn't conform to what was expected of a black man, a newspaper article would soon follow with an unflattering and untrue portrayal of my behavior during the negotiations - usually leaked to the press by the owner of whatever team I was negotiating with. The fact that I was a black man who refused to accept my "place" or hold my tongue gave me the title of a malcontent, uppity colored man, a reputation that followed me throughout my career.

The one thing I had always done during my life was stand up for what I thought was right and never caved in to pressure. The end of the UACA was the last straw. I could no longer fight the public's perception that I was in the wrong, no matter what the situation. This would be the start of a long, self-imposed exile where I spent my time reflecting on my choices in life. I would question whether I had chosen the correct times and venues to express my views regarding equal rights and benefits for athletes. If I had done something differently, would the UACA have succeeded? I'll never know the answer to these questions, but I still have confidence in my belief that the world of sports, at that time, needed the services of the UACA. In fact, almost forty years later, it still does.

For fighting for his beliefs, Cookie was ostracized and ridiculed as a crazy troublemaker. In fact, he was simply born too soon. He may have been right when he said that if he were born white, he might have just been considered "savvy." It was easier for people to dismiss Cookie's ideas about athletes suffering from drug dependency and long-term health problems from head traumas than it was to actually deal with the problem.

Cookie's arguments on civil rights, players' salaries, and the need for additional medical and mental health services are all now accepted practices in today's sports world. Some might say he fled from the public spotlight following the end of the UACA. I contend that he left a public that was not yet ready or did not want to hear what he had to say.

Jim Brown
and the First Celebrity Boxing Match

The comparisons between Jim Brown and Cookie Gilchrist were bound to come, as both were leading their respective leagues during the 1960s. Cookie was often tagged as the American Football League's version of Jim Brown. Those who really knew football would dare to say that Cookie was a better all-around football player. Few knew that off the field they had an unorthodox and sometimes volatile friendship.

When I would see Jim at an awards ceremony or media event, I would try to get under his skin by saying, "Jim, you couldn't even hold my jock," or "If I had stayed with the Cleveland Browns, people would never have heard of Jim Brown." These comments were just good-natured ribbing between two competitive spirits.

After I retired from football, I moved out to California with the hope that I would make a name for myself in Hollywood. Jim and Fred Williamson, the former Oakland Raiders defensive star, had started to make headway in the world of Hollywood, and I was hoping to jump on the bandwagon they started. Jim and I had become friendly during our time working with Muhammad Ali, and he invited me to stay at his Hollywood Hills home until I got on my feet.

The acting jobs I secured were few and far between. A few guest starring roles on The Beverly Hillbillies was the extent of my acting career. But I did love the glitz and glamour of the Hollywood lifestyle.

Jim was the life of the party and often held get-togethers at his home. On July 4, 1969, Jim was throwing a big party for the Independence Day holiday. I was in the kitchen talking to a young lady when Jim burst into the room with his shirt off and a head full of steam. Without a word Jim approached me and took a wild swing, grazing my chin. He did not connect cleanly with his fist, but as I looked on, stunned, he drew a silver handgun from his waistband.

As he raised the gun to my eye level, I moved to wrestle it from his grip. A struggle ensued, and I wrestled Jim to the kitchen floor. As I began to take the gun from Jim's grasp, he called out for reinforcements. Jim's friend Lenny Smith jumped in to help him, and he began to choke me in a headlock. In the ensuing donnybrook, Lenny was able to get me in a half nelson, and all three of us tumbled back to the floor. The entire house emptied out as this battle of the football titans went on, and the kitchen was soon in shambles with broken glass and overturned furniture littering the room.

Jim and Lenny combined were able to get me down on the floor. Once in control, Jim pointed the gun at my face. I asked him, *"Why did you pull a gun on me?"*

Jim's reply was that someone had hit on his girlfriend and I was the only person to have the nerve to do something like that. Jim was dating Jessica Cleaves, the lead singer for the musical group the Friends of Distinction. In addition to their personal relationship, he also acted as her manager. I told Jim I wouldn't disrespect our friendship by hitting on his girlfriend. I also pointed out that Jessica was black, and I preferred to date white women.

I'd had enough by that point and told Jim that if he was going to shoot me, he might as well do it. My left hand was bleeding profusely from a deep laceration, but I was more upset by the fact that my white cashmere sweater and alligator shoes were ruined during the struggle. Jim didn't go unscathed; he had a large bleeding gash on his arm.

A few seconds passed and Jim told Lenny to let me up from the floor. The panic in his face was clear. He had a good thing going in Hollywood and now, because of his jealousy, he had put everything in jeopardy. News of this incident could derail his burgeoning movie career and also put him in prison.

Jim followed me outside and apologized several times for jumping to conclusions. I told him that I had come to him for help getting into the movie industry and would never have done anything to jeopardize our friendship. Before I drove myself to the hospital I told him I wouldn't file charges against him.

The next day, the incident was all over the news wire. I had told no one. When Jet Magazine called me for a comment, I assumed that one of the other party guests had leaked the incident to the press. Several friends advised me to file charges against Jim and added that I should sue him for damages. I spoke with former Philadelphia Eagles running back Timmy Brown, who told me, *"Jim knew he couldn't beat you. That's why he pulled the gun. He thought that armed with a gun he would be able to scare you."*

I decided to follow the advice of my friends Mike Henry and Ernie Barnes, who suggested I contact Attorney Paul Caruso. Mike was a former Pittsburgh Steelers linebacker who'd found some success acting in several Tarzan Movies, and Ernie was a former Denver Broncos teammate who was now working as an artist. Ernie would eventually become world-renowned for his artwork. Since Mike and Ernie knew the Los Angeles scene better than I did, I deferred to their recommendation and made an appointment with Caruso, who was one of the top attorneys in Los Angeles and knew how to handle media-sensitive cases. I was concerned that the incident could have a negative effect on my Hollywood aspirations if I was portrayed as having culpability in this event. My reputation usually preceded me when it came to the media, and I wanted to get ahead of any negative press.

During my meeting with Attorney Caruso, I was informed that the current Los Angeles Sheriff, Peter Pitches, wanted to arrest Jim Brown, and that this incident would give him a reason. Apparently, Sheriff Pitches felt that Jim was a troublemaker, and this would be a way to knock him down a few pegs. Several prior charges brought against Jim had not stuck, and the Sheriff wanted to use me as a weapon against Jim in his personal crusade.

Caruso said that by just swearing out a complaint against Jim, I was looking at a financial windfall somewhere in the neighborhood of $250,000. I asked where the money would come from, and was told it would be from paid television and newspaper interviews regarding the incident. He also explained that the press that this would generate could catapult me into a starring movie role.

Being a compassionate capitalist, I asked Caruso what would be his interest in this endeavor, and he replied he would take a third of the proceeds. I immediately asked "*Who would pay any taxes?*"
I was told that any taxes would be my responsibility and would come out of my share.

The thought of what this would do to Jim's image and the community of young athletes who looked up to both of us was not worth the thirty pieces of silver I was being offered. I left Caruso's office with no money in my pocket, but knowing that I'd done the right thing by not kicking another human being while he was down.

Fred Williamson was finally able to get Jim and I together at the Oar House Restaurant in LA for a truce. For the moment, we settled our differences. I even moved back into Jim's house for a few more months before moving out for good in November of 1969.

In August of 1976, I drove out to see Jim with a business proposal. I had an idea for Jim and me to headline a boxing event in which former football players were the featured combatants. The funding for the event was secured when I got Houston oilman and real estate magnet Kenneth

Franzheim II to come on board with the financing. Franzheim made the majority of his fortune in the Texas oil business and was a well-respected Republican donor. He was rewarded for his support of Richard Nixon's Presidential Election when he was named the US Ambassador to New Zealand. Subsequent titles of US Ambassador to Tonga, Western Samoa, and Fiji followed soon after his New Zealand appointment.

Jim greeted me at the door and gave me a firm handshake. I jumped right into my proposal and explained that the funding and venue had already been secured. Jim said he thought we could make a lot of money, but needed a day to think it over. I said that people would be excited to see the two of us in the ring duking it out. As usual, I had to stick it to Jim and said, "You know I will win," and "At least this time we'll get paid for fighting." Before I left, we agreed to speak the following day.

This business proposal could help me get out of the financial hole I was in after I'd accrued $350,000 in financial losses from my backing of the United Athletes Coalition of America and Canada. I called Jim the next day as agreed, but received no answer. Over the next few weeks, I made numerous calls and left several messages, but to no avail.

About a year later I ran into Jim at Aunt Tilly's Health Food Store on Melrose Avenue. Jim had never returned my calls, and when he saw me, you could see the frantic and harried look on his face. You would have thought he owed me a million dollars, the way he was looking around for another exit just to avoid speaking to me.

I asked Jim if he'd thought about my proposal any further, and he said that he had to decline because he didn't think it would be good for his career. I couldn't figure out how it would be in any way detrimental to his career, and my only thought was that he had a fear of being defeated in the ring and though this would hurt his public tough guy reputation.

Jim tried to change the subject. He said he didn't think I would want to fight anyway -- he'd heard I was now a preacher. He was referring to my study of the different world religions. I replied that I was not a preacher, just a man trying to gain wisdom and knowledge regarding his spirituality.

That was the last time we ever spoke, and I thought that a great business opportunity had been missed. I was fully aware that Jim's participation was needed to make the event a success and wouldn't proceed without him.

In 2001, I happened to pick up a Sports Illustrated and, while reading it, came across an article describing a celebrity boxing match between former NFL players that was being promoted on the FX cable network.
The highlight of the event was former New York Giants linebacker Lawrence Taylor duking it out against former Cincinnati fullback Ickey

Woods. I cut out the article and mailed it to Jim with a note saying we could have made a killing with this idea. I asked him if he had any current interest because we would still put on a better show than any of the guys they dragged out for this event. I finished with, *"YOU DO KNOW I WOULD HAVE KICKED YOUR ASS, AGAIN!"*

Cookie realized that Jim Brown had been designated by many as the greatest football player to ever grace the gridiron. The fact that Cookie spent his prime years dominating in the CFL and AFL instead of playing in the media-savvy NFL obscured the depths of his talent to those who did not truly follow the game of football. Cookie knew there would invariably be comparisons due to the fact that they both dominated the game playing the same position on the field, but was confident in his abilities and felt he was the better all around player. Part of him wished for the public recognition Jim received as the star of the NFL, but he took solace in the fact that if anyone had a chance to rival Jim's position in the hearts of the nation's devoted football fans, it could only be Cookie Gilchrist.

Another Run-in with Mr. Ohio

In 1979, coach Paul Brown co-authored his life story with the help of writer Jack Cleary. Coach Brown's version of the events leading up to Cookie's signing out of high school was far from a true depiction of what had actually transpired. The book, at least as far as it had to do with Cookie, was a whitewash designed to protect the legacy of coach Brown.

Upon learning of it, Cookie was determined to prove what had truly transpired back in the summer of 1954. But he would need help from some friends in high places to get the documentation he needed to set the record straight.

The Paul Brown Story was released around 1980. Once it was brought to my attention that the book contained coach Brown's version of the events surrounding my signing out of high school, I decided to give it a read. Coach Brown's version of the event was as follows:

"In training camp that year, we were trying to sort out all the new faces when a strapping young high school fullback named Cookie Gilchrist, who had broken all of the high school records in Western Pennsylvania, came with his father to ask for a tryout. We were forbidden by NFL rules to sign anyone whose potential college class had not yet graduated, but his father insisted that the boy did not want to go to college and that we give him a tryout. We watched him run, just to ease out the situation, but never scrimmaged him, as has often been reported. Nevertheless, the boy really intrigued me, and I even called Bert Bell to reaffirm the league rule. As I expected, Bert told me not to sign him. He left us, went to Canada, where he became a star, and stayed there even after he was eligible to sign with the NFL. Later, he came back to play in the American Football League."

After reading the book, I felt that Coach Brown had lied about every aspect of my signing. What had actually happened was that Coach Brown had sent his envoy, assistant coach Ed Ulinski, to sign me in May of 1954. Coach Ulinski had warned me not to tell my family and friends about the contract until the team released the news to the press. I was surprised that, almost thirty years later, coach Brown still refused to take responsibility for what he had done. He was now considered one of the greatest football coaches of all time and had his own bust in Canton at the Pro Football Hall of Fame. I was convinced there was no way he would sully his reputation by admitting that he had cheated in order to maintain his team's winning ways.

I petitioned the NFL for their records regarding my contract with the Browns, but they refused to release the information to me. Several times I was informed that my file was misplaced and that the matter was under investigation. After getting the runaround, I was finally told that they would contact me once my file was located.

On March 15, 1983, I decided to go see Tom Carper, the newly elected Senator from Delaware. I explained my plight to Senator Carper, and he agreed to use his office to make a formal request to the NFL for the documents that I was searching for.

Senator Carper's office sent a letter of inquiry to Mr. Jim Bailey, Vice President and general counsel for the Cleveland Browns, requesting a copy of my contract. A similarly worded letter was also sent to the office of NFL Commissioner Peter Rozelle, requesting the release of the same information.

On April 9, 1983, I received a letter from Senator Carper's office with an NFL file card that read:

Gilchrist, Carlton B No College
Address: 868 Fourth Avenue Brackenridge, PA

Signed as free agent by the Browns 5/8/54- $5,500 per season (info pertaining to eligibility in his own folder).

Waivers 8/4/54: expired 8/9/54 at 9:00 a.m.

Having that card in hand confirmed my version of events. I set out and wrote a letter to coach Brown to see if an attached copy of the card would help him with his recollection of the events surrounding my time with the Browns.

Dear Mr. Brown,

On May 8, 1954, while an 18 year old junior at Har-Brack High School, I signed a pro contract with your Cleveland Browns Football Club, Inc. Since then, almost 30 years later, there has been controversy surrounding me and my illustrious football career.

The purpose of this correspondence is for direct contact with you to clear up the possible oversight and misquote on your part as stated on page 234 of your book, "The P.B. Story". You are quoted as saying my father, who is now deceased, brought me to your camp at Hiram College and demanded you give me a tryout. This is not true and knowing you as a truthful person and coach, you would not want this blemish on your great record.

In the recorded files of the NFL it states I signed a contract for $5,500 on May 8, 1954, and it was made public on May 19, 1954. As you are aware

I did not receive the money quoted or bus fare back to Brackenridge, Pennsylvania.

I think the book is great, pointing out all the great athletes you coached and fathered during your career as an innovator of coaching.

I look forward to your affirmative reply to the above.

Respectfully yours,
Carlton "Cookie" Gilchrist.

On November 2, 1983, Paul Brown answered my letter, and this was his written reply:

Dear Cookie,

I received your letter and it was good to hear from you.

Thirty years is a long time to remember some of the details of the past. It was always my understanding that the man who accompanied you to Hiram was your father. If this is not true, I apologize for the error.

I have a great admiration for you as a player over the years. There was a time we thought we might have you here with the Bengals. You were allocated to us in the player distribution by the Denver Broncos when the franchise was formed. In the meantime, however, they hired you for a promotion and a PR job that kept you with Denver, so we never had a chance to have you with use.

I wish you every success in your consulting business.

Sincerely,
Paul E. Brown

The letter was a clear slap in the face and Brown was telling me with a smile and a kind word that he would never acknowledge his wrongdoing. Even faced with the NFL's corroborating documents he chose to stick his head in the sand and decided he could change history to a version that portrayed him in a positive light. Once again, the NFL power brokers could do no wrong, and the truth would fall on deaf ears.

Having the NFL's documents and Brown's written response, I wrote to Delaware Senator Joe Biden to see if he would help bring the truth to light. I received a written response from Senator Biden, who eventually moved on from his position in Delaware to become the Vice President of the United States.

The following excerpts are from Senator Biden's written response:

"I believe that the best response to unfair treatment is through public exposure and a firm resolve to prevent similar acts in the future."

"As you know, there are situations which go beyond unfair treatment and become illegal conduct. Congress and the Constitution have established certain rights and remedies to cover such situations - in the many civil and contract laws -- to name two of the most important"

Empowered by Senator Biden's letter, I sought the counsel of my longtime friend and former quarterback with the Bills, Jack Kemp. Jack was the current Republican Congressman for New York and a powerful man within the Republican Party. I campaigned heavily for Jack when he ran for Congress and always felt he was a friend I could rely on.

On November 18, 1983, I drove to Bethesda, Maryland where Jack and his lovely wife Joanna were residing, so we could speak face to face. I spent the evening visiting with Jack and Joanna, who invited me to spend the night. Before we called it an evening Jack read the documents from the NFL, as well as coach Brown's response.

Jack's only comment was, *"You have to let Paul Brown off the hook."*

The words were stinging, especially coming from a man who I'd gone to battle with on the football field and whom I supported when he sought out public office. I always considered Jack a close friend and had expected his support in bringing my side of the story to the media.

Jack, in addition to his career in politics, maintained a strong presence in the NFL. If he became associated with a negative campaign against one of the most revered coaches in the game, it would jeopardize his standing with the league. Jack continued to try and convince me to just let it go, and added that if I played my cards right, I would eventually get into the Pro Football Hall of Fame. I refused. Now I knew where I stood with Jack. We continued to remain close after this event, but I now understood that he put being a politician before our friendship.

Cookie was determined now more than ever to get the truth out about his first venture into professional football. Only those close to Cookie knew the true events around his signing, but he wanted the world to know what went on behind the scenes in professional football. That he was again calling out those in power within the NFL may have seemed like just another round of the always difficult or "uppity" Cookie Gilchrist crying wolf. But in fact it wasn't just a case of sour grapes; it was the truth.

The CFL Hall of Fame

As with many events surrounding Cookie's life and career, the facts regarding whether or not he turned down induction into the Canadian Football Hall of Fame are a subject of public contention. The Canadian Football Hall of Fame and many of the press outlets that covered the league only have part of the story. Cookie's side of the story will shed light on why one of the best all-around football players ever to grace the Canadian gridiron is not enshrined with his peers in the Canadian Football Hall of Fame.

On Wednesday, May 27, 1983, I received a call from CFL Commissioner Jake Gaudaur, who informed me that I had been selected for induction into the next CFL Hall of Fame Class. Jake said I had been unanimously recommended for induction into that year's class, in the player category. I was told the selection was based on the qualities of character, sportsmanship, playing ability, and contributions to football in general.

I politely told Gaudaur that I would decline the honor, but would possibly consider induction in another year. I asked him to mail me a brochure about the Hall of Fame and the selection committee. I wanted to know who was sitting in judgment of my character. Was the selection committee made up of those who had mistreated me and other players of color? Were these people the gatekeepers of quality character and sportsmanship?

I loved the Canadian people; especially the fans who'd watched me play in the ORFU and CFL. But I felt that several of the CFL elite had taken advantage of me at the height of my career. I felt that if I accepted the honor from those who had mistreated me, I would be condoning what happened in the past. In addition to the poor treatment I received from several coaches and owners off the field, all of the times that I was punched, kicked, or cursed on the field just because of the color of my skin remained a vivid memory. I thought that by declining the honor, I could bring new light to what had happened to me and other players of color. At least the issue would spur on serious dialogue about player treatment now and in the past. I asked Gaudaur to keep my decision to decline out of the media until I was ready to make a public statement.

Lew Hayman had run me out of CFL when he was the general manager of the Toronto Argonauts. I had four years remaining on my contract when

I was put on waivers by Toronto prior to the start of the 1962 season. Not one team would put in a claim for me, not even for the bargain basement waiver fee of $350. I had been blackballed by Hayman and embarrassed in the press. There was a particularly offensive cartoon that ran in the newspaper the morning after Hayman placed me on waivers. The cartoon showed Hayman dressed in full pirate garb with a sword pointed in my back. He was depicted as having me walk the plank into shark-infested waters with my arms tied behind my back. I was offended on many levels. As one of the top players in the league, I knew I did not deserve what was happening to me, and as a black man, I was horrified at the way the cartoon depicted a black man being led to his death by a white man.

I had been put on waivers in retaliation for being caught out after curfew by Toronto coach Lou Agase. The night prior to my being placed on waivers we were scheduled for a preseason game. Coach Agase saw Boyd Carter and me in the lobby of the team hotel around 3:00 a.m. The coach didn't say a word to either of us, but the next day I was put on waivers for violating the team's curfew rule. Boyd only received a minimal fine, which was the customary punishment for being caught out after curfew. Agase had been losing control of the team and wanted to send a clear message that he was in charge. Unfortunately, for an infraction that would at any other time have been a fine, I became the prime example of Agase's new take-no-prisoners attitude. They say if you want to gain respect, you need to take down the biggest and baddest guy in the schoolyard. At the time, I was one of the stars of the league and the perfect target for the coach. Despite this show of power, Agase could not hold on to the team and was eventually fired three games into the 1962 season, while I moved on to Buffalo and the American Football League.

I received two more calls that summer from Commissioner Gaudaur asking me to reconsider my stance on induction into the Hall of Fame. I was steadfast in my choice to remain out of the Hall, even having my own issues with Gaudaur from our time together in Hamilton. When Gaudaur was the Hamilton Tiger-Cats general manager, he'd promised me a $500 bonus following the 1957 Tiger-Cats Grey Cup win. I had, as usual, spread myself thin financially through a combination of poor spending and business decisions, and needed that bonus to cover my rent and the home's furniture, which had been financed.

When I went to see Gaudaur to collect the promised bonus, he flatly refused. I pleaded with him and said that if he did not pay me the bonus, I couldn't make the required payments on my family's residence and furnishings. Gaudaur still refused and within days, the furniture, including the crib I'd just had delivered in anticipation of the birth of my first child, was repossessed. My family and I were embarrassed and upset by the incident and shocked with the way that Jake Gaudaur conducted business. I should have had a financial safety net, but I had assumed he would follow through with the promised bonus. This financial dispute led to me being shipped off to Saskatchewan to play with the Roughriders of the Western Division.

Following Gaudaur's final attempts to get me to reconsider, the Hall of Fame released a vague statement explaining that I declined induction. They did not give the reasons behind my decision to decline the honor, and inferred that I had talked poorly about the Canadian fans. I had asked them to remain silent until I released a statement explaining my decision, but they chose not to respect my wishes. My goal was to let the Canadian fans know that my decision to decline was not because I did not love and respect them, but was rather a matter of principle. I felt that I needed to be vocal about what had happened in the '50s and '60s now that I had a platform.

Over the years I was invited to several CFL events, which I politely declined, continuing to keep my distance from the CFL and all other football-related events. When I was diagnosed with throat cancer in 2007, the media brought my name back into the Hall of Fame discussion and the matter was revisited. The Hall of Fame contacted me and asked if I would reconsider my decision to enter the Hall. Facing my own mortality and following the births of my grandchildren, I was open to reconsidering my decision. The thought of leaving a legacy behind for my family to be proud of had started to really weigh on me. I asked the Hall of Fame whether, if I were inducted, they would allow me to sell items in their gift shop. The items would revolve around the football poem I had written with all of the profits going to charity. The proceeds would be set aside for a charity that would provide school computers and scholarships for inner-city kids. The Hall informed me that they would not agree to any special conditions for my induction. Although I had been leaning toward accepting, part of me needed them to do something positive for the old wounds to heal. Their refusal to support my charity, right or wrong, brought back a flood of bad memories, and again I walked away from the Hall of Fame.

Cookie wanted to be a part of the CFL Hall of Fame right up until the day he died. He loved his CFL teammates and the Canadian fans and could think of no greater honor than to be enshrined with the other greats of the CFL, but still the ghosts of the past haunted him. This could be a legacy he could leave for his grandchildren. The Hall of Fame would be a place where they could bring future generations and be proud of what he had accomplished.

About a week before Cookie passed, he stated his desire to get his affairs in order. The first order of business was to call the Hall of Fame to tell them that he would accept their offer of induction, no strings attached. Unfortunately, Cookie's body failed too quickly and the call was never made.

The week following Cookie's death, an email was sent to Mark DeNobile, Executive Director of the CFL Hall of Fame, stating that his family would like to have Cookie considered for the Hall. His Family wanted to know what needed to be done to nominate Cookie for the next Hall of Fame Class. Mr. DeNobile stated that he would contact the Chairman of the Selection Committee and would get back to the family. After two weeks without a response, another email was sent to Mr. DeNobile. The tone of the email's response was now less cordial, "I have talked to the Chairman of the Selection Committee. The Selection Committee last addressed the item in 2007 and the 'matter' is now closed and will not be looked at again, Regards, Mark DeNobile, CFL Hall of Fame Executive Director." In his email, Mr. DeNobile does not even address Cookie by name. Apparently, this "matter" had become personal and not just about football ability.

Some will say that Cookie had his chance and chose to thumb his nose at the CFL Hall of Fame. It's easier to judge Cookie using today's more progressive outlook toward race. Today athletes of all colors cash in on their athletic ability and do not face the obstacles that he faced playing in the 1950s and 1960s.The time has come for the CFL Hall of Fame to put their personal feelings aside and induct one of the greatest players in the league's history. The Hall of Fame should be based on what someone did on the field, and if that is the case, Cookie Gilchrist should be one of the first names in any Football Hall of Fame.

Ralph, Where's My Plaque?

The Buffalo Bills Wall of Fame has always been a passionate subject with the loyal fans of the Buffalo Bills. Every year, when the next inductee is announced, the fans begin a good-natured, passionate dialogue regarding the merits of the current inductee and a heartfelt plea for who they feel should actually be on the Bills Wall of Fame. Some of the fans feel that the award is a popularity contest and not necessarily for those that helped further the franchise on and off the field.

Many people are unaware that the Buffalo Bills Wall of Fame actually started out in 1971, as the Buffalo Bills Hall of Fame, and that I happened to be the first inductee. Bills Public Relations guru Jack Horrigan created the award. Jack was a master of promotion, not just for the Buffalo Bills, but also for the entire American Football League.

As it happened, the timing of the announcement could not have been better for the Bills, who were attempting to get public financing for a new stadium in Orchard Park. Old War Memorial Stadium seated somewhere in the neighborhood of 43,000 fans. The merger of the American Football League and the National Football League required that a team's stadium seating be in excess of 50,000 seats. The newly combined NFL felt that the stadium issue was an important aspect in the expansion of the sport's popularity. During the public debate over financing for a new stadium for the Bills, a possible move to Seattle was proposed if the new stadium financing fell through. This new award was created to honor Buffalo Bills players who'd helped lead the team to its first two AFL championships, and it would also help renew interest and fan favor for a new stadium. This would be quite helpful in the courting of votes for the new stadium, especially considering that the Bills teams of that era were losing games on a consistent basis.

The Bills informed me that the induction ceremony would be held at the Buffalo Touchdown Club during the team's kickoff luncheon to celebrate the start of the 1971 season. The entire 1971 team attended, along with my former teammates Booker Edgerson, Wray Carlton, Charley Ferguson, Ernie Warlick, Tom Sestak, and Ed Rutkowski. Even the Mayor of Buffalo, Frank Sedita, was on hand to see me presented with a plaque that signified my induction into the Bills Hall of Fame.

During my acceptance speech, I thanked the Buffalo Bills organization and the Bills fans for the honor of making me the first inductee into the Buffalo Bills' Hall of Fame. The award was the first of its kind for any team in the newly combined NFL, and would become so popular that most of the teams in the league today have some type of honor for their former players. At the induction luncheon, Bills owner Ralph C. Wilson was quoted by Buffalo News sports writer Jim Peters for an article that ran the following day with the headline, "Gilchrist Enshrined in Bills' Hall of Fame." Mr. Wilson stated, "A larger four-foot-by-eight-foot plaque will be enshrined later on in the new stadium in Orchard Park." Jim Peters put Mr. Wilson's quote in the context of the stadium funding issue, writing that it seemed more hopeful than prophetic in referring to the proposed 80,000-seat stadium in Orchard Park.

Today people ask me if I feel I should be inducted into the Bills' Wall of Fame and I tell them I already was. Many people don't remember that I was the first inductee or that the honor started as the Bills' Hall of Fame before the name change to the Bills Wall of Fame. The funding for the stadium was ultimately approved and the new stadium, now known as Ralph Wilson Stadium, or the "Ralph," was built in Orchard Park.
The plaque was never put up as promised and the honor long forgotten.

Many years later, I was approached by the organization regarding being inducted into the Bills Wall of Fame. I replied that I was already bestowed with this honor, but the plaque was never put up as promised. I considered this an insult, and as far as I was concerned, the Bills used my name in 1971 just to garner support for a new publicly financed stadium. Once they received approval for the stadium, they discarded my name when it was no longer useful. I felt a second induction ceremony would only be for their benefit, and I wouldn't attend unless I was able to promote my charity projects. The Bills refused my request to promote my charity projects, which were going to fund educational programs for inner-city youths.
I countered that I wouldn't be opposed to the team erecting the original plaque as promised at the 1971 ceremony, but added that I would not attend a new ceremony and re-write history just to increase their ticket sales.

The team ultimately walked away and, through the press, floated the story that I refused the honor, never mentioning that I had already been inducted in 1971. Once I took this stance, I knew the team would never agree to my name being added to the wall because it would be a public relations nightmare if I refused to attend the ceremony. When team reunions were held, I refused to attend, holding the same line I had drawn in the sand regarding the Wall of Fame.

Throughout my life, those who wielded the power of the press or were in positions of power used their influence to change history to a version that was kinder to them. My refusal to re-write history just for Mr. Wilson's financial gain now made me persona non grata with the Bills organization. Despite having a plaque that said I was the first inductee into the Bills Hall of Fame, the dispute with Mr. Wilson resulted in my being erased from team history.

In December 2010, during the writing of this book, Cookie softened his stance regarding the Wall of Fame and told family and friends that if the Bills announced his name for the Wall of Fame, he would attend. Very ill and facing his mortality, Cookie felt the Wall of Fame recognition would be part of the legacy he could leave behind for his family.

Shortly before his passing, Cookie and Mr. Wilson spoke and both described the call as being positive. Cookie held on to the hope that they had settled their differences and that he would be well enough to attend a Bills game with Mr. Wilson during the 2011 season, but this never came to pass. Cookie passed away a few days after their conversation.

Following Cookie's death in January 2011, many including family and friends thought that the Bills would use the 2011 Wall of Fame announcement to honor Cookie. Unfortunately, Cookie Gilchrist was not the name announced for the 2011 Wall of Fame ceremony. The Bills had the perfect opportunity to right a wrong and bring Cookie back into the Bills family, but chose not to.

Buffalo Bills Wall of Fame Inductees:

1980 - O.J. Simpson
1984 - Jack Kemp
1985 - Patrick J. McGroder
1987 - Tom Sestak
1988 - Billy Shaw
1989 - Ralph C. Wilson Jr.
1992 - The 12th Man
1993 - Elbert Dubenion
1994 - Mike Stratton
1995 - Joe Ferguson
1996 - Marv Levy
1997 - Joe Delamielleure
1998 - Robert James
1999 - Edward Abramoski
2000 - Bob Kalsu
2000 - George Saimes
2001 - Jim Kelly
2001 - Fred Smerlas
2002 - Kent Hull
2003 - Darryl Talley
2004 - Jim Ritcher
2005 - Thurman Thomas
2006 - Andre Reed
2007 - Steve Tasker
2008 - Bruce Smith
2010 - Booker Edgerson
2011 - Phil Hansen

Facebook Friends

After the early 1980s, Cookie withdrew from the limelight due to what he felt was racism and indifference to the wellbeing of athletes. The professional athlete was a commodity to be traded and sold when no longer useful to their owner. Cookie's refusal of enshrinement into the Canadian Football League Hall of Fame in 1983 was one of the last events Cookie commented on publicly before embarking on a long self-imposed exile.

This is the part of the story that Cookie did not write or record in his journals. It will be told through the eyes of our unlikely friendship.

In 2007, I retired from the New York City Police Department due to several injuries I suffered in the line of duty. Nothing as serious as being shot, but a combination of injuries to my neck, back, and shoulder suffered while trying to make an arrest. I retired as a detective and had attained that rank while working numerous dangerous assignments within the narcotics and homicide divisions of the department. Once I retired, I spent my free time reading and researching my favorite sport, football. I now used the investigative skills I once used to track down criminals to learn all I could about the game I loved.

A common thread ran through many of the books I read, especially those that chronicled the history of the American Football League. That common thread was that Cookie Gilchrist was the first marquee star of the AFL prior to the Jets' signing of Joe Namath. All of the books talked about Cookie being outspoken, but also an enigma. The more I read about this great of the AFL, the greater my desire grew to know more about his story.

Cookie Gilchrist stories varied greatly and many read like a child's game of telephone. His physical appearance would sometimes be exaggerated, as well as his exploits on and off the field. The fact that he had such great athletic ability and that he disappeared from the public eye for so many years only added to the mystery of Cookie Gilchrist. Almost all of the stories written about Cookie after the early 1980s were just a rehashing of old stories with attributed quotes from old articles and interviews.

As I read about Cookie and the other greats of football, I sometimes mailed out requests for their autographs. Most of the players I mailed requests to replied graciously, even answering questions I had posed to them in my letters. The one player who never responded was Cookie. On the Internet I read articles describing Cookie as an extremely private person who rarely granted interviews or responded to autograph requests. I became resigned to the fact that he would never respond to my letter.

In late August of 2010 I started to use the social networking site Facebook to communicate with family and old friends. As I was searching out friends to add to my Facebook circle, I wondered what were the odds that Cookie Gilchrist was on Facebook. This was a man who was known for being reclusive and would now be seventy-five years old. With the name plugged into the search engine, one possible match came back, but provided no picture and no information to determine if this was in fact the great AFL player.

On a lark, I sent a friend request with an added a message saying that I thought he was one of the greatest players to ever grace the gridiron; and asking if he was going to ever do any autograph appearances. A day or two passed, and I assumed that the person on the other end of the computer was not the famous Buffalo Bills player. Then one afternoon, to my amazement, I received a response notifying me that my friend request was accepted. The return message stated that I was talking to "The Original Cookie Monster and Peck's Bad Boy." He added that he had to respond because of the cute picture of my baby daughter Olivia that was my Facebook avatar. He also stated that he wanted the children of today to know the truth about what football really does to its forgotten heroes.

That first day or two we emailed back and forth, and I mentioned to Cookie the other AFL greats like Charlie Hennigan, the record-setting receiver for the Houston Oilers, who I had become friendly with that past year. Out of nowhere Cookie asked for my telephone number and asked if he could call me. As a football fan, there was no way I could pass up the chance to speak to one of the football greats and ask questions about the glory days of football.

Cookie called me almost immediately after I emailed him my number. When I answered the phone, somewhat nervously, I heard this booming voice on the other end. The first thing Cookie asked me was how old I was. He also wanted to know my date of birth. Cookie had a real interest in astrology and was trying to figure out my astrological sign. During the conversation, which went on for over two hours, I felt like I was on the most difficult job interview ever. The myriad of questions Cookie asked regarding race, religion, politics, etc., were exhausting. Cookie described the difficulties of being in an interracial marriage in the 1950s and how it affected his playing career. I mentioned that I too was in an interracial marriage, and couldn't imagine the way that he and his wife had been treated during the unrest prior to the passage of the Civil Rights Act.

Following my disclosure about my marital situation, Cookie's tone softened and the conversation became less of him preaching and more of a back-and-forth dialogue. I still don't know if he felt that I somehow understood where he was coming from. The only thing I could tell was that he wanted to keep the dialogue going, because after the completion of the two-hour call, he said, "Great call. Let's do it again tomorrow!"

The next day, like clockwork, my phone rang and the caller ID read, "Cookie Gilchrist." During our first conversation he had made several statements about race and astrology that I thought were controversial, but I didn't know if this was just his personality or a sign of something else. All of the stories I had read about Cookie talked about him being an outspoken and over-the-top individual, so at the time I just assumed that this was Cookie being Cookie.

I have to admit I was becoming enamored with the "cool factor" of having Cookie on my speed dial, but during our second call, I could tell that he seemed lonely. Truth be told, I was also lonely, missing the camaraderie of my fellow NYPD Officers, and I enjoyed the telephone conversations very much. These conversations gave me the opportunity to draw a parallel between the end of Cookie's career in football and mine with the NYPD. Cookie talked about being a stranger in the locker room after he retired, having to ask for a pass if he wanted to enter and see friends. Areas where he had once held court he now had to get permission to even get past the door. I explained that I felt the same way: when I wanted to return to the police facilities to see friends, I would be stopped as if I were an intruder. In both professions, and I am sure many others, time goes on. Those who've left are quickly forgotten, and this may have been the reason we both seemed to have fallen out of contact with our work colleagues. This new friendship seemed to fill the void for both of us.

This second phone call also brought up some concerns. Cookie mentioned that he was surviving on about $610.00 per month from his player pension plus his social security benefit. He said he was renting a room in Norfolk and that he had someone who came to check on him from time to time. This was when Cookie relayed the fact that for almost forty years he'd locked himself away and lived as a recluse. He said he'd spent this time alone studying the world's religions and looking for answers to life's greatest questions. I brought up the idea of Cookie doing an autograph signing to help with his finances. Cookie's tone quickly became agitated, and he said that he would never sign autographs. He became uneasy and couldn't explain his reasons for not wanting to do a paid appearance.

Then, as quickly as he became angry, he changed the subject and asked about my family.

I went with the sudden and different directions he took during the conversation, but it was almost like Jekyll and Hyde how quickly his mood and tone shifted. As the conversation was ending, he asked me, *"What do you think my autograph is worth?"* It was as if he did not remember that we just discussed this subject a few minutes earlier. I told him I would be willing to pay $150 for his autograph. He said that for me there would be no charge, but he would take doing a public signing under advisement. I soon found that Cookie used the term *"taking it under advisement"* in almost every conversation we ever had.

Before ending our chat, Cookie said that he was ready to get back out into the public eye after being a recluse for so long and wanted me to become his manager. While I was clearly honored that he thought enough of me to ask after just two conversations, I knew I was not qualified for that type of position. I was beginning to realize that Cookie needed a friend now more than ever because it was clearly more than just a difficult attitude that was controlling his behavior.

Cookie began calling daily, usually two to three times a day. There were more than a few calls at midnight where I would think that something was wrong and he would just reply that he couldn't sleep and wanted to see if I wanted to chat. These were the times when I appreciated my wife's understanding nature regarding my friendship with Cookie.

At the time, I thought I was just being kind to an old football player, especially on the days when he called me five or six times barking orders at me like I was a paid employee. The fact was that this relationship filled a void that I'd had since I left the NYPD. There were many days of feeling down due to continued back and neck pain, but the relationship with Cookie gave me focus because I now felt a sense of responsibility for him. I tried to discuss his family with him, in an attempt to find out why he was all alone. Cookie was cryptic and gave little information about anything he did not want to voluntarily disclose. If I pushed on an issue, he became angry. I decided it was more important to listen and be there for him than it was to drive him away with more inquiries. I hoped the information would present itself as our conversations progressed.

Cookie began to ask me computer questions and started to show signs of paranoia. He sent me several email exchanges he had with other people and said, "Can't you tell they are on my computer watching what I do?" At first I thought that he just did not understand some of the things written in the emails and had become confused, but this became a recurring theme. I knew if I told him that I thought he was wrong, he would just hang up and disappear. I went along and said that I would straighten out his computer situation for him, and this kept him calm for a few days.

One day he called in a panic and said that the NFL and the Bills were trying to trade upon his name. I knew that a lot of retired athletes had been taken advantage of when it came to their intellectual property rights and often were not paid for the use of their likeness in films and video games. At first glance, I didn't know what to make of his remarks. As he explained the situation, I realized what had him so upset. A company had purchased the domain name "www.cookiegilchrist.com" and had set up links to NFL sites, including the Buffalo Bills website. I tried to explain how domain names worked, and that advertising links could be added to any website. For several days he continued to call and became distraught about the domain name. I couldn't listen to him get upset any longer and contacted the company in the Netherlands that owned the domain name. I negotiated the purchase of the domain name in the hope that I could help ease his fears. I then called Cookie and explained that I had purchased the domain name and would help him construct a website that chronicled his career.

As our relationship progressed we had conversations in which Cookie vividly detailed stories from fifty years ago, but couldn't remember what we'd discussed a day earlier. Every time I became concerned about his mental state, we would have an hour-long conversation that went without a problem. There were even times where he would correctly recall to me things that I had forgotten. These good days were usually followed by several bad ones - like the day that Cookie called me three times and we had the same conversation each time as if it were for the first time. He had absolutely no memory of the previous calls. Cookie also once sent me an email that was just a long rambling of abstract thoughts and Bible quotes, without any real purpose. When I did not respond immediately to the email he called and left me a voicemail that said, "I hope I did not blow your mind with my email. I did not want to scare you off." I called Cookie and reassured him that I was his friend and that he could never scare me off. This was around the time that Cookie mentioned that he was starting to worry that he might be getting Alzheimer's disease. Cookie even stated that he wanted to donate his brain to the concussion study in Boston because he wanted the world to know how football damages those who played the game.

Not all of our conversations were gloom and doom. There were many times when Cookie would recall in great detail his days in football. As a football fan, I enjoyed hearing his stories and getting the behind-the-scenes information that wasn't available in the old newspaper articles recounting these events. As a friend, I just enjoyed hearing the joy in his voice when he talked about his greatest achievements on the football field.

In mid-September, Cookie told me he had decided to move back to his hometown area just outside of Pittsburgh. He said he wanted to reconnect with friends he had in the Pittsburgh area and that he also needed to follow-up with the doctor who had treated him for throat cancer in 2007. While not saying who was taking him, Cookie said he was having someone drive him from Norfolk to Pittsburgh and would call me the next day to let me know that he arrived safely. He had made arrangements to rent an apartment in a federally subsidized senior apartment building just outside the Pittsburgh city limits.

The next day came with no phone call from Cookie, which was unusual at this point. I called his cell phone and in a barely audible whisper, Cookie said he was in the hospital. The first thing I asked was what had happened in the twenty-four hours since we last spoke. Cookie said that the doctors told him his heart was racing and that they wanted to keep him for monitoring. I knew how boring time spent in a hospital could be, so I called the hospital gift shop and made arrangements to send balloons, magazines, and candy to Cookie's room. A few hours later, Cookie called and said that a gift shop worker had come into his room to deliver the package, which was a huge basket adorned with several "Get Well" balloons. He said he told the man making the delivery that he was in the wrong place because he had no one who would be sending him a package. Cookie told me that once he found out the package was actually for him, he felt moved with emotion because my family had thought of him, adding that he especially appreciated the chocolates, which he had already finished.

Cookie spent several days in the hospital, but we continued our daily calls. He even had the nurses call me when they needed answers to questions about his medical history or to discuss medical treatment. I explained to the nurses that I had limited information about his past because our friendship was relatively new, but offered any help I could provide. Cookie often refused to give blood or take his medication, and I would receive calls from the nurses' station asking me to get him to comply with the treatment schedule. Cookie was a believer in holistic medicine and a practicing vegetarian, so his time in the hospital did not go smoothly. I had somehow gone from a Facebook friend request to becoming his emergency medical contact, and was unsure how I'd become so involved in his life.

The day that Cookie was released from the hospital, he called me and said he just received a call from Verizon advising him that his cell phone was being turned off because his bill was past due. Cookie asked me to pay the bill and said he would reimburse me once he cleared up his banking situation. This was because his pension and social security checks came through direct deposits, which had not been moved from his Norfolk bank to a new bank in Pittsburgh. I thought to myself how much could his cell phone bill be and agreed to help him. That's when he said, "Just call the guy at Verizon and give him the $710 for the bill." I repeated the amount to Cookie, thinking I had heard him incorrectly.

After some investigation, I discovered that Cookie had been using a Verizon Wi-Fi card for the Internet and had numerous overage charges. Now I had a dilemma. I did not have the extra money, but I was concerned for his mental and physical well-being. What if he had no phone and could not call for help? Cookie and I placed a three-way call to Verizon and he had me added to his account. I paid half of the bill over the phone and arranged a payment plan, while changing the terms of his account so this wouldn't happen to him again.

I called the apartment building where Cookie had moved and spoke with the manager, Larry Cooper. Thankfully, Larry was a kind man who became my local contact to help Cookie. I lived in Staten Island, a borough of NYC, which was a six-hour drive from Cookie's apartment. With Larry's help, I arranged for Cookie to get home phone, cable and Internet service set up in his apartment. Knowing that he did not need any extra expenses, I bought a wireless router and mailed it to Larry so he could install it in Cookie's apartment. Cookie's mental state seemed fine following his hospitalization and I began to think that maybe the treatment he received at the hospital cleared up a condition I was unaware of. I hoped that brighter days were ahead for him.

Unfortunately, my hopes were soon dashed when he called to say that he was bleeding everywhere and needed help. I asked him to explain to me what he was talking about and he replied that he pulled his colostomy bag out. This was the first mention of him having a colostomy bag and I didn't know why he needed one. As far as I knew, he had just been hospitalized for a heart condition.

Cookie was again rushed to the hospital, where he would spend the next several weeks. During this next stint in the hospital, he seemed to alternate between good and bad days. On the good days we would speak for an hour or more and on the bad days we were limited to conversations of less than ten minutes. Again I became the contact for the nurses at the hospital and ran interference when they needed him to comply with any of the doctor's orders.

Cookie called me in a panic one night saying that he needed the locks changed on his apartment immediately. I asked him what was wrong, and he said he'd had a falling out with a friend who had a key to his apartment and was now worried that this person would steal his possessions while he was in the hospital. All he kept yelling over the phone was that she was after his archives and was trying to steal his legacy. Cookie almost seemed paranoid. To calm him, I made arrangements for Larry to change the locks on the apartment. Larry explained that the person Cookie was so worried about was a female friend named Bariki, who was also a resident in one of the buildings Larry managed. Larry doubted Cookie's claim because from his vantage point, she did nothing but look out for Cookie and was the person who'd helped him move back to Pittsburgh.

My wife and I discussed Cookie's situation, and I decided to drive out to see him in person to get a true read on what his situation was. I told him that after he was discharged from the hospital on November 11, I would come out to visit him on the fifteenth to take him out for lunch. He again reminded me that he was a vegetarian, so I offered to take him out for Italian.

On the fifteenth, I woke early and left my home at 4:00 a.m. for the six hour trip to Pittsburgh. I stopped for food and fuel and arrived just before 11:00 a.m. The apartment building where he was living looked well maintained, and I rang the doorbell so I could be buzzed into the building. I was nervous about this meeting on many levels. Cookie and I had had some deeply personal conversations, but this was going to be our first face-to-face meeting. I was finally meeting this legend of the gridiron whom I admired; that alone was enough to make me nervous, but I also feared what I might find.

After ringing the bell several times and getting no response, I called Cookie's cell phone and advised him I was downstairs. A few minutes later, a tall, gaunt man with a long grey beard came to the door. Cookie let me in and shook my hand quite firmly. I couldn't help but notice that his hands were huge and looked like catcher's mitts. He shuffled back to the elevator while motioning for me to follow him. Cookie had been known for being this larger-than-life football player, but by my estimate he looked like he weighed less than 140 pounds. He was wearing an old t-shirt adorned with his football poem, "U Are "A" Superstar," on the back of it.

Cookie and I sat in his sparsely furnished apartment and just talked about life. He'd had no real opportunity to set up his new apartment, and other than a used couch, an old '70s-style television and a Rubbermaid container with some old clothes, there was little else to be seen. Several hospital discharge reports, a phone book, and a McDonald's cheeseburger wrapper were on the floor next to the television. The cheeseburger wrapper made me question the whole vegetarian issue. When I asked Cookie about it, he said, “It wasn’t me, someone must have left it there.” I got a chuckle out of his response, because he looked like one of my children when they break something and somehow never know how it happened.

I’d brought a wall phone with me for Cookie’s apartment and set it up while I surveyed his living situation. The bathroom still had dried blood on the walls and floor from the colostomy bag incident that forced his last hospitalization. I asked Cookie if he wanted to go to lunch, and he said that he was not feeling up to it.

We spoke for several hours, and he recounted in great detail the events behind the boycott of the 1964 All-Star Game, just as if it happened yesterday.

I don’t think it was an issue of Cookie not being able to afford items for his apartment, but rather an issue of not being able to manage with the day-to-day activities of life. I asked him what he needed and took down a list of items that he required, including clothes and toiletries.

Cookie had never discussed family with me, other than mentioning that his two sons lived in Canada. During my visit he unexpectedly said that he needed to leave soon for an appointment he had with his doctor. I was confused, because he hadn’t mentioned the appointment when I called him the day before to confirm my trip. He also never told me that he had any family who lived locally, but now I found out he had a nephew who was taking him to this appointment.

When his nephew arrived, I walked Cookie down to the car and noticed how weak he was. He had great difficulty walking and looked nothing like the titan of football I had read about. As we parted, we shook hands and I promised to come back in a few days with the items he had requested.

This had been a long day for me because I’d driven all morning, and after spending several hours with Cookie, was now headed back home. I was about halfway home when my phone rang. It was Cookie. He said that he just wanted to make sure I was doing all right and then dropped a bombshell on me. He had been told at his doctor’s appointment that he had bladder cancer and now required surgery. I didn’t know how to respond to that. Cookie told me he was taking the need for surgery under advisement, but wanted to also explore holistic remedies. I told him I would be there for him, and that I would call him in the morning to discuss his options.

The next day I started looking for help for my friend. I started by searching the Internet for help within different NFL organizations. I contacted the NFL Player Care Foundation and spoke with Dana Lihan. I explained Cookie’s situation, and she moved quickly to get him evaluated for benefits. Dana asked me about Cookie's mental status and inquired if he had been diagnosed with Alzheimer's disease. She explained that the 88 Plan, named after Baltimore Colts tight end John Mackey, supplied benefits for players suffering from Alzheimer's. I gave Dana all of the information I had regarding Cookie's cancer diagnosis and added that I suspected he did have some form of dementia based on his behavior. The Player Care Foundation emailed me the paperwork and set up Cookie's evaluation for the program. Dana added that even if Cookie did not qualify for the 88 Plan, he might be eligible for some other type of benefit. Online I had read horror stories about former players being denied benefits or given the runaround, but my interaction with the Player Care Foundation was very straightforward. I arranged to travel back to Pittsburgh that Friday with Cookie's supplies and the paperwork he needed to sign for the 88 Plan. The sooner the paperwork could be completed, the sooner I could get him the help he required.

As I was doing my best to fill out Cookie's paperwork for the 88 Plan, he called me in distress. Cookie was saying that he had just seen something on CNN that talked about foreign objects in the body causing cancer. Cookie was alleging that a catheter, which had just been attached, was causing his bladder cancer. He talked about being in extreme pain from the catheter so I knew something was wrong. I called the office of his treating physician but received the answering service. My next call was to the nursing unit at the hospital from which he had just been released. The nurse I had been dealing with was off duty and no one else would discuss the matter with me. I explained that there was a person in distress and I needed to see whether I should call for an ambulance. After several transfers to different departments within the hospital, I found a social worker willing to help. She pulled up Cookie's file and said that once he left the hospital, the visiting nurse service was assigned to follow-up on his case, but there was no record of them ever visiting him. She arranged to get a nurse to immediately go out and evaluate his condition. I arranged for Larry to be present so he could let the nurse into the building.
Less than an hour later, I received a call back from the social worker, and she informed me that the nurse had determined that Cookie had a blockage in the catheter. She said that he had over a liter of urine backed up into his system and if left unchecked, he would have died. Cookie was now being transported by ambulance back to the hospital for treatment. After further investigation, I found out that the visiting nurse service had attempted to visit Cookie that past Friday, but he'd refused to let them in, even screaming through the door for them to leave. I asked Cookie about

this and he had no recollection of them ever coming to see him. The one positive that came from this incident was that Cookie agreed to have the surgery and decided against looking for holistic alternatives.

The next call I made was to the Player Care Foundation to advise them of how the situation had changed. At this time I put them in contact with the hospital social worker, and they determined that he could no longer live alone. The hospital would keep him admitted until his bladder surgery, and once he became cleared for release, he would be transferred to a skilled nursing facility that the 88 Plan would pay for.

That Friday morning, I drove back to Pittsburgh and brought Cookie the items he requested, along with the forms for the 88 Plan. The robe and slippers I brought him would become his daily wear and were the only thing I ever saw him wear from that point on.

During my conversations with Cookie, he talked about how he felt football had ruined so many lives, including his own. He told me that once he retired, he did away with everything related to football and even stopped watching the game. Before I returned home that Sunday, I stopped in to spend a few hours with Cookie. I arrived at his hospital room and found him smiling like a little kid while watching a football game between the New England Patriots and the Indianapolis Colts. This was in clear contrast to what Cookie had told me about how he felt about the game of football. In the bed next to Cookie was another patient, who just had total knee replacement surgery and was unconscious from the pain medication he had been given. I asked Cookie if he was enjoying the game and he replied, "I'm not watching it, he is," referring to his unconscious roommate. He just couldn't bring himself to admit that he still enjoyed watching the game he professed to hate so much.

Cookie and I continued our daily telephone conversations, and as each day passed, we became closer. His surgery was performed on December 2, and I remember waiting by the phone for word that he had survived the procedure. I had my concerns that due to his frail physical state, the surgery would be too much for his body to handle. This was the day I realized that I was worrying about Cookie like he was one of my family members. I discussed with my wife how I was feeling and asked her, "When did this go from a cool phone call with a football icon to something that has me so emotionally involved?"

She said it changed when I followed my heart and did what was right instead of what was easy.

The next few days, Cookie was very weak, but we continued to speak on a regular basis. He called me a few days post-surgery and told me that his surgeon had informed him that his condition was now considered terminal. The doctor told him he had eighteen to twenty-four months to live because the cancer had metastasized throughout his lower organs. The surgeon had discussed hospice care with him, but Cookie was unsure of what he wanted to do. In the meantime, he was preparing for his transfer to the skilled nursing facility the 88 Plan found for him in the area.

The week before his transfer was one of the worst I could remember during our friendship. Several times a day Cookie called me and said the nurses were photographing him and listening to his conversations. I called the nurses' station to let them know that he was upset in the hope that they would be better prepared to deal with him. Later the same day Cookie called and said that the nurses had handcuffed him to the bed, which made no sense. Again I called the nurses' station. They informed me that he had just caught his IV on the side of the bed, but he continued to yell out throughout the day that the nurses were restraining him.

In the last call I received that day, Cookie asked me how long it would take for me to get to the hospital because he needed my help to escape. I tried to calm his fears and said it would be at least six hours before I could get to the hospital. He said that he would set traps for the nurses in an effort to keep them at bay until I arrived. I told Cookie I couldn't get there that evening, but would be there within the week. He kept talking about the nurses having him arrested and was starting to worry that he was going to be put in jail or on the street. The only thing that calmed his fear was my promising him he would never be put on the street, and, if need be, he could come live with me. Once I made that statement, he dropped his request for my immediate arrival and said, *"That's why I love you, my friend."*

Cookie's transfer to the skilled nursing facility happened a few days later, and I drove out to visit him for the upcoming Christmas Holiday. The facility was very clean, and the staff appeared helpful. I brought Christmas gifts for Cookie and also arrived with cookies and pastries for the staff. I thought if I left the staff with a good impression, they would go out of their way to help Cookie, who could be difficult. He had spent the past few decades as a recluse and was now being forced into a setting where he shared communal recreation and dining areas. The first person I met when I arrived was the facility's social director, Sylvia. She explained that Cookie was spending every moment in his room, including all of his meals. I explained his previous living situation and said that I would talk to him, but that Cookie was only going to do what he wanted to do.

That visit was magical. We had the best conversations we ever had. Cookie was completely aware of his surroundings and had no lapses in memory. Unfortunately, while he was doing well mentally, his physical appearance was getting worse. Cookie looked so thin that every bone in his body was visible, and he looked as if he were starving to death. That night I was able to get him to eat, and we even dined together in the cafeteria, to the surprise of the facility's staff. Sylvia later whispered to me that my visit was having a positive influence on his behavior. After dinner, Cookie and I talked for hours and I gave him several Christmas gifts. The gifts included another robe and a few sweat suits he'd asked me to bring.

That evening, Cookie asked me to help him get his affairs in order before he died. Among other things on the list of things to do was to get his biography finished, settle past differences with Buffalo Bills owner Ralph Wilson, and to straighten things out with the Canadian Football Hall of Fame.

The first thing I told Cookie was that most kids today didn't know who he was. They only knew the names of the players in the Madden Football video games or on their fantasy football roster. I explained that getting into the CFL Hall of Fame and reconciling with the Bills would go a long way with getting his name back out into the public and would generate interest in his story. Cookie agreed with what I had to say, but added that, more importantly, he needed to talk with Ralph Wilson to set things right before he died. Now faced with his own mortality, he looked at the CFL Hall of Fame as a way to secure his legacy. This would be a place where his family could go and reflect on his accomplishments on the field.

During our conversation I could see that these issues were weighing on Cookie, and I promised him I would do everything in my power to help him. Cookie said he wanted to make me a partner in any projects regarding his life story. He asked me what I wanted in return for working on the project. I replied that I didn't want anything, and that all proceeds should go to his family. He kept asking me what I wanted, and I finally said, *"Cookie, you can buy me a gift if you wish."*

He replied, *"I guess I will buy you a mansion then."*

Always dreaming big, right until the end.

When our visit ended, I realized that a handshake would no longer do, and I reached in to hug his frail body. Looking upon him now was like watching Superman waste away before my eyes. He said he loved me and asked me when I would be coming back. I told him I would come back right after the New Year holiday, and added that I would bring my youngest daughter to visit. I could tell during our talks that he loved children and thought that by bringing my daughter I would lift his spirits.

As I drove back to New York, I had several hours to contemplate Cookie's situation. This was not supposed to be the end for a football hero.

He was supposed to be carried off the field on the shoulders of his teammates, not left to suffer alone and forgotten in a nursing home. Where had it all gone wrong for Cookie?

I kept in touch with Sylvia because she was now my eyes and ears at the nursing home. During one of our conversations she said Cookie had taken her off guard with a request. I asked what he requested, and she replied that he wanted to see if Sylvia could hire a girl for him. Sylvia told him she was the social director, but that did not include procuring escorts for the residents. He'd told her what he wanted was someone to sit with him at the end because he feared dying alone. I told Sylvia that I would make sure that I was there with him at the end and made a promise to myself that I would not leave him alone.

Those last few months, Cookie also tried to repair his relationship with his family. He had estranged himself from his family and now, facing his mortality, was attempting to reconcile with them. A series of phone calls between Cookie and his son Scott started to help repair their relationship.

Cookie and I still had our daily phone calls, and he still seemed to be doing well. On Christmas Eve, after playing Santa Claus for the children at our family get-together, I excused myself and had a two-hour conversation with Cookie. He told me that he was spending the evening watching television in the nursing facility's sitting room. I was happy that he had left the solitude of his room and was starting to venture out a bit. Now when our conversations ended, he would say, *"You know I love you,"* and I would respond, *"I love you, too."* I even joked after one exchange that I would have to love him to put up with his grumpy ass. His reply was a simple: *"I know."*

Right after New Year's Day, I noticed a stark change in Cookie's behavior. The phone calls were becoming shorter and shorter, and he was not sharp mentally. I began to rely on speaking with his nurses in order to determine how he was doing. On January 3, sensing that the end was near, I called the office of the Buffalo Bills to ask Ralph Wilson to call Cookie so he could say goodbye. After no response from Mr. Wilson, I called again the next day and made a pest of myself. I pleaded with Mr. Wilson's office and said Cookie was coming to the end, and if the phone call were not made immediately, it would never happen.

After my last call, Mr. Wilson agreed to call Cookie. I advised him that Cookie was not doing well and he should not be surprised if he seemed off with his time frames. That past week he was having conversations as though he were back in the 1960s and 1970s. Mr. Wilson placed the call, and Cookie called me right after to tell me they had made up. The joy in his voice could not be mistaken, and he even added that he was going to go up to Buffalo to see a game with Mr. Wilson that season. He sounded as if a great burden had been lifted from his soul and just kept repeating that he was back in the Bills family.

I knew based on his current condition he would never make it to that game in Buffalo. I just relished the fact that I had been able to help him ease his pain. Sadly, that was the last productive phone call Cookie and I would have.

I do not know what Cookie and Mr. Wilson discussed that day, but it does not matter. What mattered was that Cookie was happy with the results. The day after their call, I received a call from the Buffalo Bills Alumni director, Andy Major, who thanked me for reaching out to Mr. Wilson. I told Mr. Major how happy Cookie was about the call, but I could not tell what they had discussed. Mr. Major said he had no details either, but was just told that Mr. Wilson called the conversation "positive." I hoped that the phone call would heal the rift between Cookie and Mr. Wilson and that he would now be added to the Bills Wall of Fame.

On January 6, I called Cookie's phone several times but received no answer. In a panic, I called the nurses' station and heard the news I had been dreading. I was told Cookie was failing and that he was now in the final stages of life. The nurse said he had stopped eating and had lost a lot of weight. I could not fathom him being able to lose any more weight because he was just skin and bones when I last saw him. The last thing the nurse told me was that if I wanted to say goodbye, I needed to come there immediately; she estimated he would be gone within the next few days. I made arrangements to leave for Pittsburgh and sent word to Cookie's son Scott that he needed to make his way to Pittsburgh as well.

That evening as I packed for my trip to say goodbye to Cookie, I found myself crying. This was not the customary welling of tears that comes whenever I watch the final scene of Field of Dreams. The feelings of loss and pain I felt that evening rivaled the emotional intensity of anything I had ever experienced in my life.

The next morning I left my home at 4:00 a.m. for the drive to Pittsburgh. The New York City area had been hit by several severe snowstorms, with the latest rolling in that morning. About halfway to Pittsburgh, the weather became so severe that I had to abandon my trip and returned home for safety reasons. Once at home I paced around all day upset with the fact that I had not made it to Cookie's side, feeling that I had let him down. I feared that he would die alone and that I would not be able to keep my promise to him. Thankfully Scott was able to make it into Pittsburgh, and I was grateful that Cookie was not left alone. That evening I decided to take another run at making it to Pittsburgh after the snowstorm passed.

Again I set off early in the morning for Pittsburgh, but this time my wife Estrella and our youngest daughter Olivia accompanied me. It seemed poetic that Olivia accompanied me on my final trip to see my Cookie, as it was her photograph that had prompted the start of our friendship.

When we arrived at the nursing home, I asked Estrella to take Olivia and wait in the sitting room where the other residents were watching television. I knew Cookie was in no condition for them to see him, and I also wanted to spend some time alone with him.

His bedroom door was ajar, but I still knocked before entering. After receiving no response to my knock, I opened the door to find Cookie lying in bed. He immediately recognized me and called my name as I sat down beside him. I held his hand and told him that I wished we had met sooner. In a whisper he weakly replied, *"We met when we were supposed to meet."*

Tears now streaming down my face, I told him he was a good friend.

He replied, *"It goes both ways,"* and he then tried to move his fingers back and forth to symbolize what he was saying. Those were the last words he spoke to me. I sat there crying and thinking that it wasn't supposed to end like this.

Scott then came into the room. It was the first time we had met. I can't explain it, but we spent the weekend together and talked hours on end as if we had known each other our whole lives. There was not an awkward pause during the entire time we spent at Cookie's bedside.

Late Sunday night I sensed that Scott and Cookie needed time alone. I said my goodbyes to Cookie and kissed him on the forehead. Scott walked me to my car and thanked me for helping his Dad. I thanked him for allowing me to stay and say goodbye to my friend. I told Scott that I was going back to the hotel to get a few hours sleep and would stop in for a few minutes on my way back home. Scott and I hugged like old friends, and I drove back to the hotel.

Once back at the hotel, a flood of emotion came over me. I started sobbing as my wife tried to comfort me. I kept crying and saying over and over, "It's not fair!" A simple Facebook message had opened me up to this intense emotional pain and sense of loss. I had become accustomed to reading a little notation in the sports section of the newspaper whenever a former player died. When reading of these deaths I, like most football fans, would think how sad it was that another former great had left us, while just filing it away in my mind as another football fact. These deaths, while sad, were just something for that day's general conversation, but there was no real emotional attachment to the event.

Our friendship, while short, had become so intense that I knew I would have a hard time dealing with his death. Shortly after returning to the hotel, the phone rang. It was Scott telling me to immediately come back to the nursing home. When I arrived, Scott was crying at Cookie's bedside. He was gone, and, I'd like to think, off to his next great adventure.

Scott and I sat in Cookie's room waiting for the funeral home to arrive. After the crying ended, we told funny stories about Cookie's life while polishing off a bottle of Crown Royal Whiskey that Scott had given me earlier as a thank you gift. I told Scott that Cookie's passing felt more like a chapter closing in history than the passing of a man. The rest of the night became an impromptu Irish wake, and it was then that we made a pact to get Cookie's story told.

As I set out to tell Cookie's story, I went through Cookie's journals and manuscripts of his life. The first thing I read was the screenplay version of his life that he wrote around 2001. The opening scene was Cookie at his deathbed recounting his life to his closest friend. He was prophetic about his own death, just as he had been about so many things in life.

He was gone, but he will never be forgotten, because he left his mark not just on the game of football, but on history as well.

Cookie, you gave all of yourself to try to change the lives of others for the better. You can add my name to the list of people on whose life you had a positive impact. I've kept my promise, and now others will know how dearly that effort cost you.

Love you my friend.

Epilogue

The morning after Cookie's death, I headed back to New York to bring my family home and to grab a suit for the funeral services. When I arrived home, another snowstorm rolled in making it difficult for me to make my way back to Pittsburgh. It appeared that I would not be able to return for the funeral and called Scott to let him know I was unable to attend the services.

As if by divine intervention, when I awoke the next morning, the sun was shining and the roads had already been cleared of the previous night's snowfall. I quickly packed and headed back to Pittsburgh. When I arrived in time for the wake, I took Scott and his family completely by surprise because they hadn't expected me to make it through the storm.

Following the wake, Scott and I sat down and discussed Cookie's final wishes. He showed me several unfinished manuscripts Cookie had written over the years. As I read the manuscripts, Scott and I had a dialogue regarding what we each thought would be the best way to get Cookie's story told.

During the conversation, Scott mentioned that the funeral home had received a call from the Sports Legacy Institute in Boston asking if he would agree to donate Cookie's brain to the Institute. The Sports Legacy Institute was an organization formed in 2007 by Christopher Nowinski and Dr. Robert Cantu to research the effects of repeated head trauma from contact sports. The Sports Legacy Institute had partnered with Boston University's School of Medicine in 2008 to create the Center for the Study of Traumatic Encephalopathy, where Cookie's brain would be studied. Only post-mortem could the study determine the level of damage in the brain and then confirm a diagnosis of Chronic Traumatic Encephalopathy, or CTE, as it is commonly known.

CTE is a progressive degenerative disease of the brain found in athletes and others with a history of brain trauma. This trauma, which includes multiple concussions, triggers progressive degeneration of the brain tissue, including the build-up of an abnormal protein called tau. These changes in the brain can come months, years, or decades after the end of an athlete's career. The brain degeneration is associated with memory loss, confusion, impaired judgment, paranoia, impulse control problems, aggression, depression, and eventually progressive dementia.

I made Scott aware of Cookie's desire to participate in the study, and he agreed to the donation, wanting to fulfill his father's wishes. We both felt that the study's findings might shed some light on Cookie's sometimes-erratic behavior. I often wonder, if I had not made it back to Pittsburgh, would Cookie have become part of the study? As in everything else related to my relationship with Cookie, this appeared to just be another instance where I was in the right place at the right time. This chance conversation would later become an important factor in putting the puzzle that was Cookie's life together, as well as in the continued fight for better health care for NFL retirees.

Scott and I continued to speak on a weekly basis as I worked to complete a website chronicling Cookie's life and career. During this time, Scott and I formed a bond, and he asked me to finish Cookie's biography. While I was honored that Scott entrusted me with bringing Cookie's story to the general public, I was quickly overwhelmed by the thought of writing a book. I had never written anything other than homicide reports during my time with the NYPD. I expressed my concern to Scott, and he understood my reluctance, but said that he believed I would be the best choice for the project due to my relationship with Cookie. He felt that whatever I may have lacked in writing experience would be made up for by the connection and feelings I had for Cookie and his story.

In June of 2011, the Center for the Study of Traumatic Encephalopathy contacted Scott and informed him that Cookie had indeed suffered from CTE. Cookie's test results found that he suffered from stage IV CTE, which is the most severe classification of the condition. This meant that large parts of Cookie's brain had suffered severe damage from playing football. Scott was also told that a lot of the paranoia and other erratic behavior that Cookie exhibited were classic symptoms of CTE. Based on the level of damage to Cookie's brain, it appeared that he started suffering the effects of the condition as early as 1971. All of the stories of Cookie being difficult or acting odd in the past now needed to be viewed through the prism of knowing he was suffering the effects of CTE.

When Scott tried to explain to me the level of damage in Cookie's brain, he said that the left and right sides of his brain were held together by tissue that looked like cheesecloth. Scott's layman's description of the damage sent home a vision of the lasting effects of playing football. ESPN and the NFL highlight the explosive collisions on the field in order to sell the speed and violence of the game, but never show the lasting effects of these hits. Now I know, and I hope that Cookie's story becomes a cautionary tale for others.

Unfortunately, Cookie's story is not an anomaly. He was only one of the many former gridiron greats who suffered in silence. For years, he championed the need for better health care and research regarding head trauma, but he was continually dismissed by those with the power to make these changes. I hope that Cookie's death won't be in vain and that his story, along with the work of the Sports Legacy Institute and the Boston University Center for the Study of Traumatic Encephalopathy, will finally bring about the changes needed to protect the athletes who entertain us every Sunday on the gridiron.

Acknowledgments

There are so many people who helped to get this book made, and I will do my best to thank them all. First, I would like to thank several accomplished authors who helped direct me through the writing process: Todd Tobias, Jeffrey J. Miller, Tom Mackie, Ken Crippen, Larry Felser, Jeff Miller, Mark Gaughan, Ed Bouchette, Murray Olderman, Matt Warren, and Robert Mladinich. Their patience and words of encouragement kept me going and gave me the confidence I needed as a first-time writer. Thank you all for being gracious with your time and for your friendship.

To my editor, Megan Milks, thank you for your steady hand and fresh perspective during the editing process. Your work on this project was invaluable in helping me find my voice as a writer.

Robert L. Smith, the former Buffalo Bills team photographer, took the majority of the photographs for the book. His photographs beautifully capture the glory years of Buffalo Bills football. This book would not have been complete without many of the iconic photos Robert took during his storied career. Thank you for agreeing to allow me to use your vision to bring Cookie's story to life.

Many of the franchises that Cookie played for during his career have been helpful in tracking down the statistical information that was needed to complete this book. I would like to specifically thank Andy Major of the Buffalo Bills, Jim Saccomano and Rebecca Villanueva of the Denver Broncos, Jonathan Rubinoff of the Toronto Argonauts, and Joe Horrigan from the Pro Football Hall of Fame.

Several of Cookie's former teammates and friends were indispensable in the completion of this book, and I cannot thank them enough for their willingness to share their memories with me. I want to specifically thank Billy Shaw, Ernie Warlick, Charley Ferguson, Butch Byrd, and the Hon. Samuel Green.

A special thank you has to be given to Ange Coniglio, the foremost authority on the Buffalo Bills and the American Football League. His love for the little league that could helped to spark my interest in the AFL and led to my desire to learn more about the great Cookie Gilchrist. Ange, thank you for all you do and for being the person who makes sure we all… Remember the AFL.

There are many great organizations that are fighting for better financial and medical benefits for retired athletes, and I cannot possibly name them all in this limited space. I do want to thank the following organizations in particular for the work they do: the NFL Player Care Foundation, the Gridiron Greats, Brent Boyd's Dignity After Football, and the Gay Culverhouse Players' Outreach Program.

An organization that has to be mentioned and thanked is the Sports Legacy Institute in Boston. Their staff, led by Chris Nowinski, Dr. Robert Cantu, and Lisa McHale, tirelessly works to warn athletes and their families of the severe and negative health effects that come from repeated head trauma. Their research has changed the way in which head injuries are being treated in the world of sports, and this will undoubtedly save the lives of future generations of athletes. The Institute also provides the needed closure for the families of former athletes who have left this world well before their time. The SLI, through their postmortem brain study, has shed light on why many former athletes have difficulty functioning with day-to-day life or suffer from early onset dementia. I want to thank the SLI staff for the kindness they have shown to the Gilchrist family and the other families who have sadly lost their love ones, too often years before they actually passed away.

Booker Edgerson graciously wrote the foreword for the book and I thank him for that. More importantly, he was Cookie's closest friend and stood by his side right until the end. For that, the Gilchrist family and I will always be indebted. I am honored and humbled to now call you my friend as well. Thank you.

I want to thank the Gilchrist family for making me feel like a member of their family. Gwen and Jeffrey, thank you for your patience and for allowing me to get an inside look into your family history. Hillary, I just wanted to let you know how much I appreciate your friendship and love when our families get the opportunity to spend time together. Matthew and Sarah, your grandfather loved you more than you could ever know, and he was so proud of you both.

Scott, when your dad passed away, I mourned the loss of his friendship. Little did I know that his passing would bring another unexpected friendship, with you. Thank you for treating me like a brother and for seeing the ability in me to finish Cookie's story, even when I did not initially see it myself.

I need to thank my family for allowing me to follow my heart and fulfill my promise to Cookie. Thank you for allowing me to spend the time I needed to devote to the completion of this book. To my mother,

Denise, thank you for your input, which was greatly appreciated. I bet you never thought I would thank you for your opinion. To my four beautiful daughters, Alexis, Nicolette, Julianna, and Olivia, I love you very much and am so proud of the young women you have become.

To my wife, Estrella, your love, patience, guidance, and support are what helped me to complete this journey. Well before the writing of this book was a consideration, your understanding about my friendship with Cookie and your faith in my judgment has meant the world to me. Allowing me to look out for another, even if it meant time away from you and our family, was a giant leap of faith. Thank you for your continued love, faith and friendship. All of my love to you.

Lastly, I want to thank my friend Carlton Chester Cookie Gilchrist. Our friendship was brief, but it has changed my life forever. When you asked me to tell your story, I was moved that you entrusted me with this great responsibility. I still do not know why, after years of seclusion, you chose to confide in me, but I am honored that you called me your friend. Thank you for your trust and I hope that I have made you proud…. your friend always…Chris

Photo courtesy of the Denver Broncos